Peter Trudgill
East Anglian English

Dialects of English

Editors
Joan C. Beal
Karen P. Corrigan
Bernd Kortmann

Volume 21

Peter Trudgill
East Anglian English

DE GRUYTER
MOUTON

ISBN 978-1-5015-2147-8
e-ISBN (PDF) 978-1-5015-1215-5
e-ISBN (EPUB) 978-1-5015-1201-8
ISSN 2164-7445

Library of Congress Control Number: 2021940477

Bibliographic information published by the Deutsche Nationalbibliothek
The Deutsche Nationalbibliothek lists this publication in the Deutsche Nationalbibliografie;
detailed bibliographic data are available on the Internet at http://dnb.dnb.de.

© 2023 Walter de Gruyter GmbH, Berlin/Boston
This volume is text- and page-identical with the hardback published in 2021.
Cover image: stevendocwra/Moment/Getty Images
Typesetting: Integra Software Services Pvt. Ltd.
Printing and binding: CPI books GmbH, Leck

www.degruyter.com

In memory of my Grandad, George Trudgill (1887–1976), a fluent Norwich dialect speaker, who first interested me in the language and history of East Anglia.

Acknowledgements

I gratefully acknowledge the help I have had over the years in the writing of this book from very many people indeed, including Keith Briggs, David Britain, Peggy Britain, Neil Brummage, Andy Butcher, David Butcher, Kerri-Ann Butcher, Richard Coates, Anne-Marie Ford, Javier Ruano García, Tom Geddes, Carol Geddes, Ian Hancock, Jean Hannah, Norman Hart, Ernst Håkon Jahr, Juan Manuel Hernandez-Campoy, Stephen Laker, Margaret Laing, Roger Lass, Ken Lodge, Terttu Nevalainen, Hans Frede Nielsen, David Parsons, Diana Rackham, Carl Sayer, Keith Skipper, David Taylor, Zena Tinsley, Stephen Trudgill, Milton Tynch, Anna-Liisa Vasko, Bert Vaux, David Willis, and Laura Wright. Of these, I would particularly like to single out David Britain, who is the world's leading authority on the English of the Fens; and Anna-Liisa Vasko, who has the same kind of unique authority on the grammar of Cambridgeshire English. Very many thanks, too, to Karen Corrigan for her editorial brilliance.

Last but most, I would like to acknowledge the contribution made to this book by my mother, Hettie Trudgill née Gooch (1918–2013), who grew up in a number of different North Norfolk villages and who helped me in many ways over the decades, not least by compiling a list of dialect words, many of which appear in Chapter 5.

Contents

Acknowledgements —— VII

List of Maps —— XIII

1	**East Anglia: a linguistic history** —— 1	
1.1	Brittonic —— 1	
1.2	Latin and Northwestern Romance —— 6	
1.3	West Germanic and Old English —— 7	
1.3.1	The beginnings of English —— 9	
1.3.2	The first East Anglia —— 10	
1.4	Old Danish —— 12	
1.5	Anglo-Norman and Middle English —— 20	
1.6	Flemish and Walloon —— 22	
1.7	Romani —— 25	
2	**East Anglia as a linguistic area** —— 27	
2.1	East Anglia as an Old English dialect area —— 27	
2.1.1	Northern vs. Southern East Anglia —— 29	
2.2	East Anglia as a Middle English dialect area —— 31	
2.2.1	Northern vs. Southern East Anglia —— 35	
2.3	East Anglia as an Early Modern English dialect area —— 37	
2.4	East Anglia as a 19th-century dialect area —— 40	
2.5	East Anglia as a modern dialect area: the 1930s —— 45	
2.5.1	Phonology —— 46	
2.5.2	Morphology and lexis —— 49	
2.6	East Anglia as a modern dialect area: the 1950s —— 50	
2.6.1	The overall picture —— 56	
3	**East Anglian phonology** —— 59	
3.1	Stress and rhythm —— 60	
3.2	Segmental phonology —— 62	
3.2.1	Vowels —— 62	
3.2.2	Consonants —— 83	
4	**East Anglian grammar** —— 90	
4.1	Verbs —— 90	

4.1.1	Third-person present-tense singular zero —— 90	
4.1.2	Present participles —— 92	
4.1.3	A-verbing —— 92	
4.1.4	Progressive aspect —— 92	
4.1.5	Irregular verbs: past tense forms and past participles —— 93	
4.1.6	Imperatives —— 95	
4.1.7	Presentative be —— 95	
4.1.8	The past tense of be —— 96	
4.1.9	Have —— 96	
4.1.10	Auxiliary and full verb do —— 96	
4.1.11	Causative/non-causative pairs —— 97	
4.1.12	Borrow/lend —— 97	
4.2	Negation —— 98	
4.2.1	Multiple negation —— 98	
4.2.2	Negatives of *have* and *be* —— 99	
4.3	Noun plurals —— 99	
4.4	Numerals —— 100	
4.5	The definite article —— 100	
4.6	Demonstratives —— 101	
4.7	Pronouns —— 101	
4.7.1	Personal pronouns —— 101	
4.7.2	Pronoun exchange —— 101	
4.7.3	Weak forms —— 102	
4.7.4	East Anglian *that* —— 103	
4.7.5	Possessive pronouns —— 107	
4.7.6	Reflexive pronouns —— 107	
4.7.7	Relative pronouns —— 108	
4.8	Adjectives —— 108	
4.9	Temporal adverbials —— 108	
4.10	Intensifiers —— 108	
4.11	Prepositions —— 109	
4.12	Conjunctions —— 110	
4.12.1	*Time* —— 110	
4.12.2	*Do* —— 111	
4.12.3	*(nor) yet* —— 114	
4.12.4	*(no) more* —— 115	
5	**East Anglian lexis and discourse features —— 116**	
5.1	Origins —— 118	

5.1.1	Brittonic —— **119**	
5.1.2	Old English —— **120**	
5.1.3	Old Danish —— **126**	
5.1.4	French —— **128**	
5.1.5	Dutch —— **129**	
5.1.6	Other languages —— **132**	
5.2	East Anglian Fishing vocabulary —— **132**	
5.3	Agricultural terms —— **134**	
5.4	Archaic East Anglian vocabulary —— **134**	
5.5	Discourse features —— **136**	
5.5.1	Terms of address and greetings —— **136**	
5.5.2	Answer particles —— **137**	
5.5.3	Intensifiers and interjections —— **138**	
5.5.4	Truce terms —— **139**	
5.6	Conversational style —— **139**	
6	**East Anglian English in the world —— 140**	
6.1	Bermuda and the Caribbean —— **140**	
6.2	New England —— **141**	
6.3	The American South and African American English —— **144**	
6.3.1	The 'Southern drawl' —— **144**	
6.3.2	Conjuction *do* —— **144**	
6.3.3	Third-person singular present-tense zero —— **147**	
6.4	Australasia —— **147**	
7	**East Anglian texts —— 150**	
7.1	Mautby, Norfolk, 1448 —— **150**	
7.2	Swanton Morley, Norfolk, c. 1799 —— **153**	
7.3	Potter Heigham, Norfolk, 1946 —— **158**	
7.4	North Elmham, Norfolk, 1957 —— **162**	
7.5	Southwold, Suffolk, c.1930 —— **165**	
7.6	Pakefield, Suffolk, 1980 —— **168**	
7.7	Tuddenham, Suffolk, 1957 —— **171**	
7.8	Colchester, Essex, c.1894 —— **175**	
7.9	Tillingham, Essex, c. 1917 —— **179**	
7.10	Cornish Hall End, Essex, 1961 —— **181**	
7.11	Little Downham, Cambridgeshire, 1958 —— **184**	
7.12	Over, Cambridgeshire, c.1950 —— **187**	
7.13	Ramsey Heights, Cambridgeshire, c. 1938 —— **190**	

8	**The dynamics of East Anglian English: past, present and future** —— 193
8.1	The expansion and contraction of linguistic East Anglia —— 193
8.2	Exogenous innovations —— 197
8.2.1	The v-w merger —— 197
8.2.2	H-dropping —— 199
8.2.3	STRUT fronting —— 202
8.2.4	Long-mid diphthonging —— 203
8.2.5	L-vocalisation —— 207
8.3	Endogenous innovations —— 210
8.4	East Anglia versus the Home Counties —— 214

References —— 215

Index —— 227

List of Maps

Map 1.1   Early East Anglia —— 11
Map 2.1   Fisiak's Old English East Anglia —— 32
Map 2.2   Kristensson's Old English East Anglia + Ellis's Eastern Division c.1870 —— 36
Map 2.3   Third-person singular zero —— 52
Map 2.4   Four features —— 54
Map 2.5   The START vowel —— 55
Map 2.6   Isoglosses Combined —— 57
Map 2.7   Linguistic East Anglia —— 58
Map 3.1   Rhoticity —— 88
Map 5.1   Mawther —— 124
Map 8.1   The V-W Merger —— 198
Map 8.2   H-retention & the Weak Vowel Merger —— 201
Map 8.3   The FOOT-STRUT split —— 204
Map 8.4   East Anglian STRUT in the 1970s —— 205
Map 8.5   Long-mid diphthonging —— 206
Map 8.6   The East Anglian *moan-mown* Merger —— 208
Map 8.7   L-vocalisation —— 209
Map 8.8   T-glottalling and T-glottalisation in the SED —— 212
Map 8.9   Smoothing —— 213

1 East Anglia: a linguistic history

As a modern topographical and cultural term, *East Anglia* refers to a region of England which has no official status. Like similar labels such as "The Midlands" (of England, or Ireland) or "The Midwest" (of the USA), the term is widely understood, but stands for an area which has no clear boundaries.

Most people would agree that today the English counties of Norfolk and Suffolk are prototypically East Anglian, although even here the status of the Fenland areas of western Norfolk and northwestern Suffolk is ambiguous: the Fens were for the most part uninhabited until the 17th century, as we shall discuss later, and the cultural orientations of this area are therefore less clear. The main issue, however, has to do with the extent to which all or parts of the neighbouring counties, notably Cambridgeshire and Essex, form part of East Anglia or not. As we shall see, East Anglia as a specifically linguistic area has also changed size and shape significantly over the centuries. But it is not controversial to assert that, linguistically, northeastern Essex and eastern Cambridgeshire (at least) belong with East Anglia; and in this book we will be examining data from both of these counties as well as from Norfolk and Suffolk.[1]

As we shall also see, the English of East Anglia has played an important role in the history of the English language; and East Anglia has a serious claim to be the first place in the world where English was ever spoken. East Anglia was one of the most densely populated areas of England for many centuries – until the Industrial Revolution, Norwich,[2] the major city in the region, was one of the three largest provincial cities in the country – and there was some input from the dialects of the region into Standard English. The area also played an important role in the development of colonial Englishes (see Chapter 6), notably the American English of New England.

But of course East Anglia has not always been English speaking.

1.1 Brittonic

The earliest language of East Anglia which we know anything about was Brittonic (or Brythonic). This was the British Celtic language which was the ancestor of the

---

1 The *East Anglian Magazine*, which was published in Ipswich, Suffolk, from 1935 to 1997, contained articles about, and advertising from, Norfolk, Cambridgeshire, Suffolk and Essex.
2 Pronounced /nɒrɪdʒ/, rhyming with *porridge*.

modern Brittonic languages Welsh, Cornish and Breton, and was formerly spoken all over the island of Britain.

It is not known with any degree of certainty when Celtic speakers first arrived in Britain, but Baldi & Page (2006: 2194) say that the "traditional view of the settlement of the Celts places them in the British Isles no earlier than about 2000 BC". Fortson (2010: 309) says, more cautiously, that the first identifiable Indo-Europeans who can actually be pinpointed archaeologically in western Europe are the Celts of the later stages of the Hallstatt culture in central Europe, from about 1200 BC, who according to him then arrived in southeastern England at some point after 1000 BC.

By the beginning of the first century AD, the Brittonic-speaking peoples in and around East Anglia who we have any information about included the Corieltauvi, who occupied western Cambridgeshire, Northamptonshire and areas beyond, with their major centre on the site of modern Leicester; the Catuvellauni, who lived in Hertfordshire, Bedfordshire and southern Cambridgeshire, with Verlamion (St Albans) being their major settlement; the Trinovantes of Essex and southern Suffolk, with their capital at Camulodunon (Colchester); and the Iceni. The Iceni were the core East Anglian group, inhabiting the area that is now Norfolk together with neighbouring parts of Suffolk and Cambridgeshire. They are historically well known from their uprising, under the leadership of Queen Boudica,[3] against the Romans. Their capital was known to the Romans as Venta Icenorum: *Icenorum* was the Latin genitive plural of the tribal name of the Iceni, so 'of the Iceni'; and *venta* was used in Brittonic as the name of important markets or meeting places. The same *vent-* form appears in the modern name of the Welsh town Caerwent.[4] Remains of the Romano-British town on the site of Venta Icenorum are located today on the outskirts of the Norfolk village of Caistor St Edmunds, just to the south of Norwich.

As to whether there was any kind of distinctively East Anglian Brittonic, we can only guess. As Schrijver says, we lack "any knowledge about the peculiarities of the Celtic dialects that were spoken in, say, Kent, Essex, and East Anglia", all of our information coming from a later date, by which time Brittonic was confined to the western and northern areas of Britain. But to suppose that there actually were differences between the Brittonic of eastern England and other areas would be a very good guess. Any language which is spoken over an area as large as Britain for a thousand years or more will develop significant

---

[3] *Boudīca* was Brittonic for 'victorious'. The word survives in Modern Welsh as *Buddug* 'Victoria'.

[4] *Caer* means 'fort', and derives from Latin *castra* (see below).

regional dialect differences. And indeed "the little we know about eastern British Celtic points to it being closer to the Continental Celtic language of Gaul than to western British" (Schrijver, 2014: 31): there were "strong connections across the Channel, with the . . . Celtic of northern Gaul" (2014: 58).

The suspicion has to be, moreover, that there were significant differences *within* eastern British Celtic, including – as with the later English dialects – between southern and northern East Anglia. According to Williamson (2013), the archaeology of southern Suffolk for the period prior to the Roman conquest indicates numerous contacts with the Roman world, showing links to southeastern England and Gaul and thence to the Mediterranean. There are no such indications, however, for central and northern Suffolk or Norfolk. Williamson supposes that these differences in material culture were indicative of a political division also. The northern area was the land of the Iceni, whose leading families remained hostile to Rome after the conquest. Southwestern Suffolk, on the other hand, was the land of the Trinovantes, who also held Essex and eastern Hertfordshire. Walton Rogers (2012) writes that the boundary between the Iceni and the Trinovantes "has been placed in different positions by different authors, although all agree that it lay to the south of the current county border (between Norfolk and Suffolk)" (2012: 110). Martin (1999) believes that the boundary ran from east to west along the watershed north of the River Gipping[5] and then along the valley of the River Lark.[6] Fairclough (2010: 12) suggests that it might have run through Thornham Parva, in northern Suffok south of Scole, where a "Grim's Ditch"[7] appears on medieval maps and where to this day a sunken lane by Thornham Parva churchyard runs along the same line. In any case, it would be a surprise if this political and cultural boundary, wherever it was exactly, was not also a Brittonic dialect boundary.

Surviving linguistic evidence for the centuries-long presence of Celtic speakers in East Anglia – probably somewhere between 1,500 and 2,500 years – is not especially great. What evidence there is includes several river names which are or may be of Brittonic origin, in spite of the fact that subsequent rather dense Germanic settlement (see 1.3.1) led to only "limited survival of the old British names for streams and rivers" (Fellows-Jensen, 2000: 46). The name of the Norfolk river Yare, which in Old English was called *Gerne*, is perhaps from a Celtic root *ger-* or *gar-* meaning 'babbling river' (Ekwall, 1928), or from a Celtic root meaning 'heron' cf. Modern Welsh *garan* 'heron, crane' (Breeze, 2006); in the relatively flat East

---

5 The Gipping rises near Mendlesham in Suffolk and flows through Stowmarket to Needham Market and on to Ipswich, where it becomes the Orwell.
6 The Lark rises near Stanningfield in Suffolk and flows through Bury St Edmunds and Mildenhall to the Great Ouse near Littleport in Cambridgeshire.
7 It is possible that the name *Grim* was a reference to the Devil.

Anglian landscape, the slow-moving Yare does not exactly 'babble', so the latter seems more probable. The Latin name of the Roman Saxon-Shore fort at Burgh Castle by the river estuary was the Celtic-derived *Gariannum* (Sandred, 2001).

The British name of the River Chet in Norfolk was probably *Lodn* 'muddy', which survives today in the name of the small town of Loddon which the river flows through: the ancient Celtic root *lut-* meant 'mud'. The Great Ouse and Little Ouse rivers may derive their names from the ancient Celtic word for 'water', being related to the Scots Gaelic *uisge* 'water' which, in the form of *uisge beatha* 'water of life', is the origin of the word *whisky* (Ekwall, 1928). Other possiby Brittonic river names in the area are those of the Colne (Ekwall, 1928: 89), the Nene[8] (Ekwall, 1928: 300), and the Stour,[9] which some writers have argued comes from a Celtic root *sturr* 'strong' (Ekwall, 1928: 378ff).

The evidence also includes a number of settlement names which have been retained from the time when Brittonic was the only language of the area. The *Lynn* in the name of the Norfolk town of King's Lynn is derived from British Celtic *lĭnn* 'pool', which in modern Welsh has become *llyn* 'lake'. The names of North and South Creake in Norfolk are related to Old Welsh *creic*, modern Welsh *craig*, 'rock'. Trunch in Norfolk is probably from British *trum kēd*, 'promontory wood', where *kēd* corresponds to modern Welsh *coed* 'wood' (Coates & Breeze, 2000: 174). And there are two places in Norfolk called Eccles, which is cognate with Modern Welsh *eglwys* 'church'; Sandred (2001: 41) suggests that "the survival of this early Latin word in British form, **egles*" is remarkable.

The British language continued to be spoken by Celts throughout the Roman occupation, which lasted for around four hundred years (see 1.2). And after the influx into East Anglia of West Germanic speakers from across the North Sea, beginning in a significant way from the 5th century, these were for several generations a linguistic minority living amongst or alongside a Brittonic-speaking majority, with a significant period of language contact and bilingualism. According to Laker (2008: 21), "there is much agreement from scholars working in neighbouring disciplines that there was significant survival of the Romano-British population in the fifth and sixth centuries". This would probably be less true of East Anglia than of areas further west and north; but Walton Rogers (2012) nevertheless argues on the basis of archaeological evidence that reverse acculturation, of Germanic Anglians to British culture, took place. The survival of a distinctive and cohesive culture well into the 500s AD in the former lands of the Iceni also shows that Celtic societies "may not have been

---

[8] Pronounced both /niːn/ and /nɛn/.
[9] Most often pronounced to rhyme with *tower*, but also with *sure*.

entirely overwhelmed by the incoming culture" (2012: 119). Many linguists, indeed, have supposed that some features of the Old English language which distinguish it from its continental cousins are the result of Celtic influence, resulting from generations of bilingualism (see Filppula et al, 2002).[10]

It is, revealingly, also true that, as the Germanic-speaking peoples established villages in East Anglia with typically West Germanic names ending with the generic (second) elements *-ham* and *-ing*, there also developed several Old English place-names which confirm that British-speaking and Germanic-speaking peoples lived in some proximity to one other for some considerable time after the arrival of the Germanic speakers (Briggs, 2020a). The specific (first) element *Bret-* in the name Brettenham (one each in Norfolk and Suffolk) indicates that these villages were inhabited by British, i.e. Celtic-speaking, people. And the specific *Wal-* element in the names of places such as Walcott (Norfolk) and Walton (Norfolk and Suffolk) also all indicate the survival of Britons: *Wal-* came from a Germanic form meaning 'foreigner' which survives in the modern English name of Wales (Welsh *Cymru*).

Britonnic linguistic survival is also perhaps indicated by the name of the area of central Norwich known as Coslany. This has been argued by Coates & Breeze (2000) to derive from a Late British[11] form *köslönnī*, from Early British *ko-slunn-ijā*, which was the form ancestral to Modern Welsh *cystlynedd* 'kindred, affinity, alliance', so in this case probably 'place where people live together, community'. Coates & Breeze suggest that the name was adopted by Old English speakers around 550 AD as the name of "a place of some significance in the geography of Celtic eastern Britain" (2000: 158).

However, it then seems that the Britons of East Anglia suffered a more organised and larger invasion by West Germanic peoples in 527 AD, and that a period of actual warfare followed between these invaders and the native Celts, descendants of the Iceni (Williamson, 1993). The Late British language did then eventually disappear from East Anglia, though it is thought to have survived in the Fens longer than elsewhere in southeastern England – until perhaps 650 AD or even after: Morris writes that "near Peterborough Guthlac was troubled about 705 by the still independent British of the Fenland" (1973: 314).

---

10 See Coates (2018) for a more sceptical view.
11 The Late British period is conventionally dated as starting from around 450 AD.

1.2 Latin and Northwestern Romance

The first language after Brittonic to arrive in East Anglia was the Latin of the Romans, who invaded England in 43 AD, pushing northwards and reaching the edge of the Scottish Highlands by 80 AD or so. They appear to have taken control of East Anglia by around 47 AD.

By the time the official Roman occupation of England ended, over 350 years later in AD 410, the Lowland zone of southern England was no longer simply monolingual Brittonic-speaking, according to Schrijver (2002). Indeed, there is evidence that some upper-class Britons had a acquired a knowledge of Latin even before the Roman invasion, through travel and trade. Certainly at the end of the Roman period, Latin was being spoken in one way or another by a good proportion of the lowland Christian Romano-British population.

In using the term *lowland*, Schrijver is referring to the Romanized area of England "which runs southeast of an approximate line that connects Dorchester, Bath, Gloucester, and Wroxeter and bends sharply eastwards towards Lincoln, then northwards past York until it hits Hadrian's Wall near Corbridge" (Schrijver, 2014: 32). It certainly includes, in other words, East Anglia.

A British form of Late Spoken Latin, Schrijver suggests (2002), was very widely used by the Celts, especially amongst the upper-classes. For some Celts, this would have been their native language, their communities having gone through a period of language shift in which they had gradually abandoned Brittonic as their mother tongue. Adams writes that "there is evidence . . . for the spread of Latin among the Celtic population" (2007: 622), and he describes "a Romanised Celtic population which had not received any sort of literary education" and mentions "lower social dialects [of Latin] as they were spoken in Britain". For other Celts, it would have been a second-language lingua franca used for communicating with Latin speakers and other language groups who were part of the Roman occupying forces.

The presence of a significant Romano-British elite in East Anglia is strongly indicated by the discovery in the Suffolk village of Hoxne, just south of the River Waveney and the border with Norfolk, of what is now known as the Hoxne Hoard. This is the largest hoard of Roman silver and gold ever found in Britain: it includes 200 pieces of sliver tableware, gold jewelry, and the biggest collection of gold and silver coins from the 300s and 400s AD ever found anywhere in the Roman Empire.

The British version of Late Spoken Latin disappeared from East Anglia along with British Celtic. Jackson (1953) cites Pogatscher (1888) as believing that there were Latin speakers in England until about 600, though this is more likely to have been in the north of the country than in East Anglia. According to Schrijver

(2002), if this British Late Spoken Latin had survived somewhat longer, it would have ended up being very like Old French – he links together the Late Spoken Latin of Britain and northern France as *Northwestern Romance*: "the little that is known about the way in which Latin in Britain developed after the first century suggests that it did not differ substantially from the late Latin of Gaul, which ultimately became French" (2014: 33). He argues this point on the basis of a detailed phonological analysis of what British Latin was like as revealed by evidence of its influence on the Late British Celtic of Southeastern England.

In spite of the important role of Late Latin, however, the language of the Romans has left few traces in modern East Anglia. The place-names of Caister, near Great Yarmouth; Caistor-by-Norwich (Caistor Saint Edmund); Brancaster, in north Norfolk; and the *-chester* in Colchester, Chesterton (Cambridgeshire) and Godmanchester (Huntingdonshire), all go back to Latin *castra*, singular *castrum*, which originally referred to Roman military encampments. There are also place-names derived from the Latin word *campus* 'field', probably meaning 'enclosure', as in Bulcamp and Campsey, both in Suffolk (Briggs & Kilpatrick, 2016; Briggs, 2020a). And *vicus* 'Roman settlement' survives in the name of the two Wickhams in modern Suffolk.

The Romans were famous for their construction of long straight paved roads, and the names of Stratton Strawless, Long Stratton, and Stradsett in Norfolk, as well as Stradbroke, Stradishall, and Stratford St Mary in Suffolk, go back to Latin *strata* 'paved road'. Long Stratton and Stratford St Mary both lay on the important East Anglian Roman road which led from Caistor St Edmund southwards towards the Roman capital of Camulodunum (the Latin form of the Brittonic name), modern Colchester, which now forms the basis of the modern A140 Norwich-Ipswich road and the A12 road from Ipswich to Colchester.

1.3 West Germanic and Old English

The English language which gradually replaced British Celtic and British Late Spoken Latin in East Anglia is today most closely related historically to four other modern languages: Frisian, Dutch, Low German, and – somewhat less closely – German. These languages are all descended from a common parent language now known to linguists as West Germanic, which was spoken in what are now the Netherlands, Northern Germany and southern Denmark about 2,000 years ago.

During the 300s and 400s AD, boat-loads of West-Germanic-speaking people – no doubt particularly men – started crossing the North Sea to the eastern shores of Britain. Some arrivals, in fact, had almost certainly come well before that: since the second century AD, the Romans had been employing Germanic mercenaries in their garrisons in Britain (Nielsen, 1998: 160). These Germanic people were members of the tribal groupings we now refer to as the Jutes, Angles, Saxons, and Frisians. They were mainly from coastal districts just across the North Sea from Britain. The Jutes came from the furthest north, from northern and central Jutland; the Angles lived in areas to the south of them in southern Jutland and Schleswig-Holstein; the Saxons were located to the west of them, along the North Sea coastal areas of northern Germany in the Elbe-Weser region; and the Frisians inhabited the area of coastline between the Saxons and the mouth of the River Rhine in the modern Netherlands.

As the name *East Anglia* suggests, the heathen Germanic peoples who arrived in and eventually came to dominate the area were mainly Angles. The Saxons did give their name to the areas of southern England known as Wessex, Sussex, Middlesex and Essex, the names referring respectively to the West, South, Middle and East Saxons. But the rest of England, and southeastern Scotland, were dominated by Angles, with the easternmost of these people being located in Norfolk and Suffolk.

Unsurprisingly, there are therefore no place-names in East Anglia indicating occupation by Angles, because there would have been nothing distinctive about that. For place-names showing an Anglian presence we have to travel west to areas which were predominantly occupied by Saxons, where Angles were unusual. For example, the name of the Wessex settlement of Englefield, now in Berkshire, meant the 'field of the Angles' – which tells us rather clearly that most people in Wessex were not Angles.

East Anglia, however, did have something of an ethnic mix: there were not only Angles there. The name of the Suffolk village called Saxham, near Bury St Edmunds, meant 'the home of the Saxons' (Briggs & Kilpatrick, 2016; Briggs, 2020a). The village was obviously called that because there was something a bit different in Suffolk about being a Saxon. There were also Frisians: we can see this from the Suffolk village names Friston and Freston, 'village of the Frisians'. Indeed, in his paper "The Frisians in East Anglia", the American sociologist George C. Holman argues that "Frisians invaded East Anglia in the fifth century", and that East Anglia "is culturally more closely related to Friesland than it is even to its nearest English relative, Kent" (1962: 181). There were also other Germanic peoples present: Swabia today is the part of Germany around Stuttgart, but some Swabians must have been part of the cross-North Sea migration because the name of the Norfolk town of Swaffham meant 'the home of the Swabians'. Flempton in Suffolk, also near Bury St Edmunds, may indicate the presence of Flemings, who came from areas inland from the Frisians.

In addition, Hines (1984) argues that there is archaeological evidence to show that colonists from southern and western Norway also settled on the east coast of England from around 475, thereby opening up the way for later widespread Scandinavian influence on 6th-century Anglian England. Hines (2013: 38–9) writes that "the Germanic cultures appearing in East Anglia come from right around the North Sea, from the southern littoral – the areas of Frisia and Saxony – to Jutland and well up the west coast of Norway".

1.3.1 The beginnings of English

If we were to ask when English first came into being as a language, what we would really be asking is when it started breaking away from the other West Germanic languages, and especially from Frisian, which is its closest relative: linguists have postulated a possible earlier common language, Anglo-Frisian. The West Frisian language is still spoken today in West Friesland, the northwesternmost part of the Netherlands,[12] and it was long recognised as being a language rather similar to English: East Anglian fisherman had a rhyme which went

> "Bread, butter and green cheese
> Is good English and good Friese."

Frisian sea-faring folk, too, still have a version of the same rhyme:

> "Bûter, brea en griene tsiis
> Is goed Ingelsk en goed Fries."

A reasonable answer to the question about the beginnings of English would then be that the language began to acquire a separate identity of its own once the speakers of West Germanic, who had originally crossed the North Sea from mainland Europe as mercenaries during the Roman occupation and as raiders, first started to overwinter and then settle permanently in Britain. It was the permanent settlement of these people in eastern Britain which was eventually to lead to the break-up of the West Germanic dialects into separate languages, and thus to the development of the English language.

East Anglia lay immediately across the North Sea from the coastline of the original area occupied by these West Germanic peoples, and it was therefore one of the very first British places where they settled. It is also the area with the lowest level of survival of Romano-British place-names (Cox, 1975), which can

---

[12] The related North Frisian language is now spoken along the western coastline of Schleswig-Holstein, Germany, immediately to the south of the Danish border, and on the neighbouring off-shore islands. This area was settled from the Frisian homeland in the Middle Ages. East Frisian also still survives as a tiny language island in the Saterland, Lower Saxony.

be interpreted as being due to much heavier Germanic immigration to the region than to elsewhere in the English southeast (Nielsen, 1998). East Anglia is, too, the area where the largest concentration of early Old English (pre-650 AD) runic inscriptions has been found, for example at Binham and at Spong Hill by North Elmham in north Norfolk; and at Undley, near Lakenheath, in Suffolk (Page, 1999). We can say with some assurance that East Anglia was one of the earliest English-speaking places in the world, and very possibly even the very first place. Certainly, the oldest piece of written English ever discovered anywhere – a runic inscription on a piece of bone – was found in the Anglo-Saxon graveyard in Caistor just outside Norwich. It dates from the 400s AD, and consists of the single word RAIHAN 'roe deer'.[13]

1.3.2 The first East Anglia

East Anglia was an independent Anglian kingdom for more than three centuries, from the mid-500s onwards (Hines, 2013). The earliest Germanic rulers of East Anglia were members of the Wuffingas dynasty, which seems to have emerged from the military struggle against the Celts which took place during the course of the 6th century (see 1.1). The name of the dynasty supposedly comes from the name of the – probably historical – King Wuffa. The – definitely historical – Rædwald, who was probably Wuffa's grandson, became King of East Anglia from about 599. Rædwald, who was regarded as the overlord of the whole of Germanic England, was converted to Christianity; and he is widely thought to be the figure who was buried in the famous Scandinavian-style ship burial at Sutton Hoo, by the banks of the River Deben near Woodbridge, in Suffolk.

Politically, the independent Anglian-dominated Anglo-Saxon kingdom of East Anglia, once it became established, had somewhat indeterminate boundaries, as was typical of the time. These fluctuated "with the fortunes of war and the vagaries of dynastic policy, embracing at times Ely and its dependencies in the Fens, but perhaps excluding – at least initially – the south-west of Suffolk" (Williamson, 2013: 60). Williamson says that it is not known when southern and southwestern Suffolk became fully integrated into East Anglia – he suspects not until after the 9th-century Danish invasion. But in the event, East Anglia was eventually bordered to the west by the Kingdom of the Middle Angles – which included Cambridgeshire, Huntingdonshire and Northamptonshire as well as Lincolnshire, and later became part of the Kingdom of Mercia; while to the south lay the

---

[13] The engraved bone can be seen in Norwich Castle Museum.

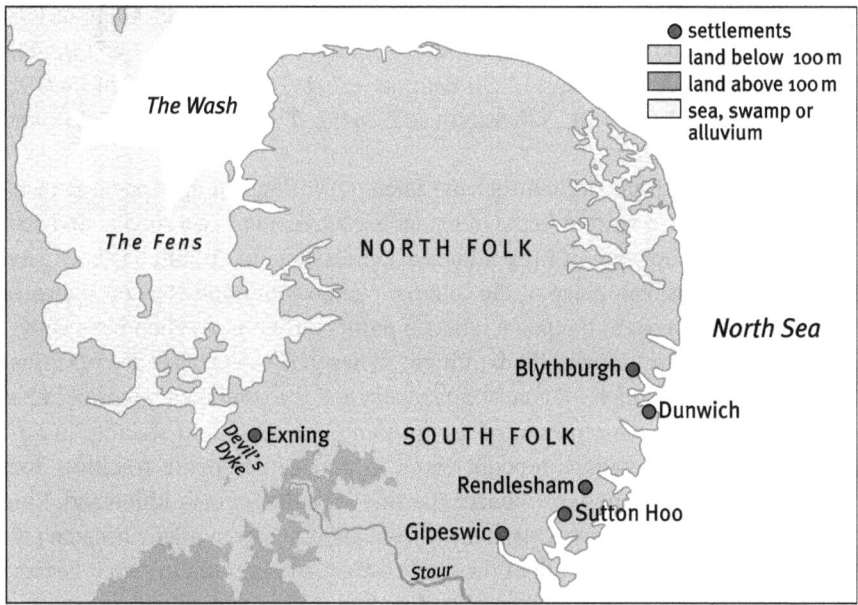

Map 1.1: Early East Anglia.

Kingdom of Essex, which also included eastern Hertfordshire and Middlesex. Williamson (2013: 58) suggests that the Kingdom of Essex might also initially have included southern and southwestern Suffolk.

Topographically, East Anglia was bounded on the east, north and northwest by the North Sea, the Wash, and the more or less impassable Fens; and elsewhere, ultimately, by "the hard, definable lines provided by rivers" (Williamson, 2013: 62) – the Ouse, Lark and Kennett to the west; and the Stour, which still forms the boundary between Suffolk and Essex, to the south. The Kingdom of East Anglia later expanded further west as far as the River Cam, which runs through Cambridge. The area between the Cam and the headwaters of the Stour, where there was no river to demarcate a boundary, was eventually protected by defensive dykes, whose still visible surviving remains have been known in modern times as the "Devil's Dyke" (see Map 1.1). These defences seem to have been aimed mainly at preventing incursions from the neighbouring and much bigger and stronger Anglian kingdom of Mercia.

After Rædwald's death in about 624, East Anglia came increasingly under attack from Mercia, which had acquired control of the Midlands of England stretching from the Thames in the south to the Humber in the north, with its capital in Tamworth, Staffordshire. A number of Rædwald's kingly descendants were killed in battle with the Mercians, including Sigeberht (d. 641). Other kings of East Anglia who we know of (Naismith, 2013) include Ealdwulf (663-c.713), Ælfwald (713–749), Æthelberht I (749), Beonna (c.749–760?), Æthelberht II (779?-794), Eadwald (796-c.800), Æthelstan (c.825–845), Æthelweard (c. 845–55), and Eadmund (c. 855–869).

Newton (1993) has argued that the famous Old English epic poem *Beowulf* may well have been written in the independent kingdom of East Anglia, and specifically during the reign of King Ælfwald. Rendlesham in Suffolk has been suggested as the possible place of the original composition; and Newton indicates that certain passages in the poem reflect a particularly East Anglian perspective. Ælfwald was the last king of the Wuffingas dynasty. He had succeeded his father Ealdwulf, who had ruled for almost fifty years; and the combined reigns of father and son seem to have represented a long period of peace and stability in East Anglia, which was perhaps brought about in part by prosperity resulting from commerce between Gipeswic (modern Ipswich) and the German Rhineland. King Æthelberht was killed by the Mercians in 794, and the region briefly became part of Mercia until, after the death of the famous Mercian king Offa in 796, it became independent once again, initially under King Eadwald.

The East Anglian kingdom continued in independence for a number of decades until the Great Viking Army of Danes invaded the region in 865: the army of the East Angles was defeated by the invaders in 869, and the East Anglian king Eadmund, who had been ruling since about 855, was killed. The onomastician Keith Briggs (2011) has argued that *Hægelisdun*, where Eadmund was slain, was situated near Maldon in Essex.[14] A shrine supposedly containing Eadmund's remains was later constructed at Bury St Edmunds in Suffolk. The East Anglian kings Oswald and Æthelred then "probably ruled as Viking quislings after Edmunds martyrdom" (Naismith, 2013: 137).

1.4 Old Danish

Large-scale Viking settlements took place in England during the 9th and 10th centuries, leading to many eastern and northern areas of the island containing a heavily Scandinavian or Scandinavianized population, as famously witnessed by the hundreds of Norse place-names (see below). The numbers of Scandinavians who actually arrived and settled in Britain is unknown and the subject of

---

[14] A widespread assumption has been that Hægelisdun was Hellesdon, near Norwich. I find Briggs's argument in favour of the Essex site persuasive.

much controversy (Härke 2002; Holman 2007). But from about 890 onwards, East Anglia became officially part of the Danelaw – the area of England which had been signed over to the Danes by Alfred, the King of Wessex. After the East Anglian defeat, parts of East Anglia were "shared out to Danish Viking soldiers, who were thereby transformed into settlers" (Nielsen, 1998: 167); large numbers of further settlers subsequently arrived from Denmark in a secondary wave.

Prior to 869, the Anglian-origin English language of East Anglia had developed gradually, with little outside influence, for about four hundred years, but now the area became bilingual again, although there remains the interesting question as to what extent bilingualism as such would actually have been necessary. The original parent language of Old Danish, North Germanic, was a close relative of West Germanic; and indeed many linguists postulate an earlier language which was ancestral to both, Northwest Germanic, which would have split up into North and West Germanic around 450 AD (Kuhn, 1955).[15]

It is therefore quite possible that English speakers and Danish speakers could still understand one another reasonably well during the 9th, 10th and 11th centuries even without becoming particularly bilingual as individuals. Indeed, Townend (2002) has shown that there is plenty of evidence to suggest that there must have been a considerable degree of comprehensibility, and that communication may not have been too difficult, especially after long periods of contact had made each group familiar with the speech patterns of the other. Townend asks, when the 9th-century Stockholm Codex Aureus was recovered from Viking hands by the English: "what were the linguistic means by which Ealdorman Aelfred negotiated with the Vikings for the recovery of the gospel-book?" (2005: 4). He cites very many other examples of contacts between Norse and English speakers where the individuals involved use language to do things like making treaties, buying land, negotiating contracts and marriages, and settling disputes, to the extent that it is impossible to conceive that they would have been able to do this without being able to understand one another to a fair degree. No interpreters or translators are ever mentioned, as they often are when communication between speakers of other languages is being described.

Bidialectalism, then might well be a better description than bilingualism for the situation in 10th-century East Anglia. It was probably mostly passive bidialectalism, however. Townend argues that the situation was one of *adequate intelligibility,* meaning "amongst other things, the ability to understand individual words, if this ability was sufficiently widespread and sufficiently successful

---

[15] The other branch of the Germanic language family was East Germanic, which was the family to which the Gothic language belonged.

to permit face-to-face and day-to-day transactions, and so to preclude the need for one or both of the speech communities in the Danelaw to become bilingual, or for interpreters to be habitually used for the purposes of Anglo-Norse communication" (2005:183).

In spite of the fact that the Danelaw soon came back under English control (in 917 – see 1.5), very large numbers of Danes stayed on in East Anglia; and according to Sandred (2001: 45), "the Scandinavian impact on the language [of East Anglia] must have been considerable". There was certainly also considerable influence from Danish culture on English culture: archaeological finds "demonstrate the clear impact Viking forms of culture exerted in East Anglia" (Pestell, 2013: 255). But it is an interesting question as to how much Danish was spoken in East Anglia, and for how long. Very many words of Scandinavian origin are in general use in modern English, but in East Anglia, as in other parts of Britain where Norse settlement was heavy, an even larger number of words from Old Norse survive to this day in local speech (see more on this in 5.1.4).

One example from Norfolk and Suffolk[16] is *beck* 'stream' – the modern Danish word is *bæk*. Another is *staithe*, from Old Norse *stǫð* 'landing stage' cf. modern Norwegian *stø*: in central medieval Norwich there were eleven landing stages called *staithes*, which "throws particular light on the role of the city as an early market and port" (Sandred, 2001). There are also many Old Norse-origin place-names in the area: for instance, *toft*, as in Lowestoft,[17] meant 'plot of land' cf. modern Norwegian *tuft;* and the Old Danish form *kirk* 'church' is also found in Norfolk (Kirby, Kirstead) and Suffolk (Kirkley).

These Scandinavian place-names can help to provide us with evidence concerning the geographical and chronological extent of the usage and survival of Danish in East Anglia. When the first Danes arrived, the Angles had of course already been occupying many of the most productive areas of the region for many centuries; and the linguistic evidence suggests that Vikings often therefore had to settle in areas which were less desirable in some way. Fellows-Jensen tells us that "the only areas from which Old English place-names are absent are the most marshy and inhospitable ones so that Danes arriving in the late ninth century cannot have found much easily exploitable vacant land". Marshy and inhospitable areas were certainly to be found around the estuary of the River Yare, and "a marked concentration of Scandinavian names is to be found at the eastern end of the Norfolk/Suffolk boundary, in the hundreds[18] of Flegg and Lothingland"

---

16 Cambridgeshire and Essex saw lower levels of Danish settlement.
17 The specific element of this name comes from the Scandinavian personal name *Hlóðvér*.
18 'Hundred' was the old Germanic label for a subdivision of a county, in use in England until 1894.

(2000: 48). Lothingland was originally an island which was bounded to the north by the River Yare and Breydon Water; to the west by the River Waveney; and to the south by what is now Oulton Broad and Lake Lothing (near Lowestoft) but which was then another branch of the Waveney.

According to Fellows-Jensen, the Danish place-names in Lothingland are quite varied, with forms in *-holmr* 'island of higher ground in a marshy area' being the most frequent. On the north side of the Yare estuary, Flegg too was an island at that time. The rather dense settlement of Flegg by Danes is revealed in the extreme concentration, unparalleled anywhere else in the region, of place-names ending in *-by* 'settlement': Ashby, Billockby, Clippesby, Filby, Hemsby, Herringby, Mautby, Oby, Ormesby, Rollesby, Scratby, Stokesby, and Thrigby (*by* is now the Danish and Norwegian word for 'town' and the Swedish word for 'village'.) *Flegg* itself is also an Old Danish word referring to a boggy area overgrown with marsh-plants such as iris (flag).

Place-names in *-thorpe* originally indicated smaller outlying Danish villages dependent on a *by*. A number of Norfolk names with the generic *-thorpe* have specifics derived from Old Danish personal names: Ashwellthorpe, Pockthorpe (there are several of these, including one in Norwich), Ingoldisthorpe, Glosthorpe (in Denmark there are two places with the same name, Glostrup), Calthorpe (cf. Kallerup in Denmark) and Freethorpe. This pattern is also found in Akethorpe in Suffolk. However, *thorpe* was later borrowed into Old English, and Besthorpe in Norfolk may well have an Old English specific (Fellows-Jensen, 2000).

A complicating factor, though, is that some Vikings also seem to have taken control over already established Anglian settlements. The linguistic evidence for this is thought to be provided by the so-called "Grimston hybrid" place-names: Grimston in Norfolk has the Old English ending *-ton* prefixed by the Danish man's name Grim. Suffolk Grimston hybrids include Thurlston, from the Scandinavian name Thorulf, and Thrandeston from Thrond. But what exactly do these hybrid names signify? Does the hybrid name of Aslacton in Norfolk signify an established Anglian village which was seized by a Viking called Aslak, who renamed it after himself? Or did Aslak simply establish a new village and give it a partly English name which fitted in with the names of the other settlements he now found around him (Parsons, 2006)? It certainly seems to be the case that in terms of soil quality and habitability, when it comes to villages with Scandinavian names, Grimston-hybrids are found on the most desirable sites; the *-by* names on the second best sites; and the *-thorpe* names on the least desirable.

The possible take-over by Danes of English settlements may also be suggested by other types of hybrid such as the two Ashbys (one in Flegg, one in south Norfolk), which derive from Old English *æsc* 'ash-tree'; Wilby (in southwest Norfolk), which derives from English *wilig* 'willow'; and Aldeby (on the north bank of the River Waveney), which contains the Old English adjective *ald* 'old'. Fellows-Jensen also suggests that the names of the Norfolk villages of Kirby Bedon and Kirby Cane indicate the taking-over by the Danes of English settlements which already had churches, and adds that "there is certainly Anglo-Saxon fabric in the church at Kirby Cane" (2000: 49).

The Danes also established a considerable urban presence. Norwich was actually ruled by the Danes from 870 to about 925 (Campbell, 1975); Thetford in Norfolk also became a mainly Viking town; and there were a high proportion of Scandinavians in Ipswich. There are still many streets in Norwich whose names end in *-gate*, the Scandinavian word for 'way, street': Bishopgate, Colegate, Cowgate, Finkelgate, Fishergate, Pottergate, Mountergate, and Westlegate. There were formerly a number of others, as recorded by the Swedish scholars Karl Inge Sandred & Bengt Lindström (1989), such as Hundegate, Neugate, and Saddlegate. Tombland, an open space by Norwich Cathedral, which was the site of the Anglo-Danish market until the Norman invaders (see below) moved it, takes its name from Scandinavian *tom* 'empty'.[19] In Thetford there are streets called Eastgate, Minstergate, and Redgate.

Another interesting set of clues as to the longevity of Danish comes from the numerous field-names of Nordic origin to be found in East Anglia (Sandred, 2001), including names in *wong* 'meadow', *sty* 'path', and *how* 'hill' (the modern Norwegian equivalents are *vang*, *sti*, and *haug*). In fact, studies of field-names, and other minor names of different localities, seem to suggest, for Norfolk at least, a wider, stronger and perhaps more persistent Scandinavian linguistic presence than the major town and village names alone might indicate. Sandred writes that the study of minor names reveals "Scandinavian influence in an area [of western Norfolk] where there are no traces of Scandinavian influence in the major names" (Sandred 1979: 115).

Parsons (2006) similarly writes that the relative richness of Old Norse field-name evidence in Holt and North Erpingham, North Norfolk, is an important indication that Scandinavian influence there was greater than might be deduced from the village names alone. He used Sandred's research to carry out a fascinating study of minor names in which he compared forms in the two Flegg Hundreds in eastern Norfolk with those in the northern Hundreds of Holt and North Erpingham. The northern Norfolk hundreds have names with *kjarr* 'carr, boggy wood' and *lundr* 'grove', as well as *tveit* 'clearing'; and Parsons' statistical work shows that there were not significantly fewer Old Danish names in north Norfolk

---

19 The in the modern spelling is unetymological. The name is most often pronounced /tu:m'lænd/.

than in the more obviously Danish-influenced Flegg: in both areas, Old Norse forms provide the generic element of nearly 20% of minor place-names. Amongst Scandinavian-origin specifics in earlier minor place-names, Parsons notes Old Norse *steinn* 'stone' in the name Magna Steyndale in Plumstead near Holt, from around the year 1300; and the form *mikill* 'much' in Myklecrundell, also from around 1300, in nearby Edgefield. Edgefield also had a traditional Old Norse personal name as a specific in the name Gunilduscroft, and there is another, Hethincroft, in nearby Sharrington.

This usage of minor names of Danish origin alongside English-origin names suggests at least a very considerable amount of language/dialect contact between speakers of Old English and speakers of Old Danish, probably lasting for many generations. In fact, place-names in eastern Norfolk indicate that Old Danish speakers in Flegg were probably surrounded by people who spoke Old English. To the north of the Flegg Hundreds was the Hundred of Happing, an Anglo-Saxon name meaning 'the followers of a man called Hæp', whose name also appears in Happisburgh,[20] dating back to an Anglo-Saxon settlement which had been there for four centuries before the Vikings arrived. And Flegg's other neighbour across what is now the River Bure, Walsham Hundred, also had an English-language name: it meant the *hām* (modern 'home') or homestead of an Anglian leader called Walh or Wæls (Ekwall, 1960: 494).

The Scandinavians perhaps did not even have Flegg all to themselves. It looks like there may have been an ethnolinguistic dividing line across the island since, immediately to the north of Hemsby, Rollesby and Ashby, there are places with names like Bastwick and Martham which go back to the original Anglo-Saxon settlement period.

It is not possible to be sure about the exact location of any ethnolinguistic boundary: Repps, in the Danish-English borderlands between Bastwick and Ashby by the river Thurne, is thought by some experts to be an English name related to the Anglo-Saxon word *ripel* meaning 'a strip of land'; but others maintain that it is from Old Danish *rep* meaning 'community'. The name of the nearby River Thurne is also linguistically ambiguous. The river is named after the village of Thurne, which comes either from Old English *thyrne* meaning 'thorn bush', or from Old Norse *thyrnir* with the same meaning. In any case, it is reasonable to assume that there was communication between the two language groups in Flegg; and that the sort of bilingualism/bidialectalism developed which must also have occurred in other areas in order to lead to, for example, the maintenance of Old Norse-origin field-names.

---

20 The modern pronunciation of Happisburgh is /heɪzbrə/.

Also in favour of the presence of Old Danish–Old English bilingualism/bidialectalism is Perridon (1997: 360), who writes that, while it is well known that Old Norse had a major impact on English, it has not been so usual to suggest that "dialect contact in the Danelaw might have had some consequences for the invaders as well". The point is that there are a number of similarities between English and the Danish dialects of West Jutland which might well have such an origin: Perridon specifically mentions the fact that varieties on either side of the North Sea both lost grammatical gender. He explores the interesting possibility that these two gender-simplification events, in Britain and in West Jutland, might be linked in the sense that the former may in some sense have exported it to the latter. Russ (1982) has made a similar suggestion.

In discussing how this carrying back of linguistic innovations from England to the Danish homeland might have taken place, we can note the relative geographical proximity of East Anglia and Jutland: from Yarmouth in Norfolk to Esbjerg in Denmark is 297 nautical miles, a distance which could be covered by some Viking ships in less than 24 hours under favourable conditions (Winroth, 2014: 72). Perridon also mentions (1997: 261) that "West Jutland mainly consists of barren moorlands, which in the past could hardly sustain its population", which might have led to a large number of people from this area emigrating to England, and "it is not unreasonable that those who returned to West Jutland, after having accumulated some wealth in England" could have been, as successful bilingual/bidialectal remigrants, rather influential.

Townend (2002) suggests that Old Norse probably died out in northern England in the 1200s, and it is therefore likely that Old Danish as such had disappeared from East Anglia, which was less heavily Scandinavianised than the north, before that. But it is not at all impossible that Old Danish, or at least an anglicised contact-form of the language, continued to be spoken in East Anglia to an extent until the 12th century (Dance, 2014; Parsons, 2001; Kisbye, 1992). As Parsons says, however, "we are very poorly informed on the crucial question of how long Norse survived anywhere in eastern England" (2006: 175).

We do know, though, that eventually the speakers of Norse did abandon it in favour of English – an English, however, which by then had as a consequence of English-Danish bilingualism/bidialectalism become considerably Norsified. In fact, "abandon" might well not be the most appropriate word here at all. In view of the at least quasi-dialectal nature of the relationship between Old English and Old Danish, we would probably do better to think of the descendants of the Viking invaders gradually modifying their Old Danish over the generations in the direction of Old English. Especially if Old English speakers in a bilingual town like Norwich also gradually modified their dialect in the direction of Old Danish, then there would have come a point where the two became no longer distinguishable.

Emonds & Faarlund (2014) claim that the Germanic language which eventually emerged out of language contact between Old English and Old Norse in early medieval England was in fact not Norsified English but Anglified Norse – a Scandinavian language heavily influenced by Old English. Modern English, they argue, should therefore be considered to be a Scandinavian language. They argue their case using mainly syntactic data, citing the Norse character of a number of Middle English[21] syntactic constructions as compared to Old English. They point out, for example, that van Riemsdijk (1978) makes the strong claim that the only languages in the world which permit grammatical constructions with fully developed preposition stranding[22] are, firstly, members of the North Germanic language family and, secondly, English: Danish *Reven ble skutt på* ['Fox-the was shot at'] is entirely paralleled by English *The fox was shot at* (Holmberg & Rijkhoff, 1998). According to Emonds & Faarlund, most languages disallow this construction completely; and West Germanic Dutch allows it only "under very restrictive conditions" – which was also the situation in Old English. According to Hoekstra (1995), it is also disallowed in Frisian.[23]

However, in view of the scenario we have outlined above of the gradual melding of the two Germanic dialects into one, the opposition between Anglified Norse and Norsified English would seem to be a distinction without a difference. Le Page & Tabouret-Keller pointed out (1985) that languages can be sociolinguistically more or less *diffuse* or *focussed*. In diffuse linguistic communities, little codification has taken place; there is little agreement about norms; little concern for demarcating the language variety from others; and relatively little importance is accorded to what the language is called. In focussed communities, codification has taken place; there is a high degree of agreement about norms; speakers show concern for demarcating their language variety from others; and there is agreement about the language's name.

Viking Age England was a much more linguistically diffuse than focussed place. People walking around, say, 10th-century Norwich would just have been speaking to each other in such as way as to ensure the best possible communication. Very few of them would have had any clear notion of the sociolinguistic situation as being one of bilingualism, and there is no reason for us to have that perception either. The single Germanic language which eventually emerged in

---

21 The Middle English period is often defined as having lasted from c.1150 to c.1470.
22 In *The boy I gave it to*, the preposition to is said to be "stranded" at the end of the sentence, as opposed to in *The boy to whom I gave it*.
23 For a discussion of the work of scholars who have suggested possible Brittonic influence on the development of English preposition stranding, see Roma (2007).

medieval East Anglia really was descended from the language of the Danish Vikings; but it was also descended from the Old English dialects of Anglian Norfolk and Suffolk.

1.5 Anglo-Norman and Middle English

In 903, the East Anglian Danes allied themselves with Æthelwold of Wessex in an uprising against the King of England, Edward the Elder. They were eventually defeated, with the result that by 917 East Anglia had come under the total control of the kings of England and ceased to exist as an independent Anglo-Danish polity. As part of the Kingdom of England, however, East Anglia did then became a separate earldom.

From 1016, during the reign of King Canute, himself a Dane, the Earl of East Anglia was Thorkell the Tall, a Swedish-Danish noble from the Baltic Sea region. But he was succeeded by a series of mostly Anglo-Saxon Earls of East Anglia, including Harold Godwinson – the later King Harold who was defeated by the Normans at the Battle of Hastings. As their name suggests, the Normans themselves were originally Scandinavian Vikings. Only a few generations earlier they had been Old Danish speakers, but had subsequently shifted to French.

After the Norman conquest of England in 1066, Norwich, the capital of East Anglia and by now a rather sizeable town with a population approaching 7,000, was a rather multilingual place. In addition to the original speakers of English, there would probably still have been speakers of a form of Danish, mostly descendants of the original 9th-century influx, but also perhaps people who had come over from Denmark with King Cnut when he became king of England in 1016.[24] There were certainly also speakers of the newly arrived Norman French. And the Normans brought with them from the continent large numbers of speakers of other languages, especially Flemish (Dutch) from the Low Countries, and Breton.

Many Jews also arrived with the Normans as well as subsequently. They were probably mostly speakers of Norman French, and would for the most part have remained so until they were expelled from Britain in 1290. They also had a knowledge of Hebrew as their liturgical language and language of scholarship. One of the most famous of all medieval Jewish poets lived in East Anglia: he is known to Jewish scholars today as Meir ben Elijah of Norwich.[25]

---

[24] After his conquest, Cnut paid off his soldiers, who mostly went back home again to Denmark.
[25] His works are now available in an English translation by Ellman Crasnow & Bente Elsworth (see Pim et al., 2013).

In 1144, a 12-year-old boy called William was murdered on the outskirts of Norwich and his body found on Mousehold Heath. There was a belief at the time "– the blood libel" – that Jews carried out ritual murders of Christian children, and Norwich citizens falsely accused the Jews in the city of killing William. William was turned into a martyr through this anti-Jewish racism, and a chapel dedicated to him was built on Mousehold – the ruined foundations are still visible. This was a manifestation of the same bigotry which later led to the slaughter of Jews in Norwich in 1190, and to the expulsion of the Jews from England by King Edward I in 1290. There was also quite possibly a linguistic component to the hostility which was directed towards the Jews. William was a Christian boy who spoke English; the Jews, like the Norman overlords, were (as just noted) speakers of Norman French – they were set apart from the English by their language as well as by their culture and religion.

Following the Norman Conquest, Ralph de Guader was appointed Earl of East Anglia and began the work of building Norwich Castle. He had been born in England and was half Breton and half English, but he fought on the side of the Normans in 1066. He was also known as Ralph de Gaël, after lands he owned in Brittany, as well as Radulf Waders and Ralph Wader. We can suppose he spoke English, Breton and Norman French. In 1069, Ralph defeated a Danish force which had invaded Norfolk and briefly taken control of Norwich. It may have been in recognition of this that the King, William the Conqueror, made him Earl of Norfolk and Suffolk (he was also known as Earl of Norwich, and Earl of the East Angles). However, Ralph was later involved in the Revolt of the Earls against King William, and when this revolt was crushed in 1075, Ralph retreated to Brittany, and the Earldom of East Anglia was abolished. Ever since 1075, then, East Anglia has been a concept rather than an area with any legal or official status.

The Norman French language of England, often referred to as Anglo-Norman to indicate the extent to which it came to differ from the language of Normandy, survived as a minority upper-class spoken language in England until the 14th century. From the mid-1300s onwards, however, English started making more of an appearance as a written language, which greatly facilitates our research into the nature of the English dialects of that time. We can see, for instance, that London was gradually becoming a site of considerable dialect contact and dialect mixture. Lass (1999: 3) writes of a "demographic movement that also had linguistic effects: an internal 'invasion' of London and the Southeast, especially from the North and East Anglia, which from late Middle English times onward left in the emerging standard and related varieties a number of items which are clearly not native to" the Southeast.

A good proportion of the in-migrants into the ever-expanding city of London were East Anglians. This is no surprise, given that "from the eleventh to the fifteenth century and beyond, East Anglia was the wealthiest and most heavily populated area of the kingdom, with the walled circuit of its regional capital, Norwich, encompassing a greater area than that of London" (Liddiard, 2013: 9). Norwich for centuries had the second largest population of any city in the land. Wright (2001) shows that it was only in London and Norfolk that 14th-century guild certificates were written in English, underlining the status of (at least northern) East Anglia as an area of high population density and language contact: "the fashion for abandoning Latin and French and using English began in the centres of commodity and exchange" (Wright, 2001: 100).

Ekwall (1956) too says that many wealthy merchants (as well as goldsmiths, clerks and others) migrated to London from East Anglia; and Kristensson (2001) suggests that social-class dialects began to develop in London at about that time, with upper-class speech patterns – hence the influence on the "emerging standard" – being derived in part from East Anglia. Three of the in-migrants to London from Norfolk became mayors, and seven of them became Members of Parliament for London.

There are many Modern English linguistic forms which do not derive from the native London-type Essex or Kentish dialects but from dialects found in areas to the north of the Home Counties – and therefore in part from East Anglian speech. They include items such as *fen* rather than London *ven*; *street* rather than *strate*; *miller* rather than *meller*; *milk* rather than *melk*; *flax* rather than *vlex* or *flex*; and *old* rather than *eld*. They also include Old Norse-origin forms, which were more prevalent in the former Danelaw, such as *them* rather than *hem*, *again* rather than *ayaine*, and *give* not *yeve*, plus Old Norse borrowings such as *get*; Kristensson suggests that East Anglian incomers were one important conduit into London for these Scandinavianisms.

1.6 Flemish and Walloon

In the 16th century, a major linguistic event occurred in East Anglia which again involved immigration from across the North Sea. From the 15th century onwards, the different provinces of the Low Countries (which are for the most part now Belgium and the Netherlands) had come gradually under the control of the Dukes of Burgundy. Mary, the daughter of Charles the Duke of Burgundy, then married Emperor Maximilian of Austria. Their son Philip married Joanna, the daughter of Ferdinand of Aragon and Isabella of Castile, and so control of the Low Countries ultimately passed to their son, who as Charles V was Holy

Roman Emperor but was also King Charles I of Spain. When he abdicated in 1556, the Empire went to his brother, Ferdinand I; but the crown of Spain went to his son, King Philip II, together with control over the Low Countries.

Although Charles had been educated in the Low Countries, his son Philip was brought up in Spain and was a devout Catholic. Most of his domestic, colonial and foreign policies were focussed on stamping out Protestantism, so it was inevitable that there would be trouble in the Low Countries where Calvinism had taken root in the northern provinces (now The Netherlands). Under the control of Philip's sister, Margaret of Parma, Spanish troops were stationed in the Low Counties and "heretics" were prosecuted by the Spanish Inquisition. This led to an insurrection against Spanish domination, which even involved the still mainly Catholic south (modern Belgium), where loss of autonomy was resented.

Persecution by the Spanish led to Dutch, Flemish and Walloon refugees fleeing to Protestant England. Many of them settled in Sandwich (Kent), London and Colchester, but by far the biggest group of refugees found their way to Norwich. They were probably attracted at least partly by an already established group of Flemish weavers there.[26] The refugees themselves, although predominantly also textile workers, included ministers, doctors, teachers, merchants and craftsmen. The very high proportion of *Strangers* 'foreigners' in the city did lead to a certain amount of friction, and there was at least one attempted revolt against them; but generally, the absorption of a very large number of refugees into the population, while undoubtedly causing overcrowding, was relatively trouble-free. By 1579, remarkably, 37% of the population of Norwich, which at that time was 16,236, were not native speakers of English. Colchester at the same period had a population of around 6,700, with around 1,300 or about 19% of this number being refugees from the Low Countries (Goose, 1981).The refugees were mostly Dutch speakers from Flanders and Brabant, but there were also French-speaking Walloons from Armentieres, Namur and Valenciennes (at this period, the border with France was further south than it is today), and even some German speakers from Lorraine.

According to Moens (1888), "in the first half of the 17th century, as much Dutch and French was spoken in Norwich as English", which cannot exactly have been true. But orders for the conduct of the Strangers were certainly written in French in 1659. And the first books ever printed in Norwich were written

---

26 In 1565, the mayor and aldermen of Norwich had invited 30 "Dutchmen" and their families – no household was to exceed ten persons – to Norwich in an attempt to modernise the local textile industry, which had been lagging behind in terms of technology, design and skills: 24 Flemish and 10 Walloon master textile makers arrived and settled in Norwich.

in Dutch; their printer was Anthony De Solempne, who had been a spice merchant in Antwerp and had arrived in Norwich as a religious refugee in 1567. Soon after arriving, he was operating a printing press in the parish of St Andrew in Norwich, and he produced two books in Dutch in 1568. These were "an edition of the psalms and some prayers in metre translated by Petrus Dathenus together with a catechism for the use of the Dutch Reformed Church" and "a reprint of a Dutch translation of the *Confession of Faith* drawn up by the Swiss Reformed Church and subsequently studied by some of the Dutch Calvinists" (Stoker, 1981).

East Anglia even produced some poets of note who wrote in Dutch (Joby, 2014). The best known was Jan Cruso, who also wrote in English. He was born in Norwich in 1592 of parents who had come from Hondschoote in Flanders[27] in the 1570s, and he probably went to the Norwich School. He spent several years in London, but was back in Norwich by 1620, where he ran the family cloth business. He was also a member of the local militia, and a church elder.[28] One of his poems runs, in part:

> *Ja d'wijl ick dit beschrijv', en in de groene dalen*
> *Langst Yeri koele stroom ick gae een lochtjen halen*
> *En keere na de Stadt de dichte Bosschen door,*
> *Hoe word' ick daer onthaelt van 't Nachtegalen Choor. . .*
>
> 'And whilst I write this, and in the green valleys
> By the Yare's cool stream, I get a breath of air
> And return to the City through the thick Woods,
> I am entertained by the Choir of Nightingales. . .' [Joby, 2014: 196]

Until the 18th century, Calvert Street in Norwich was known as Snailgate, but during the 17th century the street more often went by the name of Snackegate – in older Dutch dialects *snek* was a word for 'snail'. According to Ketton-Cremer (1957), church services in Dutch and French were maintained for many decades in the churches in Norwich that had been given over to the immigrant communities, and the congregations remained vigorous until 1700 or so (Joby, 2015). The French-speaking community in East Anglia was later further strengthened by the arrival of Huguenots from France after the revocation of the edict of Nantes in 1685; and it is clear that Norwich remained a trilingual city for 150 years, into the 18th century.

---

27 Hondschoote is now in France, immediately over the border from Belgium.
28 Cruso's brother moved to London and had a son, Timothy, who is said to have given the novelist Daniel Defoe the idea for the name *Robinson Crusoe*.

Then, "slowly but inevitably the Strangers became merged into the surrounding population and the community lost its separate identity" (Ketton-Cremer 1957). By 1742 the congregations attending church services were small, and the churches decayed. Dutch and French finally died out of use in Norwich in the 1700s.

Some possible linguistic consequences of this trilingualism will be discussed further in Chapters 4 and 5.[29]

1.7 Romani

Another significant linguistic group who arrived in East Anglia during the 16th century, or soon after, were the Romani-speaking Gypsies. Romani is a language – or more accurately a group of languages – belonging to the Indo-Aryan sub-family of Indo-European, whose closest linguistic relatives such as Hindi, Punjabi and Kashmiri are found in the northwestern part of the Indian subcontinent (Matras, 2005).

According to Hancock (1984), the generally accepted date of arrival of Romani-speakers in Britain is 1505 for Scotland and 1512 for England; but Evans (1966) has them arriving in Wales before 1440, and Matras (2010) reports that they may have settled in Scotland as early as 1460. Evans (1966) describes how one of the first records of the Gypsies in England is of the Earl of Surrey entertaining a party of "Gypsions" at Tendring Hall, near Stoke-by-Nayland in Suffolk, in about 1520. And, fascinatingly, Töpf & Hoelzel (2005) also cite strong genetic evidence from excavations in Norwich for the presence of people of Romani ancestry in Anglo-Danish East Anglia as early as the 900s AD.

According to Matras (2010: 57), "much of the history of the Romani-speaking community in Britain can be traced thanks to sources that provide us both with a description of the community and with a sample of their Romani speech". One important source is an anonymous text from 1798 known as the "East Anglian vocabulary of Romani" (Sampson 1930: 136). Another early source consists of 18th-century material collected by the Norfolk clergyman, Rev. Walter Whiter, who was born in Birmingham but died in 1832 in Hardingham, near Wymondham,[30] Norfolk. He was known in his day as an etymologist, and his work was familiar to the novelist and travel writer George Borrow (1803–1881), who was born in Dereham, Norfolk, and educated at Norwich School. Borrow lived much

---

[29] The last French-language church service in Norwich was in 1832, and the last in Dutch in Blackfriars Hall in the 1890s, but by then the languages had attained the status of liturgical languages only.
[30] Pronounced /wɪndm/.

of his life in Norwich and also took a great interest in the Romani languages (Hancock, 1997), spending time with Gypsy communities in different parts of continental Europe and Britain, including on Mousehold Heath in Norwich.

During the 19th century, Romani in England was beginning to morph into the linguistic variety now known to linguists as Angloromani. Romani is a highly inflected language, but the original inflectional (though not necessarily derivational) morphology of Romani grammar was gradually being lost during this period. It is true that

> sources such as the East Anglian vocabulary of 1798 have [the genitive case] both as a word-compositional device, as in *sunekiski chiriklo* 'goldfinch', literally 'a bird of gold', or *butti iska besh* 'working season', literally 'year of work', as well as in the function of a genuine possessive, as in *ma duvlasko rokraben* 'the words of my Lord' and *e greski bošto* 'the horse's saddle'. (Matras, 2010: 71)

And the Norfolk clergyman Whiter's vocabulary has an inflected dative in *devleska* 'for God's sake'. But this kind of morphology was gradually being replaced by English syntax and grammatical words; and, in the 20th century, Way's vocabulary "collected in East Anglia in 1900 from the Cooper, Lock and Buckland families, shows only few inflected forms" (Matras, 2010: 59), most of which have now gone entirely.

Modern Angloromani, then, does descend "from an inflected dialect of Romani that was spoken in England up to the mid-nineteenth century and perhaps even a generation or two later", but it can be thought of today as a variety which consists mainly of English phonology and grammar, but with a proportion of Romani lexical items.[31] As such, it can be used as an anti-language, i.e. a language which is intended not to to be understood by outsiders. A brief example from Matras (2010: 6) illustrates the point:

> . . .that would sell its wudrus to buy livvinda. You know, they don't kom these fowkis. . . . Me dad used to say, low life fowkis don't want chichi, never will have kuvva. Be waffadi all their lives.[32]

There has been some lexical input from Romany into East Anglian English dialects, as will be discussed in 5.4.

---

[31] For an excellent in-depth analytical treatment of Angloromani, see Matras (2010).
[32] '. . . that would sell its bed to buy beer. You know, they don't like these people. . . . My dad used to say, low life people don't want nothing, never will have any things. Be bad all their lives.'

2 East Anglia as a linguistic area

As an English-speaking region, East Anglia has always been a distinctive linguistic area. Modern East Anglian English descends in good part from the Old English which grew up out of the Anglian dialects that were brought over the sea from continental Europe, as we saw in Chapter 1, during the 5th and 6th centuries AD. Many of those Angles who became known in England as the Eastern Angles arrived in England via the Wash, and then turned east, sailing up the rivers as far as possible. Groups of Saxons also arrived via the Wash, but headed south along the Ouse and the Nene and the Icknield way, occupying Essex as well as areas further west – Middlesex, Hertfordshire, Cambridgeshire and Bedfordshire (Kristensson, 2001).

2.1 East Anglia as an Old English dialect area

Norfolk and Suffolk, then, were mainly Anglian, while the areas which bordered them to the south and west were initially mainly Saxon. Any regional linguistic differences in eastern England thus reflected the different areas of mainland European origin of the migrants. Nevertheless, it is still difficult on the basis of the available evidence to establish the validity of East Anglia as an Old English dialect area.

The expert on East Anglian place-names, O.K. Schram (1961), argued that the Kingdom of East Anglia did constitute a single, mainly Anglian ethnic and linguistic unit from very early on; and he suggested that this cultural unity is indicated by the fact that Norfolk and Suffolk both have towns and villages called Barningham, Barsham, Brettenham, Elmham, Fakenham, Helmingham, Ingham, Needham, Rougham, Shimpling, Thornham, Tuddenham and Walsham. One could also add Bacton, Barnham, Barton, Downham, Easton, Gunton, Langham, Mendham, Moulton, Oulton, Walpole, and others.

But surviving Old English texts from East Anglia are sadly non-existent, and we therefore struggle with the traditional philological picture which tells us that Old English dialects were simply divided into four groups: Northumbrian, in the north; Kentish, in Kent and Surrey; West Saxon, in the south; and Mercian everywhere else. The Mercian dialect area supposedly covered the whole of England from Chester to Bristol, from the Humber to the Thames, and from the Welsh border to the East Anglian coast.

There is every reason, however, to suppose that such a large region as this must have been much more linguistically differentiated than the traditional picture suggests, and to argue that East Anglia did form a dialect area of its own. Indeed, Fisiak argues that it is possible to employ onomastic evidence, from place-names and personal names, including evidence from coins, to support this argument, although evidence is "poor for the period before the eleventh century" (2001: 25). He also demonstrates how we can employ *retrodiction* to supplement the overall picture – that is, he makes use of evidence of East Anglian distinctiveness from later periods, for which there is more evidence, to draw conclusions about earlier periods for which evidence is lacking.

In further support of this case, Smith (1956) helpfully presents a more detailed map of Old English dialect regions, based on the presumed limits of Anglo-Saxon kingdoms and bishoprics as well as on onomastic and other linguistic evidence. This also indicates a distinct East Anglian dialect area. His map shows the supposed Mercian dialect area as in reality being divided into four:

1. **Mercian** proper.
2. **Middle Anglian**: Nottinghamshire, Lincolnshire, Leicestershire, Northamptonshire, Huntingdonshire and Cambridgeshire. Hines (2013: 38) describes Middle Anglia at the time as a "culturally distinct zone". Kristensson (1995) writes that even after Cambridgeshire and Huntingdonshire had been lost militarily and politically to Middle Anglian control, they remained ethnically Saxon.
3. **East Saxon**: Essex and Middlesex. Kristensson (2001) argues that Hertfordshire and Bedfordshire also fell into this area;
4. **East Anglian** (Norfolk and Suffolk).

Kristensson (2001: 67) also gives further linguistic support. He writes "that the kingdom of East Anglia had its own Anglian dialect was made clear by Ekwall in 1917". Ekwall (1917) shows, for example, that OE <a> before <l>, which demonstrates breaking[33] to <eal> in Saxon dialects – for instance in Essex – remains as <al> in Norfolk and Suffolk, as in *eald* vs *ald* 'old'. On the other hand, Norfolk and Suffolk have OE *strēt* 'Roman road' as /stræ:t/ in place-names while other Anglian dialects consistently have /stre:t/. This can be seen in modern East Anglian place-names such as Long Stratton, Stradsett, and Stratton Strawless in Norfolk, and Stradbroke, Stradishall, Stratford St Andrews, Stratford St Mary and Stratton Hall in Suffolk, compared to Stretham in Cambridgeshire and Strethall in Essex, as well as to the Strettons which are found in Cheshire, Derbyshire, Shropshire, Warwickshire, Leicestershire, Rutland and elsewhere. We may also observe the difference in the

---

[33] 'Breaking' is the label used to describe a sound-change whereby a long monophthong becomes a centring diphthong, e.g. [e:] > [eə].

forms of place-names descended from Latin *castra* (see Chapter 1) as between the Norfolk names beginning with /k-/ (Caister, Caistor, Brancaster), and the Huntingdonshire, Cambridgeshire and Essex forms of the name beginning with /tʃ-/ (Colchester, Chesterton, Godmanchester).

2.1.1 Northern vs. Southern East Anglia

It also seems that, from early on, there were dialect distinctions within East Anglia. Kristensson (2001: 68) writes that "there were differences between the speech of Norfolk and that of Suffolk" to the extent that it is legitimate to talk, for the Old English period, of there being Northern East Anglian and Southern East Anglian varieties. Examples cited by Kristenssson include OE /y/ giving /i/ in Norfolk but /e/ in Suffolk, as in OE *mylner* 'miller' as a byname being *Milner* in Norfolk versus *Melner* in Suffolk. This difference was still extant in the Middle English period (Kristensson, 1995), and was still being cited as typical of eastern England in the 17th-century writings of Alexander Gil (see 2.3); indeed there were still traces of it in the Norfolk and Suffolk dialects of the late 20th century.

In considering internal regional differentiation within the English of the Eastern Angles, we also have to recognise that the physical landscape was very different from that of today. There were very many fewer people 1,500 years ago than now: the population density of modern England is around 1,000 per square mile (c. 400 per km^2) but, especially after the "Yellow Plague" which devastated Britain in 664 AD (Shrewsbury 1945: 9), the corresponding average figure for England in the late 7th century would have been very much lower indeed, perhaps no more than 20 per square mile (c. 8 per km^2), though it would probably not have been quite as low as this in East Anglia.

It is also important to note that, while the greatest distance between southwestern Suffolk and northeastern Norfolk is no more than about 90 miles (145 km), travel by water in those days would have been less difficult than travel by land (except for any Roman roads which had not become overgrown). A sailing vessel could travel up to 80 miles a day compared to the around 15 miles per day that could be traversed on foot (Liddiard, 2013: 10), not least because many areas were covered by large stretches of dense woodland, as indicated by East Anglian place-names containing the Old Norse element *þveit*[34] 'clearing in a wood or forest'. There are two places in Norfolk, and one in Suffolk, simply called Thwaite;

---

34 This corresponds to modern Norwegian *tveit* (see Chapter 1) and to the modern Danish place-name element *Tved* or *-tved*.

Crostwick in Norfolk was originally Cross-thwaite; and Browick, Crostwight, Guestwick, and Lingwhite in Norfolk also all originally contained the *-thwaite* element. Woodland is also indicated by the generic element of the name of Haddiscoe in eastern Norfolk, which was Old Danish *skógr* 'wood', which also appears in Sco Ruston (Norfolk).

It is difficult today to imagine that the two smallish rivers which form the boundary between Norfolk and Suffolk – the Little Ouse which flows to the west and the Waveney which runs to the east, both rising in the same marshy field – could have formed any kind of barrier to communication. And maybe they did not: Williamson portrays a division which did not lie along that line. He postulates a cultural division between Northern East Anglia – Norfolk and northeastern Suffolk – and Southern East Anglia – southern and south-western Suffolk "along the high watershed which runs to the north of the [River] Gipping (separating its drainage basin from that of the Deben), and which continues as the watershed between the Gipping and the Blackbourne, and the Gipping and the Lark" (Williamson, 2013: 59), so that the Lark Valley and Breckland were included in the North. This is the same boundary postulated to have divided the lands, and very probably the dialects, of the Celtic Iceni from those of the Trinovantes (see Chapter 1). Walton Rogers (2012: 109), too, considers on archaeological grounds that well into the 500s AD, northern East Anglia retained a distinctive identity which she believes was due to the fact that this northern area represented "the contracted remains of the tribal territory of the Iceni and the *Civitas Icenorum* of the Roman period, which was profoundly influenced, but not entirely overwhelmed, by the arrival of immigrant culture from the Continent"; so the divide between the lands of the Celtic Iceni and the Trinovantes continued to be of significance even within the Germanic Kingdom of East Anglia.

Northern East Anglia was a region relatively cut off from the rest of England and heavily influenced by contacts with the circum-North Sea world, either directly across the North Sea or via the rivers which drained into the Wash. The Southern East Anglian area, on the other hand, "looked more to the south and south-east of England – to London, the Home Counties, the Channel, and ultimately northern France and Belgium" (Williamson, 2013: 60), reminding us again of the divide between the Iceni and the Trinovantes.

But it is also true that the name "Waveney" itself comes from Old English *wagen-ea* 'quagmire-river': much of Norfolk and Suffolk were divided from one another by land that was marshy and difficult to cross, and dialect differences between the North and the South could have reflected a relatively low level of contact across the rivers Little Ouse and Waveney.

Religious boundaries were also possibly important. There were eventually two separate bishoprics in the area, one centred on North Elmham in Norfolk and the other in Dunwich, Suffolk. Today, as we shall see, the Norfolk and Suffolk dialects still differ on a number of points, although again the boundary between the sub-dialects does not entirely coincide with the political boundary between the counties: a large area south of the Waveney belongs linguistically to Norfolk rather than to Suffolk.

2.2 East Anglia as a Middle English dialect area

It is also clear that East Anglia continued to maintain its status as a distinct dialect area during the Middle English period, from c.1150 onwards: Chaucer and Langland both refer to the Norfolk dialect in their writings, and it seems that the dialect was regarded as difficult if not incomprehensible (Beadle, 1978) by outsiders.

Again, though, we suffer from the practice of scholars who conventionally divide Middle English dialects into only five areas: Northern (a continuation of the Old English Northumbrian area), West Midland, East Midland (these two together represent a continuation of Mercian), Southwestern (from West Saxon), and Southeastern (from Kentish).

Moore et al. (1935) and many other writers place Suffolk and Norfolk in the East Midland dialect area. For students of East Anglian English it is therefore very helpful that McIntosh (1976: 41) writes of the East Midland area that "there are quite clear differences marked, roughly speaking, by the Ely-Norfolk border", i.e. the border between Norfolk and Cambridgeshire. In fact, there are a considerable number of Middle English linguistic features which help to distinguish specifically between the dialects Norfolk and Suffolk as a single unit, in comparison to the other neighbouring dialect areas such as Cambridgeshire.

Fisiak (2001), in his attempt to argue retrodictively for an Old English East Anglian dialect area, presents a map (Map 2.1) based on Middle English data from the 1400s, taken from the *Linguistic Atlas of Late Medieval English* (McIntosh et al., 1986), which also shows East Anglia as a rather clearly delineated Middle English dialect area. He writes (2001: 26): "it is possible to find a number of isoglosses running along the western border of Norfolk and Suffolk and the southern border of Suffolk in Late Middle English". In addition to features mentioned elsewhere in this chapter, his map portrays the East Anglian presence of /-k/ in *work* and *seek* as opposed to the /-tʃ/ found to the west and south.

In a helpfully extensive treatment, Beadle (1978) also cites the following features of East Anglian English for the Middle English period:

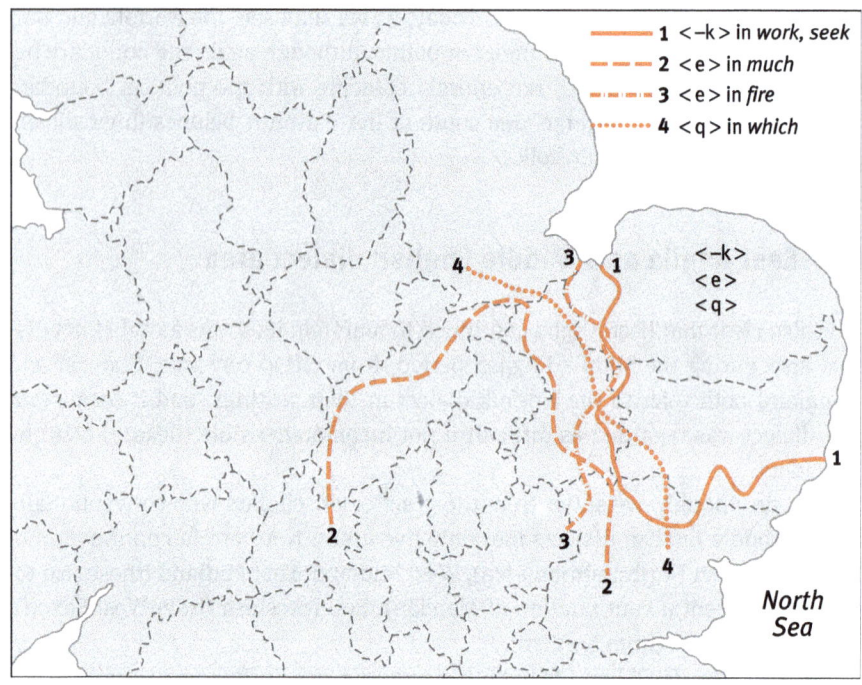

Map 2.1: Fisiak's Old English East Anglia.

1 The treatment of OE hw-

Words such as *what, where, wheel, whale, white* were spelt in Old English with <hw->. This spelling was changed to <wh-> under the Normans, even though <hw-> was a much better representation of the actual pronunciation at the time. In the 1200s, scribes in western Norfolk started writing these words with <qu-> as well as <wh->, for example *quan* 'when'. The village of Whinburgh, to the south of Dereham in west-central Norfolk, appears as *Quyneberge* in 1254 (Ekwall, 1960: 513). It is safe to assume that this was because speakers in western Norfolk had begun, at least variably, to pronounce *which, wheel* etc. with initial /kw-/ (Lass & Laing, 2016). By the 1400s, the new <qu-> spellings, and therefore presumably the new /kw-/ pronunciation, had spread to the rest of Norfolk.

Beadle shows, moreover, that it was not very long before forms in <qu> had reached Suffolk also and had become very numerous in East Anglian documents generally (see also Fisiak's map, Map 2.1). Beadle cites forms with <q> from all over Suffolk, including Beccles, which is just over the border from Norfolk, but also from Bury St Edmunds, Woolverston, Dunwich, and most notably, Long Melford in the far south of Suffolk, right on the border with Essex. He writes further that <qu> for <wh> is "indeed highly typical of the later Middle English orthography used in Norfolk and Suffolk" (1977: 60). This is confirmed by Lass & Laing (2016: 66) as being very distinctive of the whole of Norfolk and Suffolk in the 1400s. (It can also be seen in Text 1 in Chapter 7 of this book, a Margaret Paston letter.)

Today the feature has gone altogether, except that there is one small East Anglian survival in the form of the place-name of the hamlet of Quarles, which appropriately enough lies in the original birthplace of the /kw-/ < /hw-/ change, northwestern Norfolk:[35] *Quarles* comes from Old English *hwerflas* 'circles'.[36]

2 Third-person singular -t

In the Middle English period, third-person singular indicative present-tense verb forms were typically written with the ending <-th>, indicating /θ/, in the south of England. This corresponded to the <-s> which was normal in the north (extending as far south as the border between Lincolnshire and Norfolk).

Texts from Norfolk and Suffolk, however, are characterised by the large-scale presence of <-t>, indicating /t/ rather than /θ/, such as *maket* rather than *maketh* or *makes*. Beadle (1978) writes that the -t forms were fully established as the norm in writings from Norwich, Lynn (and nearby East Winch), and that they also occur in other Norfolk locations such as Thetford, Acle, Wymondham, and Ingham, as well as in northern Suffolk locations such as Beccles, Dunwich and Bury. They are also found in the production of a number of the clerks responsible for the writing of the Paston Letters (cf. Hernández-Campoy et al., 2019). According to Seymour (1968), this -t inflection is a typical feature of East Anglian; and indeed the geographical spread is impressive, from western Norfolk (Lynn) to the east Norfolk coast (Ingham), and from western Suffolk (Bury) to the Suffolk coast (Dunwich). (We shall have occasion to discuss third-person singular present-tense verb-forms further in 2.6.)

3 The early loss of the /x/ before t

The simplification of /xt/ to /t/, which is also cited by Seymour (1968), is reflected in the absence from East Anglian texts, from 1250 onwards, of <-ght> spellings e.g. *caut* 'caught', *taute* 'taught', *rite* 'right'. Beadle writes that examples are numerous

---

35 Quarles is now a part of Holkham, on the north Norfolk coast.
36 It is possible that there were some prehistoric stone circles nearby during the Old English period.

in documents from Norwich, Lynn, Wiggenhall[37] and Oxborough. Subsequently, frequent examples are found in texts from elsewhere in Norfolk – Toft Monks (on the border with Suffolk), Ingham, Westacre, Thetford, Yarmouth, Acle, Lynn, Swaffham, Tilney, Wymondham, and Fransham; and from Suffolk – Bury, Beccles, Stuston, and Dunwich; as well as from Wisbech (just over the border into Cambridgeshire). It also makes frequent appearances in the Paston Letters (see Text 1, Chapter 7).

The velar fricative /x/ was of course eventually to disappear from all of southern and central England. Dobson (1968) states very clearly that the spelling of *-ight* words with <-t> was predominantly Eastern. The orthography does not, of course, provide unequivocal evidence for the phonology, but reverse spellings[38] in the Paston Letters such as <wright> 'write' do indicate the loss of /x/ rather clearly. The phonological change /xt/ > /t/ had occurred in Old Norse by 1050 (Schulte & Williams, 2018), and it may therefore not be a coincidence that it occurred so early on in Norwich, which had a very large proportion of Old Danish speakers in its population in the 10th, 11th and possibly 12th centuries.

4 Further features

In addition to the above, Seymour (1968) cites the following features which also typify the Late Middle English of East Anglia, all of them apparently innovations:

a. The lowering of *i* to *e*: e.g. *wele* 'will', *dede* 'did', *whech* 'which', *heddyn* 'hidden'.
b. The reduction of the auxiliary *haue* to *a*: e.g. *he wolde a maried me* 'he would have married me', *here onde shulde a fayled hem* 'their breath would have failed them'. This reduction continues to be part of the modern East Anglian dialect, as in e.g. *I'a done it* 'I've done it' (see 4.1.8 and the many examples in Chapter 7).
c. The appearance of the prefix *un-* as *on-*: e.g. *onhappily* 'unhappily', *ontrowe* 'untrue'. This continues to be part of the East Anglian dialect today, although it is now confined mainly to older traditional dialect speakers (see Chapter 4).
d. The stopping of /ð/ as /d/: e.g. *federid* 'feathered'.

---

37 Wiggenhall is just to the southwest of King's Lynn.
38 i.e. spellings of words which never had /x/ with <gh>.

2.2.1 Northern vs. Southern East Anglia

It seems rather conclusively to be the case, then, that East Anglia constituted a coherent dialect area not only in the Old English but also in the Middle English period. But differences in dialect between Northern and Southern East Anglia also continued into the Middle English period, with Norfolk, as in the Old English period, maintaining /i(:)/ from Old English *y* as opposed to Suffolk /e(:)/.

Interestingly, Beadle (1978: 31) writes that:

> the significance of Jocelin of Brakelond's well-known remark about the English used by Abbot Samson of Bury[39] can . . . be taken as the earliest surviving reference to East Anglian varieties of Middle English. As early as the 1180's Samson took the unusual step of preaching to the lay people in their own language, and Jocelin's sly humour hints that the Suffolk congregation had difficulty in understanding the dialect of the Norfolk monk.

Abbot Samson came from Tottington,[40] which is across the Little Ouse on the other side of the Norfolk-Suffolk border from Bury St Edmunds, but not much more than 16 miles away.

Kristensson (1995), however, takes the north-south difference much more seriously. In his treatment of Middle English dialects from 1290 to 1350 (see Map 2.2), Norfolk lies in his East Midland dialect area, along with central and northern Cambridgeshire, Huntingdonshire, eastern Northamptonshire, Rutland, Leicestershire, southern Lincolnshire, Nottinghamshire, and southwestern Yorkshire; but Suffolk does not. Instead, it is located in Kristensson's Southeastern dialect zone along with southeastern Cambridgeshire, Essex, Kent and East Sussex.

Kristansson's arguments for his classification include the treatment of Old English *y* which we have already mentioned (2.1.1). He also argues that Suffolk shows southern voicing of word-initial /f/ to /v/ while Norfolk does not. This voicing was a medieval innovation which is still familiar to us from the modern dialects of the English southwest, in forms such as *vinger, vurrow, vlea, vloor, vrom, Vriday* (see Orton et al., 1978: Maps Ph214 – 219). The Essex place-name Vange is an example of this southern feature, coming originally from earlier Fen-ge 'fen district'. Gil (1619) also cites initial-fricative voicing as a feature of

---

[39] "Scripturam Anglice scriptam legere nouit elegantissime, et Anglice sermocinare solebat populo, set secundum linguam Norfolciae, ubi natus et nutritus erat." ["He knew how to read written English most elegantly, and he used to preach in English to the people, yet following the language of Norfolk, where he had been born and raised."]

[40] Tottington is now, sadly, a deserted and unvisitable village, the population having been expelled by the Ministry of Defence during WWII for the creation of a "battle area" and not allowed to return after the war as they had been promised – see http://www.bbc.co.uk/history/ww2peopleswar/stories/62/a3258362.shtml.

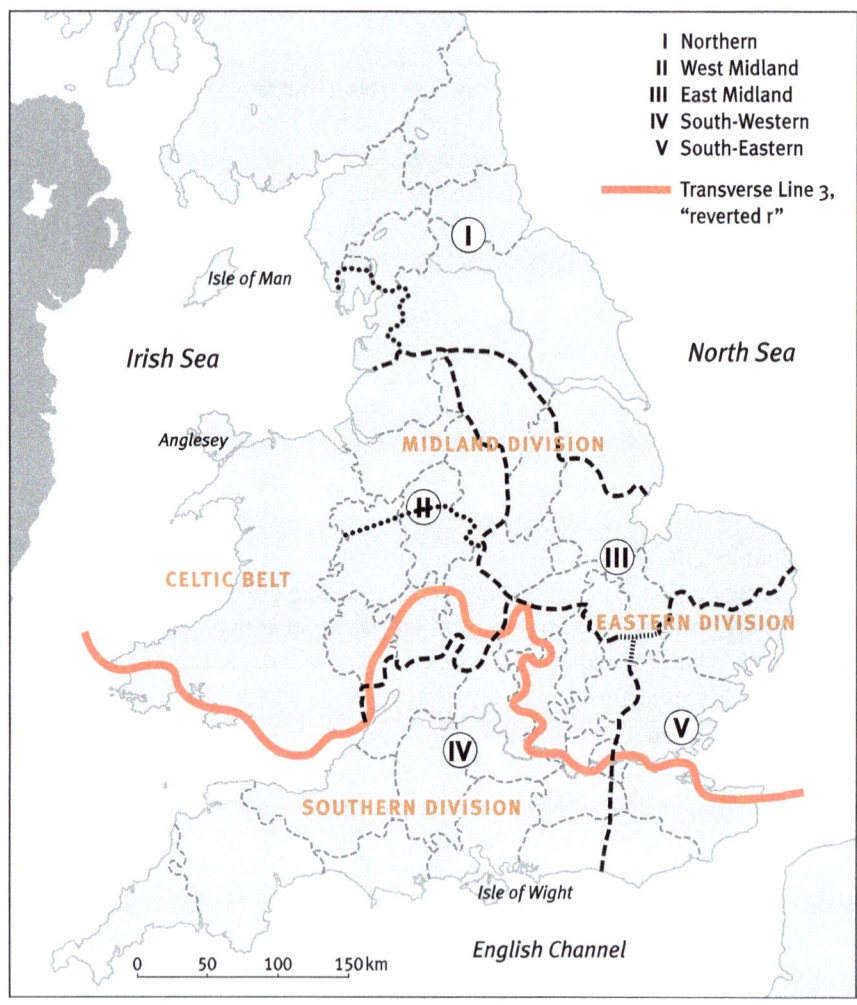

Map 2.2: Kristensson' Old English East Anglia + Ellis's Eastern Division c.1870.

the eastern dialect in the Early Modern period (see 2.5.1.1), but there are strong indications that he was writing about Essex rather than Norfolk and Suffolk. We can say that for several centuries, initial-fricative voicing was a feature which was absent from Norfolk but which became increasingly frequent as one travelled south through Suffolk and Essex towards the Thames.

We may doubt, however, whether this is sufficient reason to do away with East Anglia as a Middle English dialect region and to separate the two East Anglian counties in this way. Kristensson concedes that the evidence for *f*-voicing in Suffolk is sporadic.

Kristensson also cites the fact that Norfolk, in the first half of the 14th century, provided a large number of spellings with *qu-* and *qw-* for original *hw-*, which was not the case for Suffolk. As we have already seen, however, this was a temporary state of affairs, as the /kw-/ innovation did spread eastwards and southwards out of northwest Norfolk.

2.3 East Anglia as an Early Modern English dialect area

A major source of linguistic information about vernacular Late Middle English and Early Modern English is the well-known *Paston Letters* (Davis, 1965).[41] These were written by, and to, members of the influential Norfolk-based Paston family between 1422 and 1509.[42] The family took its name from the village of Paston in northeastern Norfolk, which is just inland from Mundesley; they eventually acquired Norfolk residences in Norwich, Caister, Oxnead near Aylsham, and Drayton near Norwich.[43] One of the best known of the Paston women was Margaret née Mautby (Hernández-Campoy, 2016), who died in 1484 and came originally from Mautby on the island of Flegg (see Text 1 in Chapter 7).

The letters give some insight into the nature of the East Anglian English of the time, though as the decades went by they were increasingly composed in a relatively regionless style, designed perhaps to go unremarked in London, where certain members of the family spent much time – hence the correspondence back and forth. Paston family letters written later than 1509 are also extant and, in particular, the letters of Lady Katherine Paston, as written between 1618 and 1627 have been collected and published (Nevalaien et al., 2001; Nevalainen & Tanskanen, 2007).

Linguistic features to be found in the Paston Letters which give some insight into the Early Modern English of East Anglia include a number of characteristics which suggest that East Anglia was often an area which was in the vanguard in terms of linguistic change (Lass, 1999b):

---

[41] See https://www.thisispaston.co.uk.
[42] Many of the letters were written by (usually male) members of the Paston family themselves, others by scribes taking dictation from (usually female) family members (Hernandez-Campoy, 2016).
[43] The Pastons were related to Sir John Fastolf of Caister, the great English soldier who achieved fame in the Hundred Years War against France and was memorialised as Shakespeare's character Sir John Falstaff.

1. Early loss of non-prevocalic /r/ is demonstrated in, for example, <cadenall> 'cardinal'. This feature did not become widespread in the southeast of England as a whole until the 1700s.
2. The change from /ŋ(g)/ > /n/ in gerunds and simplex words is found in Norfolk spellings from the 1300s, but they become commoner in the Early Modern period, as in forms from the Paston Letters such as <hangyn> 'hanging' and <hayryn> 'herring'.
3. Early examples of the assimilation of /sj/ to /ʃ/ can also be found in these Norfolk letters, as in <sesschyonys> 'sessions'.

There are also a number of early examples of aspects of the Great Vowel Shift, which is generally held to have got under way in the 15th century, so East Anglia again may have been at the forefront of these developments. These include:

4. Early raising of ME /o:/ to /u:/ is indicated by spellings such as <goud> 'good', <whous> 'whose', <owdyr> 'other'.
5. Early raising of ME /e:/ to /i:/ can be seen in <agryed> 'agreed', <appyr> 'appear', <belyve> 'believe', <kype> 'keep', and <shype> 'sheep'.
6. Early diphthongisation of /u:/ can be seen in spellings like <caw> 'cow', and <withawth> 'without'.
7. Early diphthongisation of /i:/ can similarly be seen in <abeyd> 'abide', and <creying> 'crying'.

It could also have been hoped that further information about Early Modern East Anglian English might be gleaned from the work of Alexander Gil (1564–1635). His 1619 work *Logonomia Anglia* is in Latin, but has been reported on by Kökeritz (1938) and Ihalainen (1994). Gil divided English dialects into four regional types: Northern, Southern, Eastern, and Western. He did not outline any geographical boundaries, something which, as Ihalainen says, suggests that he reckoned that his readers would already have an idea of where these dialects could be found. Gil does say, however, that Lincolnshire was part of the north, leading us to suppose that that his Eastern area must have involved only counties to the south of the Wash, so at least Norfolk, Suffolk and Essex, though surely not Kent, which would have been classified as Southern. Disappointingly, however, from the linguistic details Gil gives there is reason to suppose that he is not reporting at all on the dialects of Norfolk and Suffolk, as already mentioned.

For example, he cites as an eastern characteristic the merger of ME /a:/ as in *name*, and /ai/ as in *pay*. This was an innovation at that time, though it is today of course a feature of most English varieties; but it has not ever been a feature of the traditional dialects of Norfolk and Suffolk, with some 21st-century speakers maintaining a distinction to this day between the vowels of *daze* and *days* (see Chapter 3). Kökeritz (1938: 287) certainly interprets Gil's listing of this merger as evidence that Gil was not describing the dialect of East Anglia as such: "we may assume that Gill's notes on the eastern dialects chiefly referred to the areas adjoining London i.e. Essex and Middlesex".

Another indication of Gil's focus on Essex and Middlesex comes from the fact that he reports the Eastern dialects as having initial fricative voicing, as in *fen* /vɛn/. As we just saw, this was not a feature of Norfolk English even in the Middle English period. It was found only sporadically in Suffolk; and by the Late Middle English period, as is shown in McIntosh et al.'s (1986) *Linguistic Atlas of Late Middle English*, initial-fricative voicing was found north of the Thames only in the far south of Essex. These two features, then, are indicative of the existence of a linguistic East Anglia which is characterised by their absence and which does not include Essex.

Gil also cites as being Eastern the pronunciation of *fire* with /iː/ rather than the vowel of *fine*. Kökeritz (1938: 287) writes that this reflex represents "the south-eastern ē for OE y, which is well evidenced in Essex and Suffolk; thus Bokenam writes <fere> for *fire*, and the same spelling is found in the Bury Wills". This is the same thousand-year-old feature which we have already mentioned as making for internal north-south differentiation within East Anglia, in both the Old English and Middle English periods. Indeed, the feature has survived into the modern dialects in forms such as *mice* /miːs/. In the *Survey of English Dialects* materials from the 1950s, however, /miːs/ is found not only in Suffolk but also in the south of Norfolk (Orton et al., 1978: Ph117), which leads one to suppose that the north-south distinction may never have coincided with the county boundary.

More indicative of the status of East Anglia as a dialect area is the work of the Norfolkman Rev. Robert Forby, who was born in about 1732 and died in 1825. In his posthumously published *The Vocabulary of East Anglia* (1830), Forby starts from the assumption that there is indeed such as thing as an East Anglian dialect, and sets out to describe this dialect "as it existed in the last twenty years of the eighteenth Century", i.e. from 1780–1800. This no longer falls within the Early Modern period as such, but his observations do give us some indication of the nature of the dialect situation in East Anglia in the earlier decades of the 18th century.

In his work, Forby treats linguistic East Anglia as consisting of "the twin counties" of Norfolk and Suffolk. Essex is not considered. One complication, however, is that Forby also refers to Cambridge as "our East Anglian University". He regrets including only small amounts of dialect material from Cambridgeshire (which he tells us comes mostly from his time as a student and then

Fellow at Caius College, Cambridge University); and he apologises for "this partial application of a general name" (1830: 65). In other words, for him Cambridgeshire should have been treated more thoroughly in his book because it is also linguistically East Anglian.

This is an important departure from what we have noted from earlier periods. For both the Old English and Middle English periods, we noted the presence of significant isoglosses between Norfolk and Cambridgeshire. But Forby was born in Stoke Ferry in western Norfolk, no more than eight miles or so from the border with Cambridgeshire,[44] and he studied at the University of Cambridge and taught there: we can be certain that he was familiar with the speech of at least eastern Cambridgeshire. We can, then, surely accept the validity of his statement (1830: 66) that, although the dialects of Norfolk, Suffolk and Cambridgeshire[45] are not totally identical, they are nevertheless "varieties, and even slight ones, of the same species, and are therefore properly called by the same name", East Anglian. This has to mean that, during the Early Modern English period, there had been a significant expansion of linguistic East Anglia in a westward direction (see more on this in 8.1).

Forby does, though, recognise at least one difference between Northern and Southern East Anglia, referring to "the Suffolk whine" – a reference to the widespread perception that Suffolk speakers used different intonation patterns from those found in Norfolk.[46]

2.4 East Anglia as a 19th-century dialect area

The work of 19th-century dialectologists shows that the status of East Anglia as a distinctive dialect area was maintained into modern times.

The first large-scale systematic attempt to establish modern English dialect areas in Britain was made by A.J. Ellis (see Maguire, 2012). According to his analysis, East Anglian English formed part of a larger southeast-of-England dialect area which was marked off from other areas further to the north and west by significant phonological differences. In his pioneering publication, for which fieldwork was carried out in the 1870s, Ellis (1889) labelled this larger area the *Eastern* district (see Map 2.2); and his description of the

---

[44] However, David Britain reports that, even today, these are eight fenland miles which are not particularly easy to traverse.
[45] Note that the Isle of Ely officially became part of Cambridgeshire only in 1837.
[46] This perception remained in place a century and a half later – it was commonly said by older members of my own Norfolk family in the 1960s that "Suffolk people sing".

boundaries of the area is charmingly precise. He starts with "begin on the east coast, where the southern border of Lincolnshire falls into the sea about 3 miles east of Sutton Bridge. Go west along the Lincolnshire border to Rutland ... " and concludes " ... go by the western border of Buckinghamshire to the Thames. Go down the Thames to the coast and round Essex, Suffolk and Norfolk to the starting-point".

His Eastern area comprises the traditional counties of Norfolk, Suffolk, Essex, Huntingdonshire, Cambridgeshire, Hertfordshire, Bedfordshire, Middlesex, Buckinghamshire, Rutland, a very small area of southern Lincolnshire, and the eastern half of Northamptonshire. Ellis writes that this region is characterised by "a closer resemblance to received[47] speech than in any other division. It is the region from which received speech was taken, and contains the greater part of London." That is, East Anglia and the dialects of the other subdivisions of the Eastern area had a greater input into Standard English and Received Pronunciation (RP) than those of the other parts of Britain.

In Ellis's presentation, Norfolk and Suffolk together constitute a sub-division of the Eastern macro-dialect area which he labels *19. East Eastern*. This covers, as he says, "the whole of Norfolk and Suffolk" and nowhere else. The other subdivisions of the macro-Eastern area – whose dialects are mostly, as we shall see later, somewhat similar to core East Anglian speech – are as follows:

15. West Eastern northern Buckinghamshire e.g. Aylesbury; western Hertfordshire e.g. Berkhampstead
16. Mid Eastern central and eastern Hertfordshire e.g. Hitchin; Bedfordshire; Huntingdonshire; Essex; mid Northamptonshire e.g. Northampton
17. South Eastern Middlesex; southern Buckinghamshire e.g. Hambleden; southern Hertfordshire e.g. Rickmansworth
18. North Eastern Cambridgeshire; Rutland; northeastern Northamptonshire e.g. Peterborough; southern Lincolnshire (Stamford).[48]

Ellis's inclusion of Rutland and northeastern Northamptonshire (plus Stamford and a small area of northern Huntingdonshire) in the Eastern region is rather startling, because Rutland and northeastern Northamptonshire are separated from the whole of the south of England by what is by general agreement one of the major dialect boundaries in the English-speaking world. This is the line of

---
[47] Ellis is here using *received* in the meaning, as the *OED* has it, of "generally considered as the most correct and acceptable form of a language".
[48] Southwestern Northamptonshire lies outside the *Eastern* region altogether, being placed by Ellis together with southern Warwickshire in area D6, the Border Southern subdivision of the *Southern* macro-region. Nearly all of Lincolnshire is in his *Midland* region.

the FOOT-STRUT split (Wells, 1982), which Ellis is obviously very aware of: he refers to it as the "northern *some* line"– that is, the northern limit of the pronunciation of the word *some* as /sʌm/. This boundary is one of the ten transverse lines "passing from sea to sea" which Ellis uses to mark the limits of major dialect features. Ellis himself concedes that "the northern part of this [the Eastern] district is intersected by the northern *some* line, which passes through the length of Northampton and north of Huntingdon and Cambridgeshire" (and so south of Rutland, Peterborough and Stamford). From his text, though it is clear that, while Ellis was perfectly aware of the importance of this line, he disregarded it for classification purposes because he considered it to be unstable, with the southern variant gradually encroaching northwards.

The FOOT-STRUT split is the feature which provides the major phonological boundary between southern England, which has a system of six short vowels, and the Midlands and the North of England, which have five such vowels, with no distinction between the STRUT vowel and the FOOT vowel, i.e. words such as *foot* and *strut* rhyme, both having the vowel /ʊ/ (see Map 8.3).

The southern FOOT-STRUT split dates back to the 1500s. Middle English had a symmetrical short vowel system which consisted of only five vowels: /ɪ/, /ɛ/, /a/, /ɔ/, /ʊ/, as in *pit, pet, pat, pot, put*. This is the system which is still extant in the Midlands and North of England, as well as in the long-term anglophone southern part of Pembrokeshire in southwestern Wales (Thomas, 1994: 131), and in parts of Ireland, including Dublin (Kallen, 1994: 176; 2013: 59ff). However, in the southeast of England (Ihalainen, 1994: 261), probably starting around "the end of the sixteenth century" (Brook, 1958: 90) – it is at around this time that "foreign observers commented on the new pronunciation" (Strang, 1970:112) – the beginnings of the FOOT-STRUT split (Wells, 1982: 196) set in.

This is "one of the most unaccountable things that has happened in the history of English" (Strang, 1970: 112). According to Strang, in around 1570 the vowel /ʊ/ began to lose its lip-rounding so that a quality more like [ɣ] began to be more usual. This did not happen where the vowel occurred in certain labial environments, so that words like *put, butcher, pull* retained their original pronunciation. This eventually led to a phonemic split between /ʊ/ and /ɣ/ (later /ʌ/), which was reinforced by the shortening of /uː/ to /ʊ/ in a number of words, giving rise to minimal pairs such as *look* and *luck*. According to Ihalainen (1994: 261), "unrounded *u* was regarded as vulgar until the mid 17th century, when Simon Daines, a Suffolk schoolmaster, described it as the accepted pronunciation".

The new 6-vowel system then gradually diffused north until it came to a halt (though see Chapter 8 on continuing developments) along the line of the current FOOT-STRUT split isogloss. For the 1870s, Ellis describes the isogloss – the "northern *some* line" – as starting on the Welsh-English language border and passing through Shropshire, north of Oswestry and Shrewsbury, along the River Severn and then into Worcestershire, passing south of Kidderminster and through Warwickshire to Northamptonshire. He then continues:

> enter Northamptonshire just north of Byfield, and turn north, passing east of Weedon and Daventry and going through Long Buckley to Watford and to the west of East Haddon. Then turn east-northeast, passing by Brixworth (6 miles north of Northampton) and Hannington (5 miles northwest of Wellingborough), and then turn northeast and go between Islip and Thrapston to the border of the county about 2 miles south of Hemington. Enter Huntingdonshire just north of Great Gidding and go just south of Sawtry. Then pass just north of Ramsey and enter Cambridgeshire. Pass just north of Chatteris and, turning northeast, go east of March and west of Wisbech to the edge of the county, and then proceed by the northwest border of Norfolk to the sea.[49]

Elsewhere (p. 252), Ellis also writes: "I have placed March on the northern *some* line itself".

Interestingly for our purposes, Ellis also describes a second transverse line, the southern *some* line, which marks the southern limit of the pronunciation of the word *some* as [ʊ]. What he is doing here, by establishing two lines rather than one, is recognising that there is a corridor of variability running across parts of central England where the contrast between /ʊ/ and /ʌ/ is made only variably, and/or where the phonetic quality of the vowel in STRUT words is not always very obviously different from the vowel in FOOT words. Ellis quite correctly argues that this corridor is due to "the incomplete assertion" of the innovation: "it is only to the north of line 1 that the old state of things remains, and [only] to the south of line 2 that the new state has fully asserted itself".

Our interest here is in the part of the corridor between the two lines which runs through eastern England (see also Map 8.3). According to Ellis, the southern *some* line diverges from the northern *some* line to the east of Sawtry, Huntingdonshire, and runs eastwards south of Ramsey, entering Cambridgeshire south of Chatteris. It then goes northeast, entering Norfolk just south of the Bedford Rivers, and "pursues rather a winding course" through western Norfolk south of Downham Market and Swaffham and east of Dereham, where it turns north for about 6 miles and then, after running south of Fakenham, turns northwest and "falls into the sea" between Hunstanton and Brancaster. Ellis tells us that this information is due to his tireless fieldworker Thomas Hallam, who visited numerous Norfolk locations along the route of the line. My view, however, is that what Hallam observed in western Norfolk were vowel differences of phonetic rather than phonological significance. The modern dialect of King's Lynn,

---

49 This is my close paraphrase of Ellis's text, expanding abbreviations and omitting some details.

in western Norfolk, as investigated by me in the 1980s (see Trudgill, 1986), at that time had a STRUT vowel which was rather markedly different from that of, say, Norwich, being a closer vowel between [ə] and [ɤ] (see Trudgill, 1986). Crucially, however, it was (and is) still distinct from the FOOT vowel.

In any case, it seems that we should accept Ellis's 19th-century northern *some* line as representing the northern border of the larger Eastern region containing East Anglia (though see the discussion in 3.2.1.1 on the Fens). The eastern boundary of this Eastern region was rather obviously formed by the North Sea, so it only remains now to examine Ellis's delineation of the western and southern boundaries of his Eastern region.

It turns out that for him these boundaries were coterminous with another of his transverse lines, the line for "reverted r". This is his term (see Eustace, 1969) for retroflex /r/, i.e. for [ɻ] as opposed to [ɹ] and other variants.

There are currently three main extant variants of /r/ in the traditional dialects of England. The first is the alveolar flap [ɾ], which is today usually associated with Scotland and parts of the north of England; secondly there is the retroflex approximant [ɻ], which is most typical of southwestern England (Wells, 1982: 342); and thirdly we have the postalveolar approximant [ɹ], most usually associated with RP and south and central England. We can suppose on phonetic grounds that this reflects an ongoing process of lenition: the flap is the oldest variant and the postalveolar approximant the newest, with the retroflex variant being chronologically intermediate. This boundary of Ellis's, then, runs between the conservative western and southern retroflex form, and the more innovative eastern postalveolar form.

The division also appears (Britain, 2002c) to be identical to the division between the rhotic and non-rhotic areas of southern England, according to the records of Ellis's fieldworkers. In non-rhotic accents, /r/ occurs only in prevocalic position, as in *rat, trap, carry, car auction*, but not in non-prevocalic position, as in *cart, car, car wash*. This non-rhoticity is the result of the sound change which Wells (1982: 218) labels R-Dropping, and which is well known to have begun in England. Scotland and Ireland remain rhotic to this day (Corrigan, 2010; Kallen, 2013; McColl Millar, 2007).

The chronology of this change is of considerable interest. Wells (1982: 218) dates it to "the eighteenth century, when /r/ disappeared before a consonant or in absolute final position". Strang (1970: 112) claims that "in post-vocalic position, finally, or preconsonantally, /r/ was weakened in articulation in the 17c and reduced to a vocalic segment early in the 18c". Bailey (1996: 100) writes that in English English "the shift from consonantal to vocalic r, though sporadic earlier, gathered force at the end of the eighteenth century". Walker (1791) states that non-prevocalic /r/ is "sometimes entirely sunk", which means that the dates given by Strang and Bailey seem to be accurate for London. However, Beal (1999: 7–8) claims that Walker (1791), in saying that /r/ is "sometimes entirely sunk", is referring "only to the most advanced dialect" of his day – colloquial London English.

The other sub-divisions of Ellis's large Eastern zone which are directly adjacent to his East Eastern (Norfolk and Suffolk) sub-division are Mid Eastern and North Eastern. Omitting the places north of the FOOT-STRUT split line, the areas which might therefore be considered here for inclusion in 19th-century linguistic East Anglia, in any evaluation of the geographical extent of the dialect region, are: central and eastern Hertfordshire, Bedfordshire, Huntingdonshire, Essex, mid-Northamptonshire, and Cambridgeshire.

Essex and Cambridgeshire have to be the most serious contenders here, being immediately next to Norfolk and Suffolk. This is especially true of Cambridgeshire. We have already seen that Forby treats the Cambridgeshire dialect as East Anglian. And Halliwell, in his *Dictionary of Archaic and Provincial Words*, first published in 1847, agrees with Forby that "there is little to distinguish the Cambridgeshire dialect from that of the adjoining counties. It is nearly allied to that of Norfolk and Suffolk" (Halliwell, 1881.xi).

Ihalainen (1994: 212) analyses Halliwell's notes on English dialects and sees that "five specific clusters" emerge from Halliwell's notes. One of these clusters is core East Anglia, Norfolk and Suffolk "with links from Cambridgeshire and Essex". This is the first indication we have that at least parts of Essex should be considered as belonging to the 19th-century East Anglian dialect area.

We can therefore regard Norfolk, Suffolk, and at some least parts of Essex and Cambridgeshire as constituting core linguistic East Anglia in the 1800s. To the extent that parts of Essex and Cambridge are to be included, this indicates that during the previous three centuries linguistic East Anglia had expanded geographically towards the south as well as towards the west. We can attribute these expansions to the continuing influence of the largest urban area in the region, Norwich, as the major focal point for the outward diffusion of linguistic innovations.

2.5 East Anglia as a modern dialect area: the 1930s

The 20th century provides us with much more evidence than earlier eras for the existence, delineation and maintenance of the East Anglian dialect area. Guy Lowman (1909–1941), who was the brilliant chief field investigator for the *Linguistic Atlas of the United States and Canada* (Kurath et al., 1939–41), also conducted field interviews in sixty different locations in southern England in

1937–8 as part of the same research programme, in order to investigate correspondences between American English and English English dialects.[50] Lowman investigated three locations in Norfolk (Necton, Stiffkey, South Walsham); four in Suffolk (Ilketshall, Martlesham, Honington, Buxhall); three in Cambridgeshire (Burnt Fen, Littleport, Kingston); three in Essex (Little Sampford, Steeple, Abridge); two in Hertfordshire (Anstey, Bovingdon); two in Huntingdonshire (Alconbury, Leighton Bromswell); and one in Bedfordshire (Carlton). Also relevant were his investigations in Way Dike Bank in the Lincolnshire Fens[51] as well as those in Newborough, Warmington and Grafton Underwood in eastern Northamptonshire.

2.5.1 Phonology

In Kurath & Lowman (1961) and Kurath (1972), Kurath uses Lowman's data to investigate the patterning of dialect areas in southern England. Like Ellis, Kurath shows that southern England is divided into Western and Eastern zones. In Kurath's case, this is effected not by a single line but, more realistically, by a series of isoglosses which run approximately north-south. Figure 33 in Kurath & Lowman (1970: 34) shows seven such north-south lines forming a transitional-zone corridor which at its narrowest point ranges only from central Berkshire to eastern Buckinghamshire. Four of these lines hit the English south coast in Hampshire and Sussex, with the other three turning east to follow the line of the Thames, so along the southern boundary of Essex. The most significant of these isoglosses, as with Ellis, involves the retention of non-prevocalic /r/ to the west, with even western Hertfordshire (Bovingdon) and western Middlesex (Harefield[52]) being rhotic in the 1930s. The easternmost of the isoglosses divides western [a] from eastern [æ] in *apple*, with [æ] being found only in Norfolk, Suffolk, Essex, Cambridgeshire, Huntingdonshire, eastern Hertfordshire, and Middlesex.

Kurath subdivides the Eastern zone into three "more or less clearly marked subareas" (1970: 35). These are:

---

50 Lowman had received a PhD in phonetics under Daniel Jones at University College London in 1931. He was tragically killed in a car accident in 1941.
51 This is located at Fleet Fen, near Holbeach.
52 Harefield is now inside the M25 London Orbital Motorway.

1. The North Midland

Lowman investigated many fewer locations than Ellis, albeit with much greater phonetic accuracy, and did not visit any Shropshire locations; but his findings confirm, even if not in such detail, the location of Ellis's FOOT-STRUT-split boundary. Lowman's research shows that the boundary passes through Warwickshire and Northamptonshire and then to the north of at least most of Huntingdonshire and Cambridgeshire to reach the Wash between Norfolk and Lincolnshire. Kurath's North Midland sub-area thus includes Lincolnshire, Leicesterhire, Warwickshire and Northamptonshire – but of course in reality stretches further north into areas which Lowman did not investigate.

2. The East Central Counties

According to Kurath & Lowman, this sub-area is focussed on Middlesex, Hertfordshire and – interestingly, for our purposes – Essex. It is no doubt significant that Lowman did not visit any localities in northeastern Essex, which to this day retains clearly East Anglian features. Characteristic of this zone for Kurath & Lowman are the mergers, on an upgliding diphthong of the type [æɪ], of ME long *ā* and *ai*, as in *make* vs. *day*, which as we saw above was also treated by Gil (1619); and the corresponding merger of ME long open *ō* and *ou*, as in *stone* vs. *grown*, again on an upgliding diphthong. (We shall refer further to the retention of these contrasts in East Anglia in Chapter 3.)

3. East Anglia

Kurath writes (p. 37) that "East Anglia has a number of unique phonological features", with Norfolk being "the stronghold of these peculiarities". He singles out four of these, which we will discuss further in Chapter 3, as being typically East Anglian:
1. /eː/ in *bean*
2. /ʊ/ in *stone*
3. /ɐ/ in *thirty*
4. [ɜʉ] in *mouth*

According to Lowman's records, feature 1 is found only in Norfolk and northern Suffolk; 2 is also found only in in Norfolk and Suffolk (something which I shall dispute in 2.6); and 3 and 4 only in Norfolk, Suffolk and northern and eastern Essex. Kurath & Lowman (1970), then, have a much narrower geographical definition of East Anglia than we have seen hitherto. It is therefore probably advisable, in contemplating how far south and west we wish to consider that East

48 — 2 East Anglia as a linguistic area

Anglia stretches for our purposes, to also consider the fact that Kurath & Lowman's western [a] vs. eastern [æ] in *apple* isogloss is located a good deal further to the west than this[53] and would, if considered diagnostic, also incorporate Huntingdonshire, Cambridgeshire and eastern Hertfordshire into East Anglia, which would seem reasonable, but also Middlesex, which would not.

There are also a number of other features which Kurath & Lowman do not treat as diagnostic of East Anglia but could have. For instance, it emerges from their work that a particular characteristic of Norfolk, Suffolk, Cambridgeshire and northern Essex involves the phonetics of the PRICE vowel /ai/. Kurath & Lowman distinguish between what they very aptly call "slow" diphthongs of the type [ɑˇɪ], with a long first element, and "fast" diphthongs of the type [ɐɪ]. The "slow" diphthongs are found only to the west of a north-south line which is shown in their Fig. 34 (p. 36) as having to its east Norfolk, Suffolk, all of Cambridgeshire except the southwest (Kingston), and all of Essex except the far southwest (Abridge[54]). That is, "fast" /ai/ diphthongs are a distinctively East Anglian feature (as can be heard on the Norfolk and Suffolk recordings associated with Texts 4 and 11 in Chapter 11).

Kurath & McDavid also show very clearly that /h/-retention in *hammer, harrow, heard, hearth, hoarse* is distinctively East Anglian: their Fig. 32 (p. 33) shows /h/ for all the Norfolk and Suffolk localities, Cambridgeshire except Kingston, and Essex except Abridge. (Note that the Cambridgeshire Texts 11 and 12 in Chapter 7 show evidence of variable h-dropping.)

2.5.1.1 Northern vs Southern East Anglia

We have referred a number of times above to north-south differences within East Anglia, with the boundary between the two not necessarily coinciding with the Norfolk–Suffolk border. Lowman's materials now enable us to show approximately where the dividing line runs as far as mid-20th century dialects are concerned.

North-south differences which emerge from Lowman records include the following:

1. *The* LOT VOWEL
Unrounded [ɑ] occurs in the north versus rounded [ɒ] to the south. Lowman has the unrounded vowel in Norfolk, and in Ilketshall, northeast Suffolk, about

---

53 But see the notes to the Cambridgeshire Text given as 11 in Chapter 7.
54 Abridge is now situated inside the M25 London Orbital Motorway.

4 miles south of the Norfolk border, but the rounded vowel elsewhere in Suffolk as well as in Essex. The Norfolk North Elmham and (north) Suffolk Tuddenham recordings in Chapter 7 demonstrate this unrounded variant, as does the Cambridgeshire Little Downham speaker.

2. Yod-dropping

Yod-dropping, i.e. [ʉː] rather than [jʉː], occurs in *new, Tuesday, beautiful* in Norfolk and in Ilketshall, as opposed to [ɪʉ] in the rest of Suffolk and in Essex.

3. *Middle English long open ę*

Items such as *bean, wheat, greasy* have /eː/ rather than /iː/ in the north, i.e. in Norfolk and Ilketshall but also in Honington, northwest Suffolk, about 5 miles south of the Norfolk border. Elsewhere in Suffolk and in Essex the vowel is /iː/. Note that the Little Downham (Cambridgeshire) recording in Chapter 7 also has one instance of /eː/.

As we shall see further in 2.6, northern linguistic East Anglia continues to the present day to include the valley of the River Waveney and northeastern Suffolk.

2.5.2 *Morphology and lexis*

Viereck (1975) and Viereck (1980) use Lowman's 1930s data for a study of the regional distribution of morphological and lexical features in southern England. Viereck writes (1980: 31):

> The east can be subdivided into three areas, some of which can be delimited more neatly than others. The northern area includes the east of Warwickshire, Northamptonshire, Leicestershire, Rutland and Lincolnshire. . . .Huntingdon, Bedford and Cambridgeshire are also a transition area, most linked with the northern area just described, at least with regard to morphology.

He then continues:

> The second area to be distinguished stands out most clearly in the east – both lexically and morphologically: namely East Anglia. However, this region is much more uniform morphologically than lexically. With regard to the vocabulary, Norfolk can be further subdivided.

Finally:

> The third area that can be distinguished in the east is the eastern central region, with the Home Counties as its focus. Morphologically this area is also quite

uniform. Lexically, however, the eastern central counties are more often linked with Cambridgeshire, Bedford and Huntingdon than is the case with morphology. Furthermore, the whole of Essex is set off lexically, whereas morphologically only the northern part of the county is, being closely linked with East Anglia.

We shall look at lexis further in Chapter 5, but one interesting East Anglian morphological feature which is portrayed in Viereck (1975: Karte 175) is that there is clear regional differentiation between eastern areas which have the possessive pronouns *yours, his, hers, ours, theirs* and areas further west with *yourn, hisn, hern, ourn, theirn*. The eastern *theirs*-type forms are found in Lowman's records all over Norfolk and Suffolk, in Essex except for Abridge, and in eastern Cambridgeshire. The *theirn*-type forms are found in Lincolnshire, Northamptonshire, Huntingdonshire, Bedfordshire, Hertfordshire, and western Cambridgeshire (see the transcript of the west Cambridgeshire Text 13, Chapter 11).

Viereck (1975: Karte 60) also maps the distribution of forms with third-person singular present-tense *-s* as opposed to zero. This shows that Loman recorded *she rinse the dishes* in Norfolk, Suffolk and eastern Cambridgeshire, as against *she rinses the dishes* in western Cambridgeshire and Essex (once again, we must note, however, that Lowman did not visit northeastern Essex).

2.6 East Anglia as a modern dialect area: the 1950s

Fieldwork for the *Survey of English Dialects* (SED), as already noted, was carried out from the University of Leeds between 1950 and 1961. Of the areas which are or might be relevant to the study of the specific linguistic traits that are typical of East Anglia, there were 13 Norfolk localities which were investigated by the American linguist W. Nelson Francis between November 1956 and June 1957. In Suffolk, 5 localities were visited by Stanley Ellis[55] between August 1958 and September 1959. There were 15 localities in Essex, investigated by various workers from April 1952 to January 1962. There were unfortunately only 2 localities in Cambridgeshire and 2 in Huntingdonshire, all investigated by Ellis between March 1957 and June 1958. Bedfordshire had 3 SED localities, visited by Ellis January-March 1958. And there were 3 localities in Hertfordshire, two investigated by Ellis in 1958 and one by Marie Haslam in 1954. The two southernmost Lincolnshire localities bordering on Cambridgeshire and Norfolk,

---

[55] Stanley Ellis (1926–2009) was the main SED fieldworker, and was widely considered to be the best of them.

Lutton and Crowland, were investigated by Ellis in October 1951 and May 1953 respectively.

Phonological and morphological data from the publications of the SED were used by Trudgill (2001) in the most recent attempt to establish the extent of East Anglia as a linguistic area, which I now revise and update here. The particular geography of eastern England means that, however we are going to define linguistic East Anglia, we can be sure that it will be bounded on the north and east by the North Sea, and on the northwest by The Wash. Only to the west and south will it be bounded by other areas of terrestrial England. We are thus in the fortunate position of being able to assume that it is likely to be the case, even if not inevitably so, that those linguistic features which are most interesting and helpful for use as defining characteristics of East Anglia will lie among those which are to be found in that part of the region which is geographically furthest away from the rest of England and is therefore likely to be most prototypically East Anglian, namely northeastern Norfolk.

The SED records still show the major dialect boundary which separates southern from northern England as a line passing through Northamptonshire and meeting the sea between Lincolnshire and Norfolk: Britain (2014; 2015) gives further detailed insights into the current situation, and shows that that boundary has remained remarkably stable over the centuries. But this degree of dialect-boundary stability has not been replicated at the western and southern edges of modern East Anglia; and the further one moves away from northeastern Norfolk, the less East Anglian the English of the area becomes.

Trudgill (2001) cites the following features, many of which we have already mentioned above, as being most helpful in characterising East Anglian English on the basis of the SED materials:

1. *Third-person singular zero*
We saw above that, in the Middle English period, *-t* was the typical distinctive ending for third-person singular present tense indicative verb forms in East Anglia. Modern East Anglian dialects, on the other hand, typically have zero-marking for all persons of the verb in the indicative present tense: *he go, she come, that say.* Map 2.3 shows the extent of zero-marking on third-person present-tense verb forms (to the east of the dotted line) on the basis of the SED data. But because the SED investigated so few localities in Cambridgeshire, the map also includes data from

the pioneering dialect research into Cambridgeshire localities by Vasko (2010).[56] The map shows that third-person zero is found in all of Norfolk and Suffolk, plus all of Cambridgeshire except the far west and far south, and in northeastern Essex.

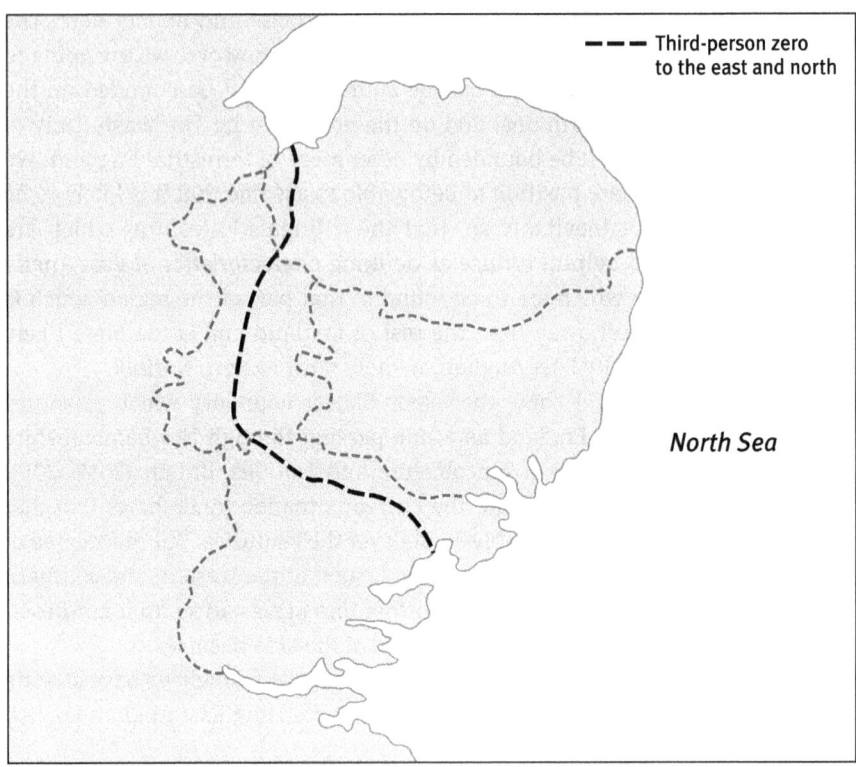

Map 2.3: Third-person singular zero.

2. H-dropping

The traditional dialects of northeastern Norfolk do not have h-dropping. The SED materials show that the absence of h-dropping is found over an extensive area which is rather similar to the third-person singular zero area. However, it also includes Outwell in the Norfolk Fens – h-dropping is infrequent in the

---

[56] Map 2.3 has been corrected from the version published in Trudgill (2001) to incorporate Vasko's Cambridgeshire data.

East Anglian Fens generally[57] – and extends much further south into central Essex.

H-dropping is of course an innovation, and so absence of h-dropping is a conservative feature. It is no surprise, therefore, to see from Ellis's records (Maguire, 2012) that in the 19th century, /h/-retention extended to all of Cambridgeshire, to the far south of Lincolnshire, and to Essex right down as far as the Thames and beyond, on into parts of Kent (see more on this in section 8.2 and Map 8.2).

Like the other phonological features presented here, this feature will be discussed further in 3.2.2.

3. The NURSE vowel

Traditional dialect of northeastern Norfolk has a vowel which is absent from most other varieties of English (see 3.2.1.1). As noted by Lowman, this is the short central open central /ɐ~ʌ/ which occurs in items such as *third, church, first*. According to the SED materials, it is found throughout East Anglia including northern Essex and southern Cambridgeshire, except that it is absent from the Norfolk and Cambridgeshire Fens. It also extends into eastern Bedfordshire (see Map 2.4).

4. The 'East Anglian short o'

In the Traditional East Anglian dialects there is a strong tendency for the /u:/ descended from Middle English ō to be shortened to /ʊ/ in closed syllables (see further Chapter 3). Thus *road* rhymes with *good*, and we find pronunciations such as in *both, toad, home, stone, coat* /bʊθ. tʊd, hʊm, stʊn, kʊt/. The SED materials show this form in all of Norfolk and Suffolk except the Fens, in southern Cambridgeshire, and in northeastern Essex extending as far south as the Dengie peninsula. It is especially interesting to note that the form also extends as far as Therfield in northeastern Hertfordshire, just south of Royston (see Map 2.4).

---

[57] David Britain (p.c.).

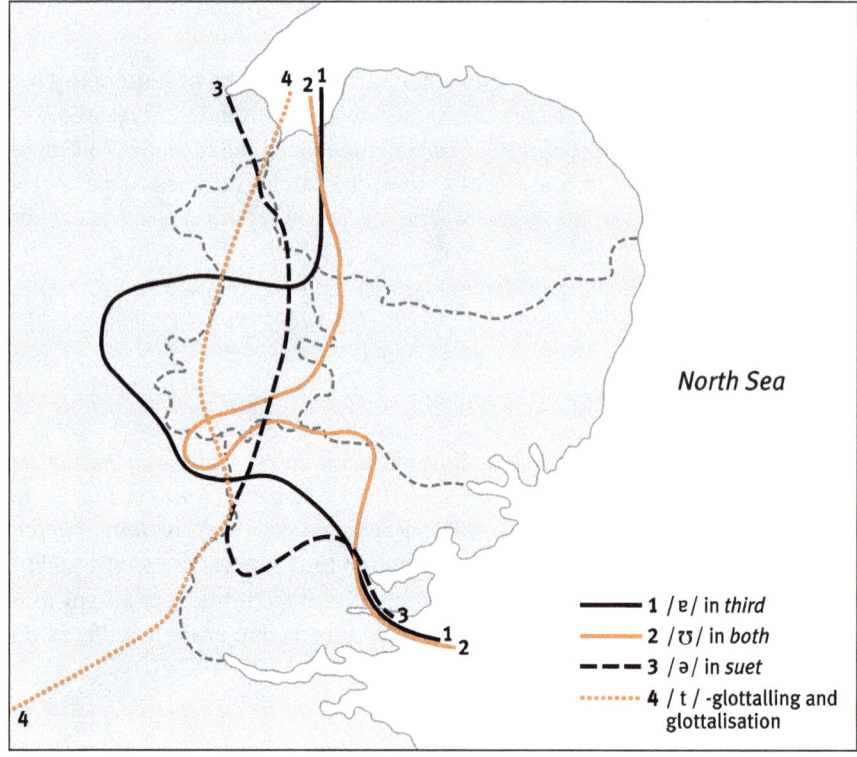

Map 2.4: Four features.

5. *The START/BATH/PALM vowel*

The vowel /aː/ in its most local realisations is a very front vowel approaching the cardinal 4 vowel /aː/.[58] This feature, which is apparent in all the recordings linked to Chapter 7, serves to mark off the southern limit of East Anglia from the point where it meets the back vowel [ɑː] of the Home Counties. The demarcation line runs from the River Crouch on the Essex coast more or less due west (see Map 2.5).

---

[58] As I have written elsewhere (Trudgill, 1982), the SED Norfolk records for this feature are incorrect, showing a back vowel instead of the front vowel which in fact occurs throughout the county.

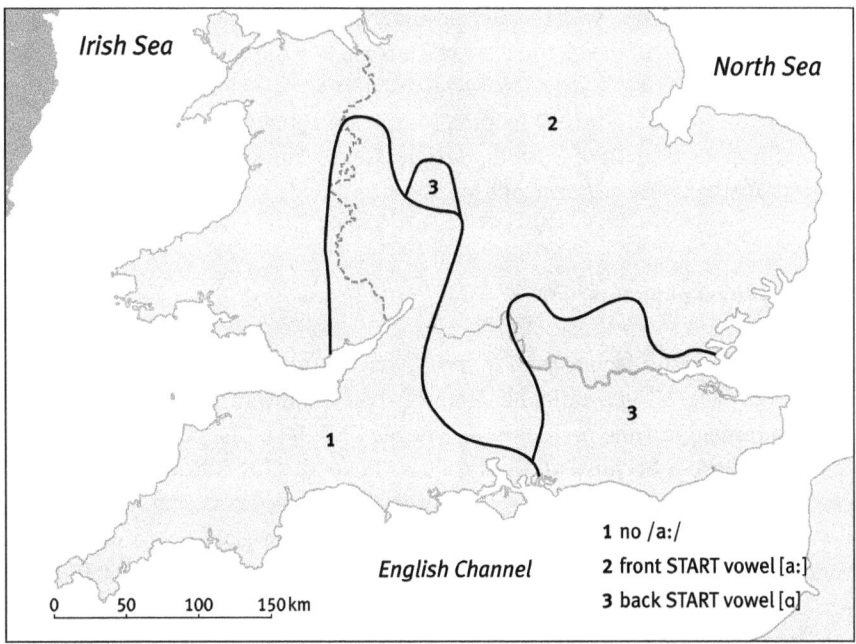

Map 2.5: The START vowel.

6. *The Weak Vowel Merger*

The Weak Vowel Merger, as it was helpfully labelled by Wells (1982), is the phenomenon which has occurred in those accents of English which have schwa rather than the KIT vowel in unstressed syllables in words such as *wanted, horses, naked, David*. In accents of this type, *roses* and *Rosa's*, and *Lenin* and *Lennon*, are pronounced identically. Areas where this merger have occurred include East Anglia: the boundaries of the occurrence of /ə/ in the word *suet* in the east of England are shown in Maps 2.4 and 8.2, derived from the SED materials.[59] Note that the merger also occurs in the southeastern Lincolnshire Fenland locality of Lutton.

7. /p, t, k/

Intervocalic and word-final /p, k/ are most usually glottalised in northeastern East Anglia. This is most audible in intervocalic position, where there is simultaneous

---

[59] Little Downham is not shown with schwa in *suet* in the SED Basic Materials, but the recording clearly shows that the speaker does have the merger.

oral and glottal closure, with the oral closure then being released inaudibly prior to the audible release of the glottal closure, thus *paper* [pæipʔə], *baker* [bæik̠ʔə]. This also occurs in the case of /t/, as in *later* [læit̬ʔə], but just as frequently t-glottalling occurs here: [læiʔə]. The SED records for the area show that glottalisation and t-glottaling occur in all of Norfolk, Suffolk, Cambridgeshire and Essex, but not in areas further west or north (see Maps 2.4 and 8.8).

2.6.1 The overall picture

Map 2.6 shows the isoglosses for the seven diagnostic features just outlined combined. Map 2.7 is a rationalisation of this. It shows the East Anglian core and the transition zone periphery, as per the SED data. The core area, which is free of isoglosses because all the localities have all of the diagnostic features, consists of Norfolk and Suffolk (except for the Fens), eastern Cambridgeshire, and northeastern Essex. The transition zone, which all the isoglosses run through, contains the localities which have between two and six of the diagnostic features, and consists of the Norfolk and Suffolk Fens including Emneth, Upwell, West Walton, Walpole St Andrew, Walpole St Peter, and Outwell, western and southern Cambridgeshire, and northeastern Hertfordshire. One locality in southeastern Lincolnshire, and one in eastern Bedfordshire, have only one of the diagnostic features each, and these have not been included in the transition zone. Neither of the two Huntingdonshire SED localities had any of the diagnostic features, although Huntingdonshire does have some other East Anglian features, as we shall see in the discussion of the texts presented in Chapter 7.

Some further phonological details about the transitional nature of the Fenland sub-area, showing differences between the western zone (e.g. Spalding), the central zone (e.g. Wisbech), and the eastern zone (e.g. Ely), are provided by David Britain (Britain, 2001; Britain & Trudgill, 2005) as follows:

Lexical set	Western Fens	Central Fens	Eastern Fens
STRUT	[ʊ]	[ɣ]	[ʌ]
one	[ɒ]	[ɣ]	[ʌ]
BATH	[a]	[aː]	[aː]
MOUTH	[ɛː]	[ɛː]	[ɛu]
GOAT	[ʌu – ɐu]	[ʌu – ɐu]	[ʊu]
hill	Ø	[h]	[h]
*buy*ING	[ɪn]	[ən ~ɪn]	[ən]
take/make	[tɛk/mɛk]	[tæik/mæik]	[tæik/mæik]

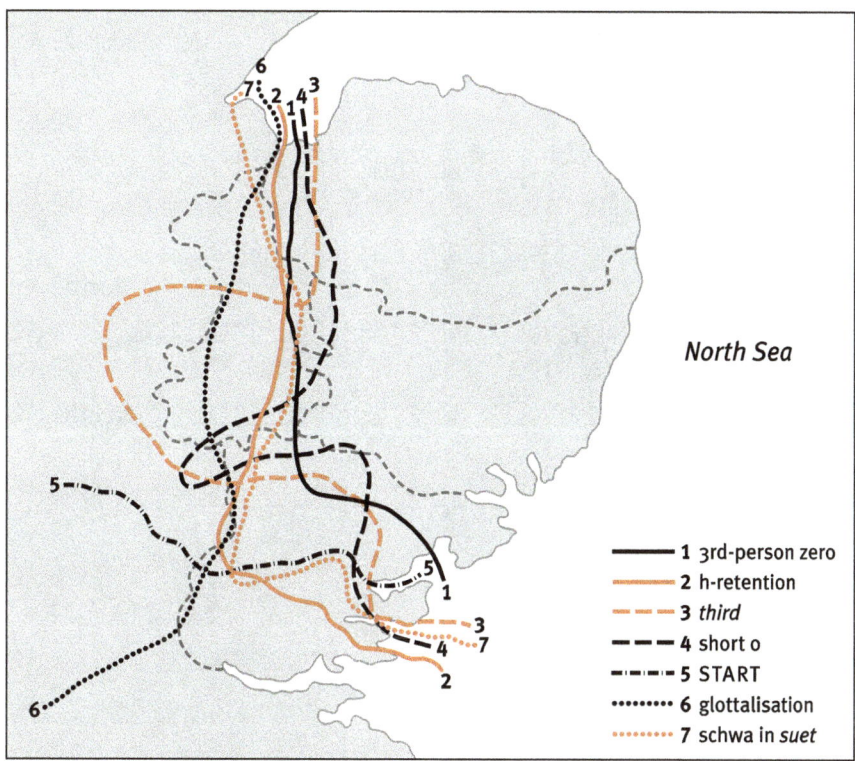

Map 2.6: Isoglosses Combined.

As already noted a number of times, the core East Anglia area can also be divided into northern and southern sub-zones, continuing a pattern which appears to have survived from Old English times, and maybe even longer than that. Map 2.7 also shows this north-south divide (as derived from Lowman's data) superimposed on the core area which we have just established. It can be seen that the northern zone consists of non-Fenland Norfolk plus the Waveney Valley and northeastern Suffolk (including Ilketshall); the southern zone includes the rest of Suffolk, eastern Cambridgeshire, and northeastern Essex. Of the major urban areas, King's Lynn, Norwich, Yarmouth and Lowestoft fall into the northern zone, while Ipswich, Bury St Edmunds and Colchester come into the southern zone. In many respects, the northern zone represents the area dominated by Norwich, and the southern zone the area dominated by Ipswich: people in northeastern Suffolk tend to look to Norwich rather than Ipswich as their local urban centre; and many of them support the major Norfolk football team, Norwich City, rather than Suffolk's Ipswich Town.

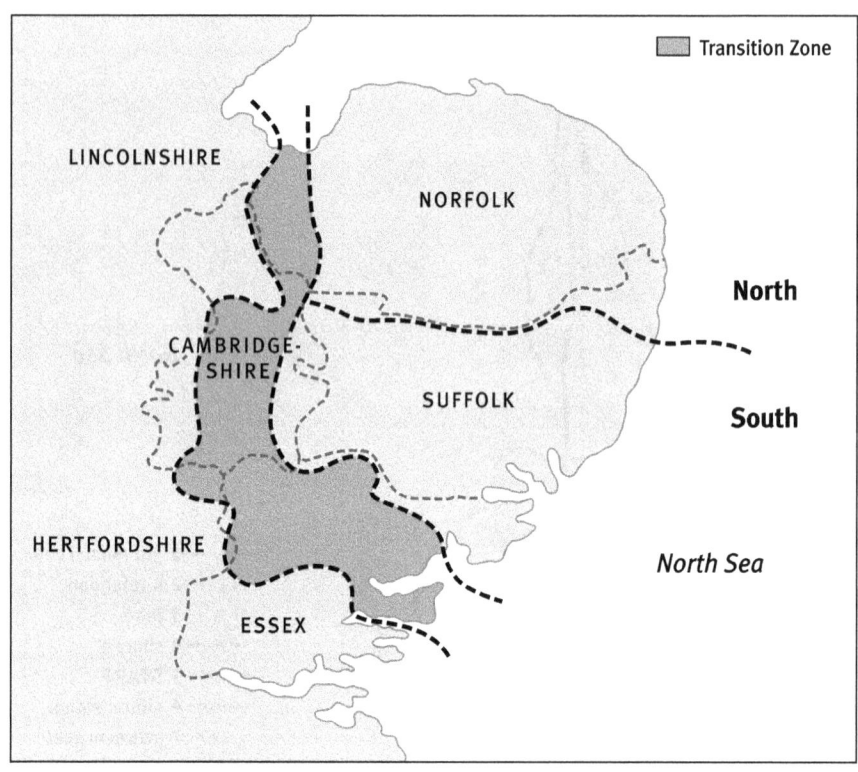

Map 2.7: Linguistic East Anglia.

3 East Anglian phonology

In the following discussion of the phonology of the dialects of East Anglia, I will be making use of knowledge gained from personal observations made over a period of more than fifty years of local dialect speakers, including some born as long ago as the 1870s, as well as from local dialect literature (see Chapter 7). I am also a native speaker of the northern variety of East Anglian English myself.

There will be frequent reference, too, to the three major surveys cited in Chapter 2:
1. Ellis (1889).
2. Kurath & Lowman (1961) – supplemented by Lowman's actual field records for Norfolk, copies of which were very kindly made available to me in the 1960s by the late Professor Raven I. McDavid.
3. *The Survey of English Dialects* (SED) – including the unpublished detailed notes made in Norfolk by the fieldworker Professor W. Nelson Francis, which were very kindly made available to me in the 1960s by the Survey. Anderson's (1987) atlas is one of a number of useful sources for these materials.

There will also be reference in this chapter to three monographs. *The vocabulary of East Anglia* by the Rev. Robert Forby (1732?-1825), as mentioned in Chapter 2, was originally published posthumously in 1830, and was intended to be a description of the East Anglian dialect as spoken in the period 1780–1800. Helge Kökeritz's Uppsala University dissertation (1932), *The phonology of the Suffolk dialect*, was based on fieldwork which he carried out between 1925 and 1930, mostly in east Suffolk[60] but also in two west Suffolk locations which, however, he did not use for his research.[61] And *The social differentiation of English in Norwich* (Trudgill 1974) was the published version of my 1971 Edinburgh University PhD thesis which was based on fieldwork carried out in the city of Norwich in 1968.

I will also be referring to the "Foxcroft-Trudgill Survey", which involved fieldwork carried out by Tina Foxcroft in the period 1975–7, in which recordings were made of casual speech from speakers in 21 towns (see Map 8.9) in the English counties of Norfolk, Suffolk, and Essex, involving 348 individual speakers.[62]

---

[60] Boyton, Woodbridge, Ipswich, Sutton, Shottisham, Bawdsey, Halesworth, Stradbroke, Southwold, Fressingfield, Chediston.
[61] Icklingham, Clare.
[62] This research was financed by a grant from the UK Social Science Research Council. The urban centres investigated were: Kings Lynn, Dereham, Cromer, Yarmouth, Thetford (Norfolk); Lowestoft, Stowmarket, Ipswich, Woodbridge, Hadleigh, Haverhill, Bury St Edmunds, Sudbury,

Throughout this book I also make frequent reference to the *English Dialect Dictionary* (EDD), which was published by Oxford University Press between 1898 and 1905. It was compiled under the direction of Joseph Wright, and is a remarkable record of 19th century English dialects. It has about 70,000 entries.

3.1 Stress and rhythm

East Anglian dialects are peculiarly, even if not uniquely, prone to phonetic reduction and erosion, with a number of rhythmic phonological characteristics of the dialect illustrating this susceptibility. These are:
1. Stressed syllables tend to be longer and more heavily stressed than in many other dialects.
2. Unstressed syllables are correspondingly shorter, with reduction of most vowels to schwa.
3. Non-utterance-final schwa tends to disappear.

Note the following illustrative examples:

Forty-two	[fɔ::ʔ: tʉː]
What, are you on holiday?	[wɑːʔ jɑn hɑːldə]?
Half past eight	[hɑ::ps æiʔ]
Have you got any coats?	[hæːjə gɑʔ nə kʊʔs]?
Shall I?	[ʃæːlə]?

This is due to the fact that the phonology of the core area of East Anglia is characterised by extreme stress-timedness, a phenomenon which I have previously referred to several times impressionistically (e.g. Trudgill, 1974; Trudgill, 1999; Trudgill, 2004). As Schiering (2006: 5) has pointed out, "stress-based phonologies show a strong erosive force in reducing and deleting unstressed syllables", as opposed to languages with mora-based or syllable-based phonologies. It is stress-based languages which show a significantly higher degree of phonetic erosion than the others (Schiering, 2010) – and it turns out that some such languages are even more stressed-based than others: "stressed-based" is a feature which admits of degrees of more or less.

Felixstowe (Suffolk); Colchester, Wivenhoe, Harwich, Walton-on-the-Naze, West Mersea, Dedham, Clacton (Essex).

My original impressionistic observations concerning the highly stress-based nature of the East Anglian dialect have subsequently received strong instrumental phonetic confirmation from the work of Ferragne & Pellegrino (2004), which uses data from speakers of fourteen British Isles varieties, including the northern East Anglian dialect of Lowestoft. Through measurements of vowel duration, Ferragne & Pellegrino show that East Anglian English is the most stress-timed of all the fourteen dialects which they investigated.

Elsewhere (2007: 1513) they note how the "comparatively great duration differences between stressed and unstressed vowels" in East Anglian English "is confirmed in a study on the rhythm of British dialects: on the vocalic PVI [Pairwise Variability Index] dimension, East Anglian falls at the most stress-timed end of a continuum". Figure 3.1, from Ferragne & Pellegrino (2007), shows that the Lowestoft dialect ("ean") has the largest ratio of length of stressed to unstressed syllables of all the 14 accents compared. It can be seen that in contrast the accent with the smallest ratio, i.e. the one which is most like a syllable-timed language, is Glaswegian ("gla").

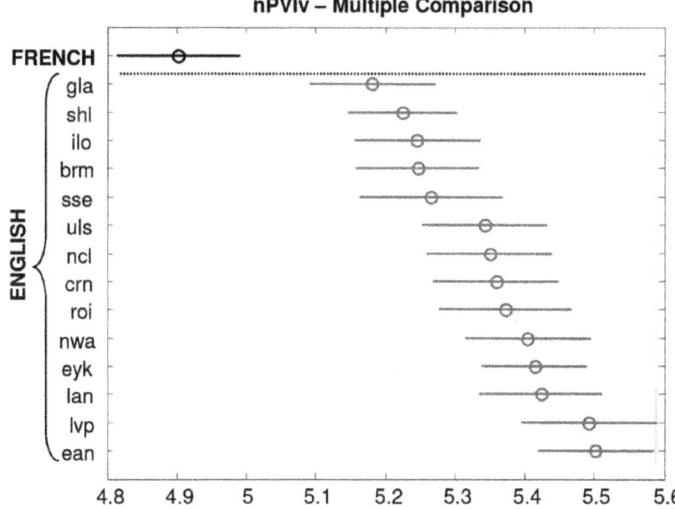

East Anglian English also has some distinctive intonation patterns. Intonation in yes-no questions is particularly noticeable. These questions begin on a low-level tone followed by high-level tone on the stressed syllable and subsequent syllables:

[wɑʔ   jɑn   hɑ▾l də]?
  ‾   ‾   ‾   ‾

"What, are you on holi day?"

3.2 Segmental phonology

The segmental phonology of East Anglia is in broad outline the same as that of the accents of the south-east of England generally. As we saw in 2.4, the accent of the region is basically non-rhotic (though see 3.2.2), which distinguishes it from the English southwest; and it has the FOOT-STRUT split, marking it off from the Midlands and North.

3.2.1 Vowels

3.2.1.1 Short vowels

The system of short, checked vowels in modern East Anglia is the usual south-of-England six vowel system involving the lexical sets of KIT, DRESS, TRAP, FOOT, STRUT, LOT. In the traditional dialect, however, there is an additional vowel in this system associated with the lexical set of NURSE.

KIT

The phonetic realisation of this vowel in the modern dialect is the same as in RP. Older speakers may have a closer realisation, nearer to but not as close as [i]. However, one of the most interesting features of the older East Anglian short vowel system is that, unlike in most other varieties, /ɪ/ does not occur at all in unstressed syllables. As reported in section 2.6, in the discussion there of the Weak-Vowel Merger (see Maps 2.4 and 8.2), unstressed /ə/ continues to be the norm to this day in words such as *wanted, horses, David, rabbit, naked, splendid, morbid*. Potter (2018) shows that the Weak-Vowel Merger currently survives very strongly in the speech of younger people in Ipswich, Woodbridge and Wickham Market in eastern Suffolk (see 8.4).

In the traditional dialect, moreover, /ə/ is the only vowel which can occur in any unstressed syllable. This is true not only in the case of word-final syllables in words such as *water, butter*, which also have /ə/ in RP; and in words such as *window, barrow*, which are pronounced /wɪndə, baerə/ as in very many other forms of English around the world; but also in items such as *very, money, city*, which are /vɛrə, mʌnə, sɪtə/. In the modern dialect, though, dedialectalisation has taken place to the extent that words from the *very* set are now pronounced with final /ɪ/ by older speakers and /iː/ by younger speakers, as is now usual throughout southern England.

Lexical incidence
In the traditional dialect, the KIT vowel occurs not only in items such as *pit, bid* but also in a number of other words, such as *get, yet, head, again*. There is little predictability as to which items have the raised vowel, but in all the words concerned the vowel is followed by alveolar /n/, /t/ or /d/.[63] This was a feature which also occurs, or occurred, in many other areas of southeastern England (see Wyld, 1953).

There is, however, no trace of the Middle English pronunciation of words such as *will, did, which, hidden* with /ɛ/ which we noted in Chapter 2.

DRESS
The vowel /ɛ/ in the traditional dialect is a rather close vowel approaching [e]. During the course of the 20th century, it gradually opened until it is now much closer to [ɛ] in modern speech. In Norwich, it is now also retracted before /l/, and in the most modern accent it has merged with /ʌ/ in this context, i.e. *hell* and *hull* are identical (Trudgill 1972, 1974, 1988).

In older forms of the East Anglian dialect, /ɛ/ occurs not only in the expected *bet, help, bed*, etc., but also in a number of items which elsewhere have /æ/, such as *catch* and *have/has/had*.

In the traditional dialect areas of northern East Anglia, /ɛ/ has also become /æ/ before the front voiced fricatives /v/ and /ð/, as in *never* /nævə/, *together* /təgæðə/, *devil* (see Text 7 in Chapter 7).

TRAP
The vowel /æ/ appears to have undergone a very considerable amount of phonetic change over the last century and a half. For older speakers who have DRESS as [e], /æ/ is closer to [ɛ], while in the modern dialect it is a good deal more open.

Before velar consonants, diphthongisation may occur, as for example in Norwich *back* [bæɛkʔ] (Trudgill 1974), and as [æɪ] in *bag, tag* in some of the SED Norfolk and Essex localities.[64]

FOOT
The FOOT vowel /ʊ/ has recently developed an increasingly unrounded pronunciation in the speech of younger speakers, as in very many other places around the English-speaking world (see Trudgill, 2003), but has traditionally always been [ʊ] in East Anglia.

---

[63] A number of examples are pointed out in the notes to the texts in Chapter 7.
[64] For more on TRAP, see also *An alternative analysis of TRAP and LOT* below.

The vowel, however, is more frequent in the East Anglian dialect than in southern English English generally, mostly because of the phenomenon of the 'East Anglian short *o*', meaning that /ʊ/ occurs in certain items from the lexical set of GOAT.

The 'East Anglian short o'
The vowel labelled the GOAT vowel by Wells (1982) has maintained two counterparts in the vowel system of East Anglia, with Middle English ǭ and ou remaining distinct to this day in the dialects of at least northern East Anglia. The distinction is between the /uː/ = [ʊu] descended from ǭ, as in *moan*, and the /ʌu/ = [ɐu], descended from ME ou, as in *mown* (see more on this under GOAT). However, as we saw in Chapter 2 (see Map 2.6), there has been a strong tendency in East Anglia for the /uː/ descended from Middle English ǭ = /ɔː/ to be shortened to /ʊ/ in closed syllables. Thus *road* can rhyme with *hood*; and *toad, home, stone, coat* can occur as /tʊd, hʊm, stʊn, kʊt/.

Kökeritz (1932) lists the following items as having the same vowel as *pull* in his Suffolk localities:

> *boast, boat, bone, choke, cloak, clover, coach, coast, coat, don't,*
> *folk, goat, hole, home, hope, load, loaf, moat, most, oak, oath, oats,*
> *over, poach, pole, post, road, rope, smoke, stone, toad, whole,*
> *wholly.*

Lowman's records (see Trudgill 1974) also show a large number of examples of the 'short *o*', although transcriptions such as [stɒn] *stone* make it unclear as to whether he regards such words as having a vowel identical to that of FOOT. Words in his records that have the 'short *o*' are:

> *froze, posts, comb, bone, oats, whole, home, boat, stone, yolk,*
> *poached, hotel, ghosts, don't, won't, woke, wrote, over, toad.*

The usage of 'short *o*' in East Anglia seems to have been in decline by the 1950s, as revealed by the *Survey of English Dialect* records, which show only the following items with a short vowel in the Norfolk localities:

> *both, broke, comb, road, spoke, stone, throat, whole.*

In his 1957 field notes, Francis mentions the occurrence of short forms, and writes of Pulham, Norfolk: "Evidence of shortened lax forms, apparently much more prevalent in the dialect 50–75 years ago, was rather plentiful in the speech . . . of the oldest informant; thus [ɹʊd, stʊn, kʊm, spʊk, tɹʊt] [= *road, stone, comb, spoke, throat*]."

The SED records also show instances of the 'short *o*' in e.g. *both* in northern Hertfordshire

Trudgill (1974) showed that by 1968 it was only the working class for whom the 'short *o*' was a strongly characteristic feature of the urban dialect of Norwich. Items on my fieldwork tapes which have this feature are:

aerodrome, alone, bloke, both, broke, Close, coats, comb, combed, don't, drove, Holmes, home, most, notice, only, over, photo, post, road, spoke, stone, suppose, whole, woke, won't.

And note that even the lower working class used only 42% of possible forms with 'short *o*', which suggests that this had now become something of a relic form. This is stressed by the fact that this figure is largely made up of a relatively small number of common lexical items, notably *don't, home, suppose, only*. On the other hand, the shortening process has clearly been a productive one – witness *photo* in the list from 1968 – suggesting that knowledge of the stylistic relationship between /uː/ and /ʊ/ has continued to be part of the competence of local speakers. In addition to the 60+ items just listed with 'short *o*', I can cite from my own experience the fact that until the 1960s Norwich had a theatre known as *The Hippodrome* /hɪpədrʊm/, and that trade names such as *Kodachrome* could also be heard with pronunciations such as /kʊdəkrʊm/. The feature survives particularly strongly in *home* /(h)ʊm/.[65]

The 'East Anglian short *o*' is a feature of some antiquity. Writing about the dialect as spoken in the late 1700s, Forby (1970: 90) says:

The long o ... has also in some words the common short sound of the diphthong[66] oo (in foot), or that of the vowel u in pull: Ex. Bone–stone–whole.

The longevity of this feature is almost certainly also signalled by the fact that 'short *o*' occurs in the dialects of Eastern New England (Kurath & McDavid, 1961), and was therefore very probably transported there from East Anglia during the 1600s and early 1700s (see 6.2).

The FOOT vowel also occurs in *roof, hoof, proof, room, broom*.

STRUT

According to Britain (2015), the traditional dialect of Peterborough does not have the FOOT-STRUT split, as discussed in Chapter 2. On the other hand, rural Fenland

---

65 I still have *home, suppose, aerodrome, Holmes* with the FOOT vowel in my own speech.
66 By "diphthong" Forby simply means that the vowel is represented by a sequence of two letters <oo>.

West Norfolk, focussing on King's Lynn and Downham Market, together with the eastern Cambridgeshire Fens around Ely and Littleport, have the fully-fledged southern system with the FOOT-STRUT split; while Wisbech, Chatteris and March form a transitional Fenland zone where the split is variable.

This is a geographical reflection of the well-known fact that, as we saw in Chapter 2, the STRUT vowel is a recent arrival in the phonological inventory of English. In the late 1500s, the vowel /ʊ/ began to lose its lip-rounding in the southeast of England in some phonological and lexical environments, giving [ɣ]. Subsequently it lowered to the back vowel cardinal [ʌ] – Gimson (1962: 103) postulates this "for the eighteenth century" – eventually producing a phonemic split between the vowels of e.g. *put* and *but*. And then by the beginning of the 20th century, a vowel a little to the front of [ʌ] seems to have been the RP norm. During the course of the 20th century it then fronted to central [ɐ], which is the pronunciation in RP today (see Roach, 1983: 16).[67] In the English of London and other parts of the southeast, however, the fronting has progressed further, giving "an open front vowel very close to cardinal [a]" (Gimson, 1962: 103). This diachronic pattern is reflected in a synchronic geographical pattern: the further one goes away from the English southeast, the further the vowel quality is located back along the trajectory the vowel has followed over the last 500 years (see Figure 3.1; and see more on this in 8.2). The phonemic distinction involved in the split is of course only lost when the vowel qualities of the two lexical sets of FOOT and STRUT completely coincide.

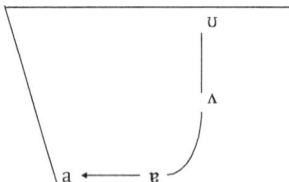

Figure 3.1: The trajectory of the STRUT vowel.

LOT

Wells (1982: 130) writes: "in Britain the predominant type of vowel in LOT is back and rounded". However, he goes on to add that we also find "the recessive unrounded variant [ɑ] in parts of the south of England remote from London". He

---

67 The practice continues, however, of writing /ʌ/ to symbolise this vowel phonemically.

further indicates (p. 347) that the vowel "often appears to be unrounded in the west [of England], being qualitatively [ɑ], much as in the Irish Republic or in the United States". The modern Southern Hemisphere Englishes typically have a rounded vowel in this lexical set. However, some Falkland Islands English speakers do have unrounded realisations; and unrounded /ɒ/ in LOT = [ɑ] is very common in the data from the *Origins of New Zealand English* project recordings of New Zealanders born in the 19th century (Trudgill, 2004): 47% of the informants use an unrounded LOT vowel either consistently or variably, which suggests that unrounded LOT was much more common in Britain in the 1800s than it is today.

Wells also says (1982: 339) that "in Norfolk the LOT vowel has an unrounded variant". This unrounded vowel must have been a distinctive feature of northern East Anglian English for some considerable time because Ihalainen (1994: 226) writes that "the term 'Norwich *a*' refers to the unrounding of the vowel in words like *top* . . . . It is one of the features exploited by Larwood in his 'Norfolk dialogue' (1800)". Lowman's data for the 1930s (Kurath & Lowman, 1970: 22) coincide very well with Wells's suggestions, indicating unrounded vowels in most of the south of England apart from Suffolk, Essex, Cambridgeshire, Hertfordshire and Middlesex. This typical pattern of geographical diffusion, with the southeast and southwest of England forming areas with unrounded vowels which are separated from one another by an intervening area with rounded variants, including London, helps to confirm the Southern Hemisphere evidence suggesting that the [ɑ] area was much larger in the mid-19th century than it is now.

The East Anglian evidence, then, suggests a rather long-standing difference within East Anglia, with Norfolk having unrounded vowels, and Cambridge, Suffolk and Essex demonstrating rounded variants. Trudgill (1971, 1972, 1974) showed that the rounded variant was also becoming increasingly common in Norwich in the late 1960s.

Like TRAP, the LOT vowel can also be phonetically long: Lodge (2001: 211) cites examples such as *want* [wɒːnʔ] (for more on this, see *An alternative analysis of TRAP and LOT* in 3.2.1.3 below).

The lexical set associated with this vowel was formerly rather smaller than it currently is because, as in most of southern England, the lengthened vowel /ɔː/ was found before the front voiceless fricatives, as in *off, cloth, lost*. This feature still survives in East Anglia to a certain extent, but mostly in working-class speech, and particularly in the word *off*. Typically *dog* is also /dɔːg/. On the other hand, traditional dialect speakers also have LOT in *un-* and *under* rather than STRUT (see 2.2 for possible medieval antecedents of this). And as a result of early non-prevocalic /r/-loss before /s/ (as in *bust < burst*), *horse* often has the LOT vowel (this can be heard in the recording of Text 11 in Chapter 7). *Nothing* also has the LOT vowel: /nɒθn/.

Church

As we saw in 2.5 and 2.6, older forms of the dialect have an additional vowel in the short vowel sub-system which occurs in items from the set of NURSE. Forby (1830: 92) wrote about this vowel:

> To the syllable *ur* (and consequently to *ir* and *or*, which have often the same sound) we give a pronunciation certainly our own.
>
> Ex. *Third word burn curse*
>   *Bird curd dirt worse*
>
> It is one which can be neither intelligibly described, nor represented by other letters. It must be heard. Of all legitimate English sounds, it seems to come nearest to *open a*,[68] or rather to the rapid utterance of the *a* in the word *arrow*, supposing it to be caught before it light on the *r*... *Bahd* has been used to convey our sound of *bird*. Certainly this gets rid of the danger of *r*; but the *h* must as certainly be understood to lengthen the sound of *a*; which is quite inconsistent with our snap-short utterance of the syllable. In short it must be heard.

My own observations, particularly of older speakers, suggest that earlier forms of East Anglian English had a checked vowel system consisting of seven vowels. The additional vocalic item, which I represent as /ʌ/, was a short open vowel, slightly front of central, which occurred in the lexical set of *church, first*, i.e. in words which had Middle English *ir, ur* in closed syllables. In open syllables, only /aː/ occurs: *fur* /faː/, *sir* /saː/ (<far> and <sar> in the dialect literature – see for example Text 3 in Chapter 7).

Dialect literature generally spells words from the lexical set of *first, church* as either as <fust, chuch> or <fasst, chatch>. If we examine representations of words from the NURSE set in 20th-century dialect literature, we find the following (for details of the dialect literature involved, see Trudgill 1996):

	Dialect spelling
first	fust, fasst
worse	wuss
church	chuch, chatch
purpose	pappus
turnip	tannip
further	futher
hurl	hull
turkey	takkey

---

68 By which Forby means the vowel of *balm*.

turn	tann
hurting	hatten
nightshirt	niteshat
shirts	shats
girl	gal
dursent (=daren't)	dussen

The reason for this vacillation between <u> and <a> is that the vowel was in fact phonetically intermediate between /ʌ/ and /æ/. The existence of this additional vowel was not picked up on by Kökeritz (1932), who identified it with STRUT.

The SED records show that in the 1950s this short vowel was also found as far afield as southern Cambridgeshire, northern Essex, Bedfordshire, and eastern Hertfordshire, for example in *first, third, Thursday*.

During the last fifty years, this short /ᴀ/ vowel has more or less disappeared from urban speech. In my 1968 study of Norwich (Trudgill 1974), /ᴀ/ was recorded a number of times, but the overwhelming majority of words from the relevant lexical set had the originally alien vowel /ɜː/. Only in lower working-class speech was /ᴀ/ at all common in 1968, and then only 25% of potential occurrences had the short vowel even in informal speech. Interestingly, the vowel did not occur at all in my 1983 corpus (Trudgill 1988).

Summary

The older short-vowel system of East Anglian English was thus:

/ɪ/ *kit, get*	/ʊ/ *foot, goat, home, roof*
/e/ *dress, catch*	/ʌ/ *strut*
/ɛ/ *trap* /ᴀ/ *church*	/ɑ/ *top, under*

The newer short vowel system is as follows:

/ɪ/ *kit*	/ʊ/ *foot, home, roof*
/ɛ/ *dress, get*	/ʌ/ *strut, under*
/æ/ *trap, catch*	/ɑ/ *top*[69]

---

[69] With /ɒ/ being the norm in the south and west of the region.

3.2.1.2 Upgliding diphthongs

In East Anglian English, it is a phonetic characteristic of all of the upgliding diphthongs – of which there is one more than in most accents of English – that, unlike in other south-of-England varieties, the second element is most usually a fully close vowel e.g. the FACE vowel is typically [æi] rather than [æɪ].

FLEECE

The /iː/ vowel is an upgliding diphthong of the type [ɪi], noticeably different from London [əi].

The modern East Anglian accent also demonstrates HAPPY-*tensing*, so that the FLEECE vowel occurs in the modern dialects in the lexical set of *money, city, party* etc. Speakers born before about 1920 had /iː/ in open syllables as in *party* but /ɪ/ in closed syllables as in *parties*. The traditional dialect had schwa: *city* /sɪtə/, *very* /vɛrə/ (see 3.1).[70]

Unstressed *they* has /iː/: *Are they coming?* /aːðiːkʌmn/.

In the traditional dialect of Suffolk, *mice* was /miːs/, as already noted; and *deaf* could be /diːf/ throughout East Anglia.

FACE

The most local modern pronunciation of /æi/ is [æi], but qualities intermediate between this and RP [eɪ] occur in middle-class speech (see Trudgill 1974).

In the traditional dialects of East Anglia, the front Long Mid Merger (Wells 1982: 192–194) has not taken place, so in these varieties the /æi/ diphthong occurs only in items descended from ME /ai/, while items descended from ME /aː/ have monophthongal /eː/ = [ẹː~ ɛː]. Thus pairs such as *days-daze, maid-made* are not homophonous (see Lodge, 2001). This distinction, which now survives – insofar as it survives at all – only in the northern area of East Anglia, is currently being lost through a process of transfer of lexical items from /eː/ to /æi/ (Trudgill & Foxcroft, 1978). The vowel /eː/, that is, is in the process of disappearing. Words that I recorded in Norwich in 1968 as having /eː/ included *face, gate, plate, take, make*.

For earlier decades, Kökeritz (1932) states that the Suffolk dialect "as spoken by elderly people clearly distinguishes between such words as *name* (pronounced with [eː]) and *nail* (pronounced with [æɪ, ɛɪ]) which in St.Eng. are

---

[70] For instance, Lady Wilhelmine Harrod, the Norfolk writer. and conservationist (see entry in the *Oxford Dictionary of National Biography*), was always known as "Billa" /bɪlə/. Men named William and James who elsewhere would have been called "Billy" and "Jimmy" were in East Anglia known as "Billa" and "Jimma".

pronounced alike". He also points out that this distinction, under the influence of RP and Cockney, is dying out, with younger people generalising the diphthong to both groups of items, as just noted. In Lowman's records, we find [æɨ] for all Norfolk and Suffolk localities in *eight, pail, they, way* and [e·ə] in *April, paper, lane, apron, bracelet, relations, make*. The distinction between the two sets is clear enough. However, Martlesham has the upgliding diphthong alternating with [e·ə], which is significantly labelled "older", in *apron, bracelet, relations, make*. The SED records show many examples of the distinction preserved, but also many more /æɪ/ from ME *ā* than in the pre-WWII records. Under Ludham (Norfolk), Francis writes of "several different variants, perhaps indicative of change" involving a merger with reflexes of ME *ai, ei*.

FACE in FLEECE items

The /eː/ vowel also occurred in the older dialect in a number of words descended from ME *ẹː*, such as *beans, creature* /kreːtə/. There are traces, quite substantial in the pre-WWII records, of a distinction between reflexes of ME *ẹː* as [iː] and ME *ę̣ː* as [eː, ɛː]. Reflexes of ME *ę̣ː* appear in some cases to have fallen in with reflexes of ME *aː*, and in others to have remained distinct. In the localities studied by Kökeritz, items of this type have the /eː/ of *name* if they do not have /iː/ It is also striking that Kökeritz records several instances of [eː] derived from ME *ē*, e.g. *deep* [deːp]. Lowman has the [e·ə] vowel in *grease* in four localities, including all three Norfolk localities; in *beast* in one Norfolk locality;| in *wheat* in both Norfolk localities which gave this item; and in two out of three Suffolk localities, in one of which it is labelled "older form". Francis states that ME *ẹː* and ME *ę̣ː* have fallen together in Ashwellthorpe but that informants were aware of older forms with /eː/ from ME *ę̣ː* and occasionally used them. The older form of the dialect, he says, appears to have had a three-way contrast:

ME *ę̣ː* > [eː] *bean*
ME *aː* > [ɛː] *name*
ME *ai* > [ɛi] *maid*

PRICE

There is considerable social and regional variation in East Anglian English in the articulation of the /ai/ vowel. As described in detail for Norwich in Trudgill (1974, 1988), the most typical realisation is [ɐi], but younger speakers are increasingly favouring a variant approaching [ɑi]. Both these variants are distinctively "fast diphthongs", as noted in 2.5.1 on the basis of the transcriptions of Guy Lowman, who was a truly excellent phonetician.

The occurrence of the newer [ɑi] variant perhaps explains why some more recent dialect writers have unfortunately adopted the practice, unknown until a few years ago, of writing <oi> to represent this vowel. This should not be interpreted as implying any kind of merger with the CHOICE vowel – there is no such merger in Norfolk. Amos (2011) did report that older speakers on Mersea Island in Essex have PRICE as [ɔi]. But this is still distinct from CHOICE, which has [ɵɪ]. Labov (1994) discovered that speakers in Tillingham, Essex, while they reported that pairs such as *line* and *loin* were identical, nevertheless did in fact keep them apart phonetically in speech, as confirmed instrumentally. A quality close to [ɒɪ] can be heard from the West Essex speaker in the recording of Text 10, Chapter 7.

Interestingly, in certain areas of the East Anglian Fens, /ai/ is involved in "Canadian Raising" (Britain & Trudgill, 2005). The phonetics are not at all the same as in Canadian English, but an identical phonological pattern occurs, with very different allophones of /ai/ occurring before voiceless consonants from those found elsewhere. In the western Fens, e.g. Peterborough and Spalding, /ai/ is typically [ɑː ~ ɑɪ ~ ɒɪ] in all environments. In the eastern Fens, e.g. Ely and Downham Market, /ai/ is typically "fast" [ɐi ~ ɜi ~ əi] in all positions. But in the central Fens, e.g. Wisbech, March, and Chatteris, there is clear allophonic variation between eastern-type vowels with central onsets in pre-voiceless environments versus western-type vowels elsewhere, e.g. *night-time* [nɐiʔ tɑːm].

In Trudgill (1985, 1986) I argued that Canadian Raising arose out of a process of *reallocation* which occurred during new-dialect formation. The suggestion is that the distinct allophones of PRICE (and of MOUTH) that are found in Canadian English – as well as, crucially for this argument, a number of other colonial varieties of English such as that of St Helena in the South Atlantic – are due to the process of new-dialect formation which led to the development of Canadian English as a new variety. Scottish-type diphthong variants of PRICE and MOUTH, with central onsets in all environments, and south of England-type diphthongs, with open onsets in all environments, were both present in the original dialect mixture which preceded the eventual focussed variety. Both variants survived, but were reallocated new functions as positional allophonic variants. This reallocation took place according to the very logical principle that the narrower diphthongs were confined to the pre-voiceless consonant environment where all English vowels have shorter allophones (Laver 1994: 446). The same thing, I suggest, happened in the Fens, although only in the case of PRICE.

Dutch engineers were commissioned to begin drainage work in the Fens from the mid-17th century onwards, and gradually this area of impassable marshland was turned into a fertile arable farming area. This reclamation led to considerable in-migration, especially into the more central and hitherto most inaccessible parts of the Fens, and thus to rapid demographic growth. Much of the in-migration (see

Britain 1997a) was from the area immediately to the west of the central Fens, and so to the west of the isoglosses discussed in 2.4 – Northamptonshire and Lincolnshire; and much of it was from the area immediately to the east of the Fens and thus to the east of the same isoglosses – eastern Cambridgeshire and western Norfolk (see 8.1). During the 18th and 19th centuries, this process of steady land-reclamation, followed by in-migration from neighbouring areas, led to considerable dialect contact and dialect mixture, and to the formation of a new central Fenland dialect. The different western and eastern diaphones or regional variants of the PRICE vowel were preserved in the new dialect, but were redistributed according to phonological environment.

CHOICE

In the speech of older East Anglians it is still possible to hear certain words from this set with the PRICE vowel, notably *boil*. This reflects an earlier absence of the CHOICE vowel from the vowel inventories of many varieties of English, due to the fact that English /oi/ occurs predominantly in lexical items borrowed from French. This usage of /ai/ in *boil* is now very recessive.

The vowel /oi/ itself ranges from the most local variant [ʊi], as in [bʊi] *boy* to a less local variant [ɔi], with a whole range of phonetically intermediate variants. Amos (2011), as noted above, reports that older speakers on Mersea Island, Essex, typically have the vowel as [ɵɪ].

In parts of the Fens, CHOICE can variably be monophthongal [ɔː].

GOOSE

The vowel /ʉː/ is phonetically a close, central diphthong [ʉʉ], with more lip-rounding on the second element than on the first. The phonetic quality of this vowel in at least the northern part of East Anglia was famously distinctive in the 19th century: Ihalainen (1994: 227) writes that "Ellis seems to have regarded it as an important characteristic of Norwich English. He calls it, rather hesitatingly, 'French (y)'." Ihalainen supposes that it was probably a central vowel – as it still is today, while no longer being particularly distinctive because of a widespread and ongoing process of GOOSE-fronting in English generally.

The vowel does occur, as one would expect, in words which had ME long close *ǫ:* /oː/, such as *soon, root, too, shoe,* but in northern East Anglia its distribution over lexical items – and its relationship to the sets of GOAT and FOOT – is complex.

First, northern East Anglian English demonstrates total yod-dropping (see Trudgill 1974): /j/ is absent before /ʉː/ not only in *rule, lute, suit* but in all environments. There is therefore complete homophony between pairs of words such as *dew-due = do* and *Hugh-hew-hue = who*.

Secondly, as we saw briefly already, a distinction has been maintained between two different GOAT vowels: an /ʌu/ = [ɐu], descended from ME *ou*, as in *mown;* and an /uː/ = [ʊu] descended from ǭ /ɔː/, as in *moan* (Butcher, 2021). The complication is that in northern East Anglia, and particularly in the region of Norwich, many or even most words from the GOOSE set can actually have this same /uː/ vowel, producing numerous homophones such as *boot-boat*,[71] *cool-coal, fool-foal, hoop-hope, mood-mode, moon-moan, soup-soap* (Lodge, 2001).[72] Thus *rood* may be homophonous either with *rude* or with *road* (which, however, will not be homophonous with *rowed*). This is variable and differs from speaker to speaker, word to word, and social class to social class: *boot* is more likely to be /buːt/ amongst urban and middle-class speakers, /bʉːt/ amongst working-class and rural speakers.

Note that this alternation never occurs in the case of those items such as *rule, tune, new* etc. which have ME *iu, eu* as their historical sources. For very many speakers, then, words such as *rule* and *school, rude* and *food*, do not rhyme.

There are two historical scenarios which could account for this rather unusual situation. First, in most forms of modern English, as is well known, the two ME front vowels ME *ẹː* and ME *ę:* have merged on the /iː/ vowel of FLEECE: both *beat* and *beet* are /biːt/. A reasonable supposition here would be that in much of Norfolk the same thing happened with the back vowels as well, so that ME *ǫː* and ME *ǭː* have merged on /uː/, with the result that both *boat* and *boot* are /buːt/. The set of *rude, tune* from /iu, eu/ remained distinct.

The problem then is to account for the fact that, in modern speech, some words which had ME *ǭ:* do not have /uː/ but rather the /ʉː/ descended from ME *iu, eu*. For what it is worth, the only GOOSE words which have /ʉː/ in my own speech are *who, whose, do, soon, to, too, two, hoot, loot, root, shoot, choose, lose, loose, through, shoe*.[73] I have no explanation as to why *soon* and *moon* do not rhyme in my speech. Note again that this alternation never occurs in the case of those items such as *rule, tune, new* etc., which always have /ʉː/. And, as just noted, *rule* and *school* therefore do not rhyme.

A more promising possibility therefore is that no merger ever occurred, and that ME *ǭ:* as in *boat* became /uː/ in Early Modern Norfolk while ME *ǫ:* as in

---

[71] As a child I believed that a *gravy boat* was a *gravy boot*. My mother was always uncomfortable about *soup* and *soap* being pronounced the same, and tried to encourage extra lip-rounding on *soup*. I eventually changed to pronouncing it as /sʉːp/.

[72] Muspole Street in Norwich was originally spelt "Muspool" Street, after an adjacent pond.

[73] There is also considerable individual variation: my mother (1918–2013) had /uː/ in *choose* and *root*, and my father (1916–1986) had /uː/ in *who*.

boot became /ʉː/. This hypothesis is supported by the behaviour of these vowels before historic /r/: CURE words such as *boor, moor, poor, spoor, tour, your* have /ɔː/, while those descended from ME /iur/ or /eur/ such as *cure* and *pure* have /ɜː/. The result is that *sure* /ʃɜː/ and *shore* /ʃɔː/ are not homophones, and neither are *you're* /jɜː/ and *your* /jɔː/.

Subsequently, perhaps because of the salience of the (at that time) unusually fronted GOOSE vowel, words were transferred from the GOOSE set to the GOAT set because the /uː/ vowel of Norfolk GOAT was very close to that of the RP GOOSE set. This is supported by the undoubted awareness Norfolk speakers have that *fool* /fʉːl/ is a more dialectal pronunciation than /fuːl/ – see the discussion of the spelling <fule> in Text 3, Chapter 7.

In certain items from the GOOSE set, the vowel /ʊ/ occurs: *roof, proof, hoof* and their plurals, e.g. /rʊfs/. It is also usual, in middle-class sociolects, in *room, broom* (working-class sociolects tend to have the GOOSE vowel in these items). In the older dialect, especially in Suffolk, /ʊ/ could also occur in other words such as *boot, goose, moon, move, noon, root, soon, spoon, tooth* as well as in compounds such as *afternoon* /aːtənʊn/.

The question then is, given the convergence in pronunciation on /uː/ of items from both the GOOSE and GOAT sets, whether the northern 'East Anglian short o' has any connection with the complicated shortening process which led to short /ʊ/ in *good, foot*, and, variously in different accents, in *look, tooth, room* etc. That is, does the change from /uː/ to /ʊ/ in *boot* represent the same phenomenon as (a putative) change from /uː/ to /ʊ/ in *boat*? This situation appears to have no parallel in the USA, and might represent a complication which postdates the emigration of East Anglians to New England.

Also in the older dialect, a number of FOOT words derived from Middle English /ɔː/ with shortening followed the same route as *blood* and *flood* and had /ʌ/: *soot, roof* /sʌt, rʌf/, as reported for example for Suffolk by Kökeritz (1932).

GOAT

As we saw under FACE, the Long Mid Mergers have not fully taken place in East Anglian dialects except in the Fens (Britain, 1997). Paralleling the vestigial distinction in the front vowel system between the sets of *made* and *maid*, corresponding to the distinction between the ME monophthong and diphthong, there is a similar distinction in the back vowel system which, however, is by no means vestigial in the northern part of the area.[74]

---

[74] In my own speech I have the merger of *made* and *maid* but not of *moan* and *mown*. This lack of symmetry as between the two subsystems is rather striking (for discussion see Trudgill, 1998).

The distinction, as we have already seen, is between /uː/ [ʊu], descended from ME ǭ: /ɔː/, and /ʌu/, descended from ME ou. Thus pairs such as *moan* ≠ *mown*, *road* ≠ *rowed*, *nose* ≠ *knows*, *sole* ≠ *soul* are not homophonous.[75] Middle English /ɔː/ plus /lC/ also gives /ʌulC/, as in *hold*. Final unstressed open syllables generally have /uː/ whatever their source, as in *billow, window*.

Amongst the traditional dialect records, Kökeritz writes [ʊː] in *alone, coal, clothes, loaves, soap, toe* etc. and [ɑʊ ~ ɒʊ ~ oʊ] in *blow, crow, grow, know, though* etc. for Suffolk. Lowman's records show a clear distinction for all three Norfolk and all four Suffolk localities between the GOAT vowels from the two different sources, with e.g. *clothes* being written with [o̞ᵛᵊ] and items such as *though, low, grow* with [ʌU]. By the time of the SED 1950s records, the distinction has been lost in Suffolk and Essex, but W. Nelson Francis records a distinction for all the Norfolk localities. He also writes in his unpublished notes that a Cardinal [uː]-type vowel is "a feature of the lower-class dialect of Norwich" in modern reflexes of ME ǭ:.

One further complication is that, in modern Norwich speech, adverbial *no* has /uː/ while the negative particle *no* has /ʌu/: *No, that's no good* is pronounced /nʌu, ðæs nuː gʊd/.

Two modern developments should also be noted. First, the phonetic realisation of /uː/ in the northern area is currently undergoing a rather noticeable change, with younger speakers favouring a fronter first element [ʉu] (see Trudgill 1988; Labov 1994). This process is more advanced in Lowestoft, Gorleston and Yarmouth than in Norwich.

Secondly, in the southern zone, the *moan-mown* distinction is now very recessive. In our "A sociolinguistic study of linguistic change in urban East Anglia", Trudgill & Foxcroft (1979) showed that the distinction survived intact in the urban centres of Norwich, Dereham and Cromer. Around 70% of the sampled populations of King's Lynn, Yarmouth and Lowestoft retained the distinction, with those who did not being mainly younger middle-class speakers. In Stowmarket, only older speakers had the distinction, and then only variably. The evidence is, however, that rural areas are retaining the distinction rather longer (see more in 8.2.4).

In the southern zone, the *moan-mown* distinction is now very recessive, so that for most speakers /ʌu/ is used in both lexical sets and /uː/ has disappeared. As a consequence, GOOSE words can no longer alternate in their pronunciation.

---

[75] Growing up with this distinction in my own speech, I was confused as a child by the abbreviation IOU. Puns such as the title of the 1965 Beatles album *Rubber Soul* also do not work in the dialect. And neither does the well-known comment on inadvertent rhyming: "You were a poet and you didn't know it".

As of the second decade of the 21st century, the distinction is also beginning to disappear in northern zone. When it has finally disappeared, this will complete a merger process which began in more central areas of England 500 years ago.

Words such as *bowl* and *shoulder* may have /au/ in the older dialect.

Kökeritz records *bought* and *thought* with /ʌu/, i.e. the same vowel as in *know, low;* and Francis has *thaw* with the same vowel in many of the Norfolk SED localities.

Mouth

This vowel is perhaps the segment which demonstrates most regional variation within East Anglia. The most typical realisation of the /au/ vowel in the north-eastern part of the area is [æʉ] although there is some variation in the quality of the first element, e.g. qualities such as [œʉ] can also be heard. In the south and west a more typical realisation is [ɛʉ] – note for example the Suffolk speaker from Tuddenham in Chapter 7 (Text 7) . The West Essex speaker in Text 10 in Chapter 7 has [eʉ]. Amos (2011) reports that the traditional pronunciation on Mersea Island in Essex is [ɛʊ].

In the central Fenland areas of northern Cambridgeshire, such as March, monophthongal variants of the type [ɛː ~ æː] occur (Lodge; 2001; Britain & Trudgill, 2005; and see also 2.6.1). In Wisbech and adjoining areas of Norfolk such as Outwell and Upwell, MOUTH and SQUARE have been merged on /ɛː/, such that *cow* and *care* are homonyms; *hour, sour* also have /ɛː/.

In the older East Anglian dialect, *enough* and *trough* had the MOUTH vowel and no final consonant: the English Dialect Dictionary (EDD) has examples spelt <enow, trow>.

Summary

The most distinctively East Anglian system of upgliding diphthongs is thus as follows:

/iː/ fleece /ʉː/ choose, rude
/æi/ day /uː/ goat
/ai/ price /ʌu/ know
/oi/ choice /au/ now

3.2.1.3 Long monophthongs – ingliding diphthongs

NEAR/SQUARE

These two lexical sets are merged in Norfolk, eastern Cambridgeshire and northern Suffolk (Butcher, 2021; Anderson, 1987: Map 60). The most usual realisation of this single vowel, which I symbolise as /ɛː/, is phonetically [ẹː ~ ɛ̣ː]. Traditional dialect speakers did have a schwa off-glide in these items, however, as shown in the SED materials: [eə̣ː ~ ɛ̣ə] (see further 8.3).

This gives numerous homophonous pairs such as *peer-pair, here-hair, tear-tear, dear-dare, beer-bear, we're-wear*.[76] Note that this merger also involves many items where no historical /r/ is involved: *idea* /aɪdɛ ː /, *Korean* /kərɛːn/, *Beatrice* /bɛːtrəs/, *creosote* /krɛːsuːt ~ krɛːsʊt/, *vehicle* /vɛːkl/ (and see further below on 'smoothing').

There is also then the interesting question as to whether the monophthongal FACE vowel of *made* (but not *maid*) in the traditional dialect, [ẹː~ ɛ̣ː], is or was distinct from the NEAR/SQUARE vowel. Dialect literature spellings such as *face* <fearce, fairce> suggest not; and Lodge (2001) concurs. I am not sure, but believe that in fact at least some speakers may have maintained a distinction, with [ẹː] in *face* and [ɛː] in *fierce*.[77]

In southern East Anglia, the vowels remain distinct as NEAR [ẹː ~ eə̣], SQUARE [ɛ̣ə].

THOUGHT/NORTH/FORCE/CURE

The /ɔː/ vowel has a realisation which is approximately [ɔː] without, however, very much lip-rounding. The East Anglian vowel is distinctively different from the closer London realisation, approximately [oː].

The vowel occurs not only in THOUGHT, NORTH and FORCE words but also in items from the CURE set such as *boor, moor, poor, spoor, tour, your*. CURE words descended from ME /iur/ or /eur/ have /ɜː/, as already noted under GOOSE. Examples of items which have /ɜː/ are *you're, pure, endurance, fury, mural, rural, Bure*[78] and *cure* itself.

---

76 On leaving Norwich and going to university at the age of nineteen, I attempted to introduce the NEAR-SQUARE distinction into my own accent, but had considerable difficulty since spelling is no help with forms such as *near* and *pear*. I am still not always sure which *tear* is which.
77 I do not have the *made-maid* distinction in my own speech, but discussed the issue with my maternal grandmother (1886–1979) who did, if only variably.
78 The name of one of the major Norfolk rivers.

In the traditional dialects of East Anglia, as is typical of more conservative south-of-England varieties generally, the /ɔ:/ vowel also occurs frequently in the lexical set of CLOTH, again as already noted. Pre-fricative lengthening (Wells, 1982: 203) occurred in the case of original short *o* but, unlike the corresponding process involving *a* as in BATH, is ultimately receding again. In addition to pre-fricative-lengthened items such as *lost, cross, froth, coffee,* /ɔ:/ can also occur in *dog* and *god*.

As already seen, in the traditional dialect *thought, brought* were pronounced with the same vowel as *mown, know,* so /θʌut/, /brʌut/. In the 19th-century dialect, *daughter* was pronounced so as to rhyme with *rafter*.

START/BATH/PALM

In its most local realisation, the vowel /a:/ is a very front vowel approaching cardinal [a:], but in more middle-class speech more central variants occur. Typical London and RP back variants around [ɑ:] are not found.

As we already saw (3.2.1.1), in the older dialect this vowel also occurs in *sir, fur, earth, her* etc.

As observed by the SED Norfolk fieldworker Prof. W. Nelson Francis in his field-notes, in the older dialect words such as *half* could also occur with the long vowel [æ:] which was distinct from the [a:] of START (see further below under *An alternative analysis of TRAP and LOT*). This can be heard on the Norfolk recording that accompanies Text 4 in Chapter 7, and on the Essex recording which accompanies Text 10.

NURSE/CURE

The vowel /ɜ:/ did not exist in the dialect until relatively recently. As already noted, words ending in open syllables, such as *sir* and *fur*, have /a:/ in the traditional dialect. This is also true of items descended from ME *er*, such as *earth* and *her*[79] (as well of items descended from *ar* such as *part, cart*). According to Wyld (1953: 216), spellings with <ar> of original <er> words such as *sermon* begin making a significant appearance in the south and southeast of England in the 15th century, but the form *parsones* 'persons' occurred in the Norfolk Guilds as early as 1389. These pronunciations were very widespread until around 1750 and then gradually receded again, with some exceptions such as *clerk*. They were retained much longer than this in East Anglia, however. The continuation of these

---

[79] In Norwich, men and boys called *Herbert* might be called *Arbo* /'a:bu:/.

forms in the region for a further two centuries and longer can be seen from 20th-century dialect-literature spellings such as the following:

	Dialect spelling
her	har
heard	hard
nerves	narves
herself	harself
service	sarvice
earn	arn
early	arly
concern	consarn

In words such as *church* and *first*, which involve Middle English *ir, ur* in closed syllables, the short open vowel /ʌ/ occurs, as noted in 3.2.1.1. There is, however, some interchange and variability. The long vowel /aː/ can also occur in such items, and there are also occasional pronunciations of forms descended from ME *er* and *ar* with the short vowel /ʌ/, notably *partner* as a term of address (see 5.6.1). Interestingly, the common exclamation *blast!* can also occur with the short vowel.

In the modern dialect, /ɜː/ does now occur, as we saw in 3.2.1.1, with a phonetic realisation a little closer than in RP. It occurs in all items from the set of NURSE, but also, as already observed, in words from the CURE set which are descended from ME /iu/ or /eu/ before /r/, so that *sure, pure, lure* rhyme with *her*, and *surely* is identical to *Shirley* (see also below on 'smoothing'). Other words which have /ɜː/ include *you're, pure, endurance, fury, mural, Muriel, rural, plural*.

Note too that, because of *yod-dropping* (3.2.2), the following are homophones in northern East Anglia: *pure* = *purr* /pɜː/, *cure* = *cur*, *fury* = *furry*.

Hour, Fire

We have already noted that earlier ingliding diphthongs have become monophthongs, especially in northern East Anglia, such that [ɪə] > [ɛː] in NEAR, and [ɛə] > [ɛː] in SQUARE. This same monophthongisation process has also produced /ɔː/ in *poor*, /ɔː/ in *pore* – both of these leading to a merger with the monophthong of THOUGHT – and /ɜː/ in *pure* – rendering this homophonous with *purr*.

A similar development has also occurred – for example in the working-class speech of Norwich and beyond – in the case of the triphthong [auə] as in *hour* /ɑː/. This back vowel, /ɑː/, occurs only in few words such as *hour, tower, power* – something which is also reflected in the SED records for Norfolk. (See below for the suggestion that this is in fact identical with the LOT vowel.) In middle-class speech, however, such words have /ɑ:/. This gives a social-class dialect distinction as follows:

	half an hour
Middle Class:	/hɑ:f n̩ a:/
Working Class:	/hɑ:f n̩ ɑ:/

The vowel /ɑ:/ can also occur as a result of smoothing of the triphthong /aiə/ in items such *fire*, *Brian*.

Smoothing

This historical process involves vowel-lowering before /ə/, followed by loss of the /ə/, plus lengthening. This is paralleled by a synchronic phonological process which carries across morpheme and word boundaries (see e.g. 4.1.8 on *we have* /wɛː/), and extends to additional vowels. The process has been labelled 'smoothing' by Wells (1982) and is particularly common in northern East Anglia, though it is currently spreading southwards: it is the only feature which in the modern dialect is diffusing in a north-south direction in East Anglia, rather than northwards from London (see more on this in 8.3; Trudgill & Foxcroft, 1979; Trudgill 1986).

In examining the following examples, recall that East Anglia has /ə/ in unstressed syllables where many other accents have /ɪ/, as a result of the Weak Vowel merger (3.2.1.1). The full facts can be summarised as follows:

Vowel + /ə/	Example	Output		
/iː/	seeing	/siːən/	>	/sɛːn/
/æi/	playing	/plæiən/	>	/plæːn/
/ai/	trying	/traiən/	>	/traːn ~ trɑːn/
/oi/	cloying	/klɔiən/	>	/klɔːn/
/ʉː/	doing	/dʉːən/	>	/dɜːn/
/uː/	going	/guːən/	>	/gɔːn/
/ʌu/	knowing	/nʌuən/	>	/nɒːn/
/au/	ploughing	/plauən/	>	/plaːn ~ plɑːn/

Thus *do it* can be homophonous with *dirt*, and *going* rhymes with *lawn*.[80]

---

[80] The song *Hev the bottom dropped out?* by the Norfolk dialect singer Alan Smethurst, known as The Singing Postman, contains the rhyme "He went away on the Monday morn/

There is area of Norwich called Heigham /hæiəm/ > /hæ:m/, though the name is most often heard in the names of Heigham Street, Heigham Park and Heigham Road. Heigham Street is often jocularly referred to as "Ham Street" – see below on the length of the TRAP vowel.

The vowel /ɒ:/ and – in basilectal varieties, the vowel /ɑ:/ – occur only as a result of smoothing.

Interestingly, basilectal Norwich speakers pronounce *towel* as /tɜ:l/. I assume that this form reflects the results of smoothing on an earlier pronunciation /tʉ:əl/, where the stressed vowel would have resembled that of the original French form *touaille*. This might perhaps indicate a borrowing or re-borrowing into Norwich English. In the form borrowed into mainstream varieties of English, Old French /u:/ had become Modern English /au/ as a result of the Great Vowel Shift. A later borrowing into Norwich English from the French of the Walloon Strangers (see 1.6), postdating the Vowel Shift, could account for this distinctive form.

An alternative analysis of TRAP and LOT

As entirely correctly pointed out by Lodge (2001), the TRAP vowel in northern East Anglia is often phonetically long. We also just noted that the vowel of items such as *half* can be [æ:] rather than the [ɑ:] that occurs in START. And the traditional rural dialect of northern East Anglia also has the interesting phonotactic feature that the TRAP vowel can be used in open syllables: in words such as *say* and *day*, where the vowel which descends from the ME *ai* diphthong occurs word-finally, it may be pronounced /æ/, e.g. *say* [sæ] Larwood writes *say* as <sa> in his *Norfolk Dialogue* (1800) (see Chapter 7); and the *English Dialect Dictionary* has *today* as <to-daa>.[81]

Given that smoothing also produces long [æ:] in e.g. *Heigham, playing*, including also in open syllables as in *player* /plæ:/, this opens up the possibility that dialectal TRAP is actually part of the long rather than the short monophthong system. The same could then also be said of LOT, basilectally [ɑ:], which can also occur in open syllables in *hour, ploughing*. If this is accepted, then the short monophthongal system should be presented as:

/ɪ/ kit   /ʊ/ foot, home, roof
/ɛ/ dress   /ə/ comma   /ʌ/ strut

Didn't tell a soul where he was a-goin". And when as a child I first heard the technical term for the fungus-like organisims *mycetozoa*, I assumed it was spelt so as to end with <-ore> or <-aw>.
81 Ihalainen (1974) guesses that this spelling represents the pronunciation [ɛ:], but in my experience of traditional Norfolk dialect speakers, it is in fact the TRAP vowel that occurs here.

And, correspondingly, the traditional-dialect long monophthong system would be:

/ɛː/ *near, square, seeing* /ɔ/ *thought, north, going*
/æː/ *trap, say, half* /ɑː/ *top, hour*
  /aː/ *start, heard*

3.2.2 Consonants

/p, t, k/
Intervocalic and word-final /p, k/ are most usually glottalised (see 2.6). This is most noticeable in intervocalic position where there is simultaneous oral and glottal closure, with the oral closure then being released inaudibly prior to the audible release of the glottal closure, thus *paper* [pæipʔə], *baker* [bæikʔə]. This also occurs in the case of /t/, as in *later* [læitʔə], but more frequently actual glottalling occurs, especially in the speech of younger people: [læiʔə]. Trudgill (1988) showed for Norwich that [ʔ] is the usual realisation of intervocalic and word-final /t/ in casual speech and that, as of 1983, it was also increasingly diffusing into more formal styles.

There is an interesting constraint on the use of [ʔ] and [tʔ] in East Anglian English in that these allophones cannot occur before [ə] if another instance follows. Thus *lit it* has to be [lɪtəʔ] rather than *[lɪʔəʔ].

In /nt/ clusters, the /n/ is frequently deleted if (and only if) the /t/ is realised as glottal stop: *twenty* [twɛʔi], *plenty* [plɛʔi], *going to* [gɔːʔə].

/d/
In traditional dialects in much of Norfolk, and at least the Waveney Valley of Suffolk, word-final /d/ has merged with /t/ in unstressed syllables, e.g. *hundred* /hʌndrət/, *David* /deːvət ~ dæivət/.

/kl, gl/
In the older form of the dialect, these clusters can be pronounced /tl, dl/: *clock* /tlɑk/, *glove* /dlʌv/.

/k, g/

Lowman's records show that palatalisation of velar consonants in the environment of front vowels, as in *cart* "kyart", was not uncommon in East Anglia in the traditional dialects of the 1930s. Lowman records *garden* as [ɟaːdn] from South Walsham in Norfolk, for instance. This was a common feature of the English of England generally in the 17th, 18th and 19th centuries (McMahon, 1994).

/θr, ʃr, θw, kw/

The older northern East Anglian dialect had /tr/ from original /θr/, and /sr/ from original /ʃr/. Thus *thread* was pronounced /trɪd/,[82] *threshold* /trɑʃl/, and *shriek* /sriːk/. Ellis recorded /tr/ from /θr/ all across Norfolk and in northeastern Suffolk (see Maguire, 2012; and www.lel.ed.ac.uk/EllisAtlas). Also, /tw/ could occur for original /θw/, as in the place-name *Thwaite* /twæit/. And /kw/ could be reduced to /k/ in certain environments: the Norfolk SED fieldworker Nelson Francis recorded a number of instances of *quarter* as /kɔːtə/.

/h/

Traditional dialects in East Anglia did not have h-dropping. Norwich, however, has had h-dropping for several generations. Trudgill (1974) showed that in Norwich in 1968, levels of h-dropping correlated with social class and style, ranging from 0% for the Middle Middle Class (the highest social class group) in formal speech to 61% for Lower Working Class informants in casual speech. It is interesting that these levels are much lower than in most other parts of England, and that hypercorrect forms do not occur. This is also true of Ipswich. Cambridge, too, has h-dropping, as do nearby locations such as Waterbeach, Toft, Harlton, Kingston, and Fulbourn (see more on this in 8.2).

/v/

In many of the local varieties spoken in the southeast of England in the 18th and 19th centuries, prevocalic /v/ is reported to have been replaced by /w/ in many lexical items. An early instance comes from the correspondence of Norfolk-born Margaret Paston (1423–1484; see Chapter 7), who has *vouchsafe* as <wochsaf> (Wyld, 1953: 292). Trudgill et al. (2003) argue that the original merger

---

[82] My own surname is an East Anglian form of *Threadgold*.

was actually on a voiced bilabial fricative or approximant [β ~ β̞] rather than [w] (see more on this merger in 8.2).

The facts concerning this merger as they were generally reported are that in many of the local varieties spoken in the southeast of England, in at least the 18th and 19th centuries, prevocalic /v/ in items like *village* was replaced by /w/. Most reports focus on word-initial /w/ in words such as *village, victuals, vegetables, vermin*; and although many writers do not actually say so, the impression one receives is that [v] then occurred only in non-prevocalic position, i.e. in items such as *love*, with the consequence that [w] and [v] were, presumably, in complementary distribution and /w/ and /v/ were no longer distinct. Ellis (1889) describes the southeast of 19th century England as being, at the traditional dialect level, the "land of wee" (as opposed to *v* "vee"). Wright (1905: 227) says that "initial and medial v has become w in mid-Buckinghamshire, Norfolk, Suffolk, Essex, Kent, east Sussex". This geographical configuration leads one to suppose that it was a feature also of the dialect of Hertfordshire, which has boundaries with Buckinghamshire to the west and Essex to the east. Wakelin (1972: 95–6) writes that the SED materials show that "In parts of southern England, notably East Anglia and the south-east, initial and medial [v] may appear as [w], cf. V.7.19 *vinegar*, IV.9.4 *viper* (under *adder*), V.8.2 *victuals* (under *food*) . . . The use of [w] for [v] was a well-known Cockney feature up to the last century". Wakelin (1984: 79) also says that "Old East Anglian and south-eastern dialect is noted for its pronunciation of initial /v/ as /w/ in, e.g. *vinegar, viper*; a very old feature, which was preserved in Cockney up to the last century".

Further examination of the published SED materials shows other sporadic instances of this merger. The spontaneous responses to VIII.3.2, for instance, show *very* with initial /w/ in Buckland and Coleshill in Buckinghamshire; and in Grimston, North Elmham, Ludham, Reedham, and Pulham St Mary in Norfolk. Many of the other SED instances of /w/ are from reports in which informants have labelled this pronunciation "older". Certainly Norfolk was one of the areas in which this merger lasted longest. In a paper on vestigial dialect variants (1999), I discussed the current high stereotype-level of awareness of this feature in the county even though it has almost totally vanished from actual usage. The merger is "remembered" by the local community decades after its actual disappearance. Most local people in the area over a certain age "know" that *village* used to be pronounced *willage* and that *very* used to be pronounced *wery*. The longevity of this folk memory is rather remarkable. As a child, I regularly associated with traditional dialect speakers who were born as early as the 1860s. However, I never heard anyone use this feature except as a joke or quotation. Discussions with older Norfolk people[83] suggest that it was in widespread normal unselfconscious use only until the 1920s. The fact that modern dialect writers still use the feature is therefore highly noteworthy. For example, Michael Brindred in his local dialect column in the Norwich-based *Eastern Daily Press* from August 26th, 1998 writes *anniversary* <anniwarsary>. This dialect feature has remained a stereotype for generations after its disappearance from actual speech.

The present-tense verb form *have* (which also occurs in the 3rd-person singular – see 4.1.1) is normally pronounced /hæ ~ hɛ ~ hə ~ ə/, i.e. without a final /v/, unless the next word begins with a vowel: *Have you done it?* /hæ jə dʌn ət/. The frequently occurring unstressed variant consisting simply of schwa means that forms involving *to have* and *to be* can be homophonous, because of smoothing (see 3.2.1.3): *we're coming* /wɛː kʌmən/, *we've done it* /wɛː dʌn ət/.

/ð/

Word-initial /ð/ in unstressed forms can in some cases be omitted, as in

'A'ss right	'that's right'
A'ss a rum'n	'that's a rum one'
Are y'comen'en?	'Are you coming then?'

In 4.7.3 we also have an example from the Essex Ballads of *that ere* 'that there'.

At least in Norwich, moreover, an intervocalic /n+ð/ cluster can also become /l/ as a fast speech phenomenon (Trudgill, 1974: 184):

[nʌʊ ə ɪʔ b dæʉ lɛ ː læiʔlɪi]
No I in't [haven't] *been down there lately.*

/l/

/l/ was traditionally clear after front vowels in northern rural East Anglian dialects, and this can still be heard from speakers born before 1920 in e.g. *well*, but modern speech now has the same distribution of clear and dark allophones as RP. Vocalisation of /l/ does not occur in the north of East Anglia but is increasingly common in the south of the region (see more on this in 8.2).

---

83 Including, very helpfully, my mother, b.1918.

/r/

Map 3.1, from Trudgill (2004), suggests that East Anglia must have been one of the first parts of England to lose rhoticity. Text 2 in Chapter 7, composed no later than 1799, has the spellings <northing> 'nothing' and <arter> 'after', which indicate the pronunciations /nɔːθɪŋ/ and /aːtə. These spellings could not have been used if Norfolk English had still been rhotic at the time.

East Anglian English today is mostly firmly non-rhotic. There are some exceptions, however, as can be seen from the same map. Lowman recorded rhoticity after the NURSE vowel in eastern Essex in the 1930s; the SED also found a few rhotic tokens on the far eastern peninsulas of coastal Essex in the 1950s – rhoticity can be heard in the recording of Text 4 in Chapter 7. There is also rhoticity on the NURSE vowel which is clearly audible on the SED recording from Little Downham, eastern Cambridgeshire, Text 9 in Chapter 7, and on the recording from Tuddenham, northwest Suffolk, Text 7 in Chapter 7.

I have also personally encountered three Norfolk people who had consistent *r*-colouring on the NURSE vowel: one Norwich woman, born c. 1910; one South Norfolk man, born in the 1920s; and one North Norfolk woman also born in the 1920s. In Trudgill (1999) I discussed this as a *vestigial variant* and suggested that, just as innovations have to start somewhere, linguistic features which are dying our will also have an increasingly small number of speakers who preserve the conservative variant longer than others.

Intrusive /r/ is the norm in modern East Anglia: /r/ is invariably inserted where the vowels /ɛː, aː, ɔː, ə/ occur before another vowel across both word and morpheme boundaries: *drawing* /drɔːrən/, *draw it* /drɔːrət/. Because of the high level of reduction of unstressed vowels to /ə/, intrusive /r/ occurs in positions where it would be unusual in some other accents: *Give it to Anne* /gɪv ət tər æn/, *quarter to eight* /kwɔːtə tər æit/.

The term 'linking r' is used to describe the same phenomenon where /r/ is etymological, which therefore occurs additionally after /ɜː/ (which derives in all cases from a vowel plus etymological /r/[84]), as in e.g. *her and me* /hɜːr ən miː/. Both intrusive and linking /r/, which are essentially the same phenomenon, are probably rather recent phenomena in some areas: the speaker from Tuddenham (Chapter 7, Text 7), for example, does not have either.

/j/

The northern zone of East Anglia, as already mentioned, has total yod-dropping (Wells 1982). That is, in items which had Middle English *iu* and *eu*, /j/ has gone

---

[84] The word *colonel* derives historically from *coronel*.

3 East Anglian phonology

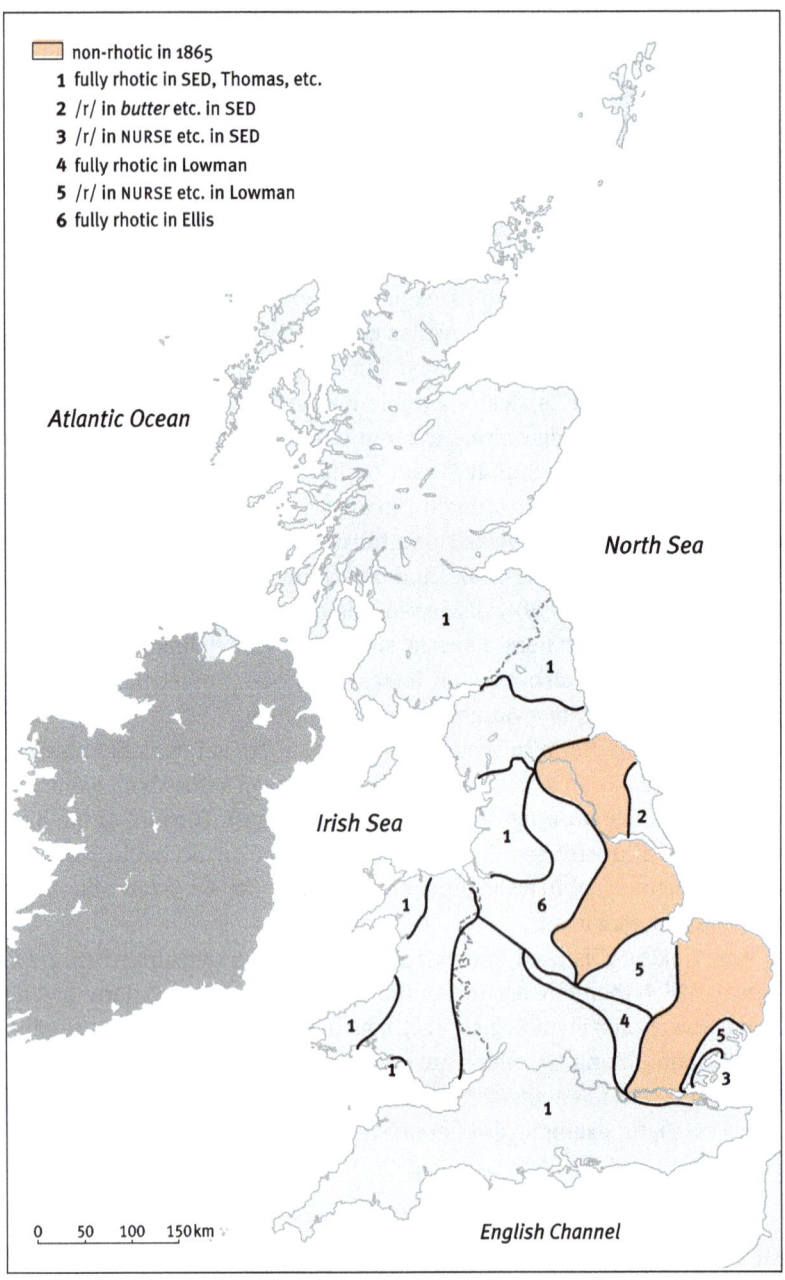

Map 3.1: Rhoticity.

missing not just after /r/, /l/, /s/, /θ/, in *rule, lute, suit, enthuse,* as in most forms of modern English; and not only after /n/ in *news,* as for example in London English; and not only after /t/ and /d/, in *tune, duke,*[85] as in many areas of North America; but after all syllable-initial consonants, so also in *pew* /pʉː/, *beauty, music, cue, argument, huge.* This produces homophonous pairs such as *Hugh-who, dew/due-do,* as well as *pure-purr* etc.. Pairs such as *feud-food, cute-coot* can be homophonous depending on whether or not the second item of the pair has /ʉː/ or /uː/ (see 3.2.1.2).

Yod-dropping is a very salient feature of the dialect for speakers of other forms of English, and outsiders trying to represent the local dialect in writing typically make attempts to indicate this pronunciation: Dickens writes *dutiful* as <dootiful> when portraying East Anglian dialect in *David Copperfield.*

Geographically, total yod-dropping extends from Norfolk on through Cambridgeshire into Bedfordshire, Huntingdonshire and parts of Northamptonshire, Lincolnshire and Leicestershire (Trudgill, 1999a). The southern area of East Anglia, on the other hand, does not have total yod-dropping but instead preserves an earlier stage, from even before the development of *iu, eu* to /juː/, so that much of Suffolk has, for instance, *pew* as /pɪu/. Trudgill & Foxcroft (1979) also found this latter variant in the Essex locations of Colchester, Wivenhoe and West Mersea.

/w/

Word-initial /w/ is often absent before /ʊ/. The availability of the 'East Anglian short *o*' (3.2.1.1) therefore means that *won't* and *wouldn't* can be homophonous as /ʊnt/.

/ŋ/

Present participles and gerunds, as well as names and other forms in *-ing,* are typically pronounced with /ən/ or syllabic /n̩/: *running* /rʌnən/, *Reading* /rɛdn̩/, *Fleming* /flɛmən/, *darling* /daːlən/. *Russian* and *rushing* are homophones.

---

[85] The traditional dialect pronunciation of *education* was /edëkeːßnY̶/.

4 East Anglian grammar

This chapter focusses on grammatical features and forms which are particularly associated with East Anglia. Nonstandard grammatical features which are found in East Anglia but are also common to a majority of other English dialects apart from Standard English are mostly not treated in much depth, there being nothing particularly East Anglian about them. These include features such as adverbs formally identical to adjectives, as in *she sing very good*; unmarked plurals after numerals as in *five foot*; so-called double comparatives and superlatives like *more nicer*; and the use of *never* for past-tense negation even for single events: *That wus never me what broke that window.*

4.1 Verbs

4.1.1 Third-person present-tense singular zero

One of the best-known morphological features of the East Anglian dialect area is *third-person present-tense singular zero*. There is now no trace of the third-person singular *-t*, as reported in 2.2. Rather, East Anglian dialects have zero-marking for all persons of the verb in the present tense, so that forms occur such as *he go, she come, that say*.

As we saw in 2.6, this feature is a major defining characteristic of East Anglian English. It occurs in all of Suffolk, and all of Norfolk except the Fenland far west: it is absent from Outwell as investigated by the SED. It is found in non-Fenland eastern Cambridgeshire, including the villages of West Wickham, Burwell, Bartlow, Swaffham Prior, Little Downham, and Witchford. The feature also occurs in northeastern Essex, but is not recorded in western Essex (Gepp, 1920). It is absent from the Cambridgeshire Fens, not being found for instance in Wisbech, nor in its Norfolk suburb of Emneth.

Unlike the urban dialects of Norwich and Ipswich, the modern dialect of the city of Cambridge itself does not have third-person zero; but Vasko's data show a few other sporadic instances of zero further west into south Cambridgeshire, for example in Little Eversden, which is 7 miles/11 kilometres southwest of Cambridge.[86] This suggests that the form previously occurred over a wider areas of Essex and Cambridge than currently. There is, however, no evidence of

---

[86] I have taken care to exclude from this analysis instances of third-person forms of *do* and *have*, which have zero in very many dialects.

zero ever having occurred in eastern England in any dialects beyond Essex and Cambridgeshire.

Third-person singular zero is a social dialect feature (see Trudgill 1974): a number of middle-class East Anglians do not use it at all, and many others use it variably. In spite of this, however, it is not involved in hypercorrection: speakers never add -s to forms other than the third-person singular (Trudgill, 1996, 2002).

One interesting question concerning this feature is why East Anglia is the only major area of Britain to have this system of zero-marking for all persons.[87] It has been argued (Trudgill, 2002; Nevalainen, Raumolin-Brunberg & Trudgill, 2001) that this East Anglian zero-marking phenomenon has to do with the large-scale immigration into Norwich in the 16th century of the remarkable group of refugees we now know as the Strangers (see 1.6). These were mostly native speakers of Dutch/Flemish, but there were also a good number of immigrants who used varieties of French.

As is well known, second-language learners of English often have difficulty with the irregularity of the third-person singular -s of Standard English and therefore omit it. And, as the language of Shakespeare shows, the 16th century was the period in the history of the English language during which northern third-person singular verb forms in -s were spreading south and gradually replacing the older southern forms in -th, with both forms occurring variably in London English.

I hypothesise that the more-or-less simultaneous arrival in Norwich of the new *he goes* form from the north of England (see Wright, 2001), and the hypothesised *he go* forms from the foreigner English of the Strangers, both of them in competition with the old southern *he goeth* forms, led to a situation where there was competition between the three forms -th, -s, and -Ø, in which the most regular form was the one which eventually won. It then subsequently spread outwards from Norwich, which was the second largest city in England at the time, to the whole of the area which the city dominated culturally and economically, namely East Anglia (see Trudgill 2002).

Wright (2001) shows that in fact northern -s did make it into the written language of Norfolk guild certificates as early as the 14th century, but this was true only of areas of western Norfolk immediately adjacent to Lincolnshire: five Norfolk scribes, all located in this northwestern corner of the county, used the -s suffix.

---

[87] The SED records show a small area of Somerset and Devon which also had present-tense zero in the 1950s.

4.1.2 Present participles

As we saw in 3.2.2, present participles typically end in /-(ə)n/. Together with the smoothing of triphthongs which was noted in 3.2.1.3, this leads to some interesting morphophonemic alternations:

be	/biː/	being	/bɛːn/
do	/dʉː/	doing	/dɜːn/
go	/guː/	going	/gɔːn/
say	/sæi/	saying	/sæːn/

4.1.3 A-verbing

As in many other dialects, it is usual in continuous aspect verb-forms for present participles in *-ing* to be preceded by *a-* [ə]:

I'm a-runn'n
She's a-sing'n.

The history of such participles as originally nominal forms – *he was a-hunting* was originally *he was on hunting,* i.e. 'in the act of hunting' – can still be seen from the fact that when these verb forms are transitive, they are normally followed in dialectal East Anglian English by *on* (which corresponds to Standard English *of* – see 4.11):

He wus a-hitt'n on it. 'He was hitting it.'
I'm a-taken on em. 'I'm taking them.'
What are you a-doin on? 'What are you doing?'

4.1.4 Progressive aspect

Older East Anglian dialect speakers have a tendency to employ the simple (non-progressive) verb forms typical of older forms of English (Wakelin, 1972) where many other dialects would use continuous (progressive) forms with *-ing* participles (Vasko, 2010: 3.1):

(The) kittle bile! 'The kettle's boiling!'
I go to Norwich tomorra. 'I'm going to Norwich tomorrow.'

Forby also has the example *Do it freeze?* 'Is it freezing?'

4.1.5 Irregular verbs: past tense forms and past participles

The East Anglian dialect shows a number of differences in verb-formation from Standard English, with considerable variability. Vasko (2010:3.3.2) writes that

> the past participle of the verb *freeze* shows great variation. In addition to the form *froze* (i.e. the StE simple-past form), the forms *frez* and *frorn* are attested in the interviews carried out for the Cambridgeshire data, as illustrated by the examples [*They*] *skate down to Ely and back, on the – the water frez over* (Waterbeach) and *we wonnt* [weren't] *satisfied at all if we – if we got . . . half-frorn apples* (Willingham).

Peitsara, too, has it that in the Suffolk dialect "the paradigm *freeze – friz – frore/froren* seems to be agreed on by most authors" (1996: 298–299).

In some cases, Standard English irregular verbs are or may be regular in East Anglia: according to Vasko (2010: 3.3.2), the past-tense forms of the verbs *blow, burst, come, draw, grow, know, run, sow, throw,* and *wake* are usually formed with the suffix *-ed* in her Cambridgeshire data; and Claxton (1968: 12) similarly cites *blow, draw, grow* and *throw* as being regular in Suffolk.

In other cases, Standard English regular verbs are irregular in East Anglia: for example, the past tense of *snow* is *snew* in the traditional dialect. In many other cases, partial regularisation has taken place, so that there are two forms instead of three (present, preterite, past participle), as with *break*, or one form instead of two, as with *come*. Typical Norfolk verb forms include:

Present	Preterite	Past Participle
begin	*begun*	*begun*
beat	*beat/bet*	*beat/bet*
become	*become*	*become*
bite	*bit*	*bit*
blow	*blew*	*blew*
break	*broke*	*broke*
catch	*catched*	*catched*
choose	*chose*	*chose*
come	*come*	*come*
draw	*drawed*	*drawed*
drink	*drunk*	*drunk*
drive	*driv*	*driven*
forget	*forgot*	*forgot*

give	give/gon	give(n)
grow	growed	growed
hit	hot	hot
know	knowed	knowed
mow	mew	mown
owe	ewe	own
ride	rid	rid(den)
rise	ris	ris(en)
ring	rung	rung
run	run	run
see	see	see(n)
shake	shook	shook
show	shew	shown
shriek	shruck	shruck
snow	snew	snew/snown
speak	spoke	spoke
steal	stole	stole
stink	stunk	stunk
swim	swum	swum
take	took	took
thaw/thow	thew	thew
tear	tore	tore
tread	trod	trod
wake	woke	woke
wear	wore	wore
wrap	wrop	wrop
write	writ	writ

Some of these forms are very archaic, especially *gon* 'gave', *hot* 'hit', and *wrop* 'wrapped'. On the other hand *shew*, as the preterite of *show*, is very widely used and is still very frequently found in the speech even of people whose English is not very dialectal. The past-participle form *frit* 'frightened', otherwise more associated with Lincolnshire and Northamptonshire, occurs in the Norfolk Fens.

For phonological reasons, *chose* and *choose* can be pronounced identically (see 3.2.1.2).

4.1.6 Imperatives

The second-person pronoun is usually explicit in East Anglian imperatives, as it was in much older forms of English:

Go you on!
Shut you up!

This is true even when the imperative is strengthened through the use the auxiliary verb *do:*

Do you sit down!

Vasko (2010) reports the use of the construction with the explicit pronoun from the Isle of Ely, northern Cambridgeshire, e.g. *Come you along and have a look* (from Haddenham, just to the southwest of Ely). She also reports (Vasko, 2005), however, that it is absent from southern Cambridgeshire (5.3.2).

As Admiral Lord Nelson, a Norfolkman,[88] lay dying on board the *Victory* at the Battle of Trafalgar, he famously said to Captain Hardy: "Do you anchor Hardy!" This has often been interpreted as a question but was in fact an instruction to Hardy to anchor.

4.1.7 Presentative be

The present tense system of the verb *to be* in East Anglia is identical with the Standard English system: *I am, he/she/it is, we/you/they are*. But there is one interesting exception. This concerns the phenomenon of *presentative be*. Speakers normally say *I am* but may nevertheless announce themselves, on arriving somewhere, by saying

Here I be!

Similarly, if they are looking for someone who they then find, they may exclaim *There he be!* That is, *be* is used for all persons when the speaker is presenting themselves or someone or something they have found or come across. These forms might perhaps reflect an earlier stage of the dialect when *be* was the

---

[88] Nelson was born and grew up in Burnham Thorpe in North Norfolk.

normal present-tense form in all meanings, as in parts of the West Country where speakers still say *I be, you be* etc.

4.1.8 The past tense of be

In the older dialect, the past tense form of *be* was *war* /waː/ for all persons in the positive. Since the mid 19th century, however, the past tense form of *to be* has been *wus* /wʊz/ for all persons in the positive, but *weren't* for all persons in the negative (see Anderwald 2002). This is also generally speaking true of the Fens (Britain, 2002), but see Text 13 in Chapter 7. East Anglian *weren't* can be pronounced in a number of different ways: /wɜːnt/, /waːnt/, /wɔːnt/, /wɒnt/.

4.1.9 Have

Unless the next word begins with a vowel, *have* is most often pronounced without the final /v/:

Ha'ya got some? / hæjə ~ hɛjə gɑt sʌm/
cf. *Have a look* / hævə lʊk/

As noted in 3.2.2., the weak form of *have* is thus often /ə/ rather than /əv/, giving *we have* /wiːə > wɛː/ (homophonous with *we're < we are*), and *he have* /hiːə > hɛː/, homophonous with *here* and *hair*.[89]

This does not apply to much of Cambridgeshire, however, where final /v/ in *have* is usual.

4.1.10 Auxiliary and full verb do

As in most English dialects, the past tense of the full verb *do* is *done* rather than *did*, but this is not true of auxiliary *do*, where the past tense is *did*:

You done it, did you?

---

[89] See 3.2.1.3 on the NEAR-SQUARE merger and *smoothing*

4.1.11 Causative/non-causative pairs

As in many other dialects, *learn* and *teach* are often not distinguished, with only *learn* being employed:

He didn't learn us too good.

Similarly, East Anglian English speakers typically *lay down* rather than *lie down* – another rather widespread feature of many English varieties: *lay* is used as an intransitive as well as a transitive causative 'cause to lie'.

A more particularly East Anglian feature is the lack of distinction between *sit* and *set*, with *set* being used in both senses. Vasko (2010) reports that in Cambridgeshire the use of *set* is almost categorical. Historically, *set* was 'to cause to sit', just as *fell* is 'to cause to fall'. English has gradually lost most of these causatives – for example *sench* 'to cause to sink' – so we can regard these East Anglian replacements of *sit* by *set* and *lie* by *lay* as part of this diachronic pattern.

Text 11 in Chapter 7, from Cambridgeshire, also demonstrates the falling together of causative *raise* with non-causative *rise:* "they've riz this bank a lot, two or three different times, this bank's riz a wonderful lot".

4.1.12 Borrow/lend

As in many other dialects, the word *borrow* occurs rather infrequently, with *lend* being used instead:

Can I lend your bike?

Here *lend* operates in the same way as, for example, Danish *låne* which can be translated into Standard English as both *lend* and *borrow*.

Dare

The archaic English past tense form of the verb *to dare* was *durst*. In the East Anglian dialect, this has become the present tense form:

You dursn't/dussn't/darsen't. 'You dare not.'

In less dialectal local speech, the negative present tense form *daren't*, is still regionally distinctive in that it is pronounced as two syllables, rhyming with *parent*, unlike in much of the rest of the country where it is normally pronounced as a single syllable. This is true even for speakers who otherwise have few regional features in their pronunciation.

Ought
Typical East Anglian forms of this verb, even in the speech of people who otherwise use few dialect forms, involve negative and interrogative forms with the past tense auxiliary *did*:

You didn't ought to do that, did you?
Did you ought to do that?

Matter
In the basilectal form of the dialect *It doesn't matter* is most usually *That don't matters*. The origin of this form with *-s* is not clear, but it probably derives from phrases, as recorded in the EDD, like *as near as (makes) no matters* 'as near as can be'; *no great matters* 'nothing to boast of'; *no matters* 'nothing out of the common'; *to be of no matters*; *to make no great matters*.

4.2 Negation

4.2.1 Multiple negation

As in most nonstandard dialects of English, multiple negation is usual. The Norfolk poet John Kett provides a nice example in his *Pome for Conservation Year* when he writes:

The Jolly Farmers pub have gone, and not a stun in't left
'. . . and not a stone is left'.

East Anglian English also extends multiple negation to constructions with *hardly* and *only*:

I couldn't find hardly none on 'em.
'I could find hardly any of them'.

We hadn't got only one.
'We had only got one.' (see also Text 11, Chapter 7)

4.2.2 Negatives of *have* and *be*

Corresponding to the more geographically widespread form *ain't*, the negative present-tense form of both *be* and of *have* in much of East Anglia is most often /ɛnt/ or, in more modern speech, /ɪnt/, for all persons:

I in't a-comen. 'I'm not coming.'
I in't done it yet. 'I havent done it yet.'

The equivalent form in much of Cambridgeshire, but not including the Isle of Ely, is *een't* /iːnt/ (Vasko, 2010: 5.1). Vasko cites examples such as:

They een't over here now, are they? (Rampton)
You're all right as long as you een't a-travelling. (Waterbeach)
Now you got taps, een't you? (Burwell)
[That artificial is not good?] – That een't.

In the older East Anglian dialect, the negative form of *have* could retain /h/: /hɛnt ~ hænt/. Forby describes the 18th-century dialect as having three different negative forms:

een't   'is not'
ain't   'am not'
heen't 'have not'

In the modern dialect, *aren't* can also occur as the negative form of *am*, not only in tag questions as in *aren't I?* but also as corresponding to Standard English *am not*, e.g. *I aren't comen* 'I'm not coming'.

4.3 Noun plurals

The older dialect had a number of archaic plurals:

house housen
mouse meece

These still survive in some areas, and Vasko (2010: 6.1) has *Only what people got on their own housen* from West Wickham in eastern Cambridgeshire. Forby

(1830) also cites *cheesen* 'cheeses', and *closen* 'clothes'. Gepp (1920) has *leece* as the plural of *louse*.

According to Gepp (1920), the traditional dialect of west central Essex around Little Dunmow also had disyllabic plurals of nouns in *-sk, -sp, -st*, so *cask-es* /kaːskəz/, *crust-es, wasp-es*.

Vasko (2010) also reports the survival in Cambridgeshire of *horse* as the plural of *horse* as in (*There were*) *two horse pulling,* from West Wickham; and *A man drove em with a plough cord, an that had sticks an that'd steer them **horse**, them **horse** go straight* (Bartlow).[90] See also Text 7 in Chapter 10;

4.4 Numerals

Although this usage was by no means confined to East Anglia, it is notable that two decades into the 21st century, many older East Anglian speakers still tell the time using *five-and twenty* rather than *twenty-five*:[91]

The bus arrive at five-and-twenty to.
Thass five-and-twenty past six.

This was formerly also used of people's ages, as in *When I was five and twenty.*

4.5 The definite article

In the traditional dialect, *the* normally appeared in the form *th'* if the next word began with a vowel: *th'old* house, *in th'oven*.

In the older 19th-century dialect, the definite article could be omitted after prepositions of motion, and before nouns denoting certain familiar domestic objects:

He walked into house.
Put th'apples into basket.
She come out of barn.
Kittle boil!

---

[90] In 1819, Byron was writing "a thousand horse".
[91] I grew up saying this and was using it well into the 1960s.

4.6 Demonstratives

As in many other dialects, the distal plural form of *that* is not *those* but *them*, e.g. *Eat you them carrots* 'Eat those carrots'. *Here* and *there* are often used as reinforcers:

This here book
Them there books.

4.7 Pronouns

4.7.1 Personal pronouns

In the older dialect *you* was pronounced so as to rhyme with *now*, and is often spelt <yow> by dialect writers.

You . . . together functions as the second-person plural pronoun in the traditional dialects of Norfolk, Suffolk, Cambridgeshire (Ellis, 1889: 249) and Essex (Gepp, 1920: 37):

Where are you together?
Come you on together!
Good night, together!

4.7.2 Pronoun exchange

In parts of the southwest of England, the pronoun forms *he, she, we, they* can occur as grammatical objects, and *him, her, us* can occur as grammatical subjects (Ihalainen, 1991). This feature is often known as *pronoun exchange*. It seems possible that what happens is that the Standard English subject pronoun forms occur as objects when the pronoun is emphasised, and object pronouns as subjects when the pronoun is not emphasised.[92] Something similar occurs in southern East Anglia.

Charles Benham's *Essex Ballads*, first published in Colchester in the 1890s, contain a number of instances of this feature e.g.:

---

[92] A good analytical survey can be found in (Hernandez et al, 2011).

Tha's where they're gooin', are they? Pas' the mill,
Along the fiel' path leadin' tard the woods.
*I'll give **he** what for some day, that I will,*
For walkin' out 'ith that ere bit of goods.

and

J'yer hear him call "Good arternune" to me?
He think he's doin' of it there some tune.
*Next time I ketch him out along o' **she**,*
*Blest if I don't give **he** "good arternune".*

The evidence of these ballads and of the SED records suggests that in southern East Anglia the phenomenon tends to be more restricted than in the southwest of England. The southwestern usage of *him*, *her*, *us* as subjects does not occur here; we see merely the use of *he*, *she*, *we*, *they* as objects. Vasko (2010: 7.4) makes the same observation about areas of Cambridgeshire "close to the Essex border", as with *Early harvest weren't no good to help **we** through the winter* from Castle Camps, which is close to both the Suffolk and Essex borders. However, Gepp (1920) cites some southwestern-style examples from the Little Dunmow area of Essex, including *We shall have to git up tidy forr'd, shan't **us**?*

Some examples from western Essex of *they* as an object pronoun can also be found in Text 10 in Chapter 7.

4.7.3 Weak forms

The personal pronouns *I*, *you*, *he*, *they* have distinctive weak forms which occur when these forms are unstressed:

I'm no good, am I?	/æm ə/
You're no good, are you?	/aː jə/
He's no good, is he?	/ɪz iː/
They're no good, are they?	/aː ðiː/

In Cambridgeshire, the weak form of *you* can be /jiː/: *You was one of'em, was ye?* (Vasko, 2010). Vasko also reports the weak form /iː/, as in *they 'd take 'ee t' Ely* 'they'd take you to Ely', which might be derived from an original *ye* or *thee*.

4.7.4 East Anglian *that*

The third-person singular pronoun *it* of Standard English corresponds to *that* in East Anglia. Vasko (2010) cites examples from Cambridgeshire; and the *English Dialect Dictionary* has the following Norfolk and Suffolk examples:

How that du snow!   'How it's snowing!'
That don't fare no better to-daa.   'It doesn't seem any better today'
That wagged that's tail.   'It wagged it's tail'

From local dialect literature, it can also be seen that *thaself* was formerly found as the reflexive (Trudgill, 2003):

The dog hurt thaself.

In contemporary East Anglian English we find forms such as:

That's raining.
That's cold today.
That was me what done it.
Where's the cat? – That's over there.
Hello, that's only me!

This is not just a traditional dialect feature – I have it quite naturally in my own speech. Geographically it extends south into areas of southeastern Essex which are no longer linguistically very East Anglian in other respects.[93]

The weather-related expletives in these examples confirm that we are not dealing with a demonstrative here, but with a genuine pronoun.

Note, however, the different apparently objective forms of the pronoun which occur as in:

I don't like it, that's no good
[ɐi dʊnʔ lɐik əʔ, ðæs nʊu gʊd]

I have used the orthographic representation <it> here, but it is not actually immediately clear how the form [əʔ] = /ət/ should be analysed. There are two possibilities:

---

[93] I have come across this usage in Southend, for example.

1. It could be that we should analyse /ət/ as *it*, with *it* functioning as the object-form of *that*, making for a paralellism with the rest of the pronominal system:

I-me, we-us, they-them, he-him, she-her, that-it.

2. Or, it could be that /ət/ is simply a phonologically reduced weak form of *that*, just as /ə/ is the weak form of *I*, and /ði:/ is the weak form of *they* (4.7.3).

There are a number of reasons for supposing that 2 is in fact the correct analysis here:
a. It is typical of Indo-European languages that they do not have distinct subject and object forms for third-person neuter pronouns.
b. As a subject form, pronominal (but not demonstrative) *that* is often pronounced without the initial /ð/ (see 3.2.2):

That's raining /(ð)æ(t)s ræinən/.

It is therefore unproblematical to interpret /ət/ as a reduced form of /æt/ = *that*.
c. There are clear examples of unstressed /ət/ occurring as a subject in tag questions: *That's no good, is it?*
d. There are examples from the older dialect of unreduced *that* occurring as an object form. For example, the *English Dialect Dictionary* (1989–1905) has *That on't hurt that* 'It won't hurt it' from East Anglia.[94]

In the older dialect, *that* also appeared as /tə/, often represented in the dialect literature as *ta* or *t'* (Trudgill, 2003): *Ta fruz* 'it froze' [tə fɹʊz]. This has now disappeared except in the concessive expression *T'is true* 'It's true'.

Forby has the following examples, where *ta* co-occurs together with *that*:

Ta freeze? Yes, and that hail too.
Do it freeze? No that don't freeze now, but ta wull at night.
(Forby, 1830: 339)

Forby interprets *ta* as a variant of *that*, but it seems equally possible that *ta* is a back-formation from /ət/ involving the change: /ət > t > tə/, as perhaps in *that was* /ətwʊz/ > /twʊz/ > /təwʊz.

This all raises the question of the antiquity of East Anglian *that*. Poussa (1997, 2001) has interestingly argued that East Anglian *that* is due to the Viking

---

[94] Note here the absence of /w/ from *won't* (3.2.2).

occupation of the area and the several centuries of Norse-English contact which followed in the region (see 1.4). She supposes that East Anglian *that* is the result of Scandinavian linguistic influence, pointing to the obvious similarity between East Anglian *that* and Old Norse *þat*, modern Scandinavian *det* 'it' (neut.). On the face of it, this seems perfectly possible: as Poussa says, if *they, them, their* could be transferred from Old Norse into the English personal pronominal system, why not *that* as well?

There are serious problems with this suggestion, however. One is that the geography and chronology appear to be somewhat anomalous. If East Anglian *that* is to be explained as being the result of a Scandinavian substratum, this development would have had to take place two or three centuries earlier than the transition to *they, them, their*. The Scandinavian third-person plural pronouns first emerged in the English of the North of England in the 12th century, and only gradually made their way south over a period of four centuries, not totally replacing the original English forms in the south of England until around 1500 (Lass, 1992: 120). Wright (2001) shows that the original Old English objective *hem* 'them' and possessive *here* 'their' had still not been replaced by the Scandinavian forms *them* and *their* in English documents written in Norfolk as late as the winter of 1388–9. And, indeed, non-Scandinavian *hem*-type forms can still be found in the Paston Letters, written in vernacular Norfolk English, in the 15th-century:

> On Friday night last past come Alexander Wharton, John Hose and John Fille, with ij. good carts well mannyd and horsyd with hem.   (Paston Letters 866, c. 1482)

Since *that* did not replace *it* anywhere outside East Anglia, it could not have spread to Norfolk from outside – it was a purely internal development. Poussa's claim necessarily therefore has to be that the modern Norfolk *that*-system dates back way earlier than the introduction of *they*: since *that* did not diffuse into East Anglia from elsewhere, it must have been borrowed into English from North Germanic while Scandinavian was still being spoken in Norfolk, i.e. before Old Danish died out in the region.

We do not really know when the language shift from Norse to English was completed in England. And in any case, the death of Old Danish is not by definition something that can be determined exactly because of the great similarity of the two languages, and the possibility this opens up for the two languages having merged with one another gradually just as the populations did (see 1.4). But Townend (2002) argues for the language death of Old Norse as having taken place in northern England during the transition period between Old English and Middle English – so by about 1200. In East Anglia it could well have been earlier, because of the lower density of the Scandinavian-origin population, even in Norfolk.

And in any case there is no evidence for Poussa's thesis concerning the (pre-)13th-century development of *that* in Norfolk. Crucially, the vernacular Norfolk English of the 15th- and 16th-century Paston Letters contains no examples that I have been able to find. It is, on the other hand, very easy indeed to find examples of subject *it* in the letters, including in weather expressions as *it reyned* in the example below. It took me about ten minutes to find the following examples from letters written by female members of the Paston family in Norfolk in the 1400s:

	Date	Letter
Qhan ze kom hom, as itt longeth to zw to don	**56**	1448
It reyned so sore	**160**	1451
It fortunyd so that he came to me	**361**	1460
It is right grete almes to help her	**707**	1472
If it happen yow to be seek	**763**	1475
It shall never neede to prykk nor threte a free horse	**802**	1477

The first actual reference I am aware of to Norfolk *that* occurs in the description of the late 18th century dialect by Forby (1830). Poussa claims that Forby does not mention it, and finds this "odd", suggesting that "we cannot draw any firm conclusions from Forby's silence" (2001: 245); but although it is true that Forby does not comment on it as such, he does actually give a few examples which contain non-demonstrative *that* (see *No that don't freeze now*, just cited). So East Anglian *that* has been in existence at least since 1750 or so; but there is no evidence of it being used before that; and there is actually evidence of it not being used in the 1400s.

A much more likely explanation for how East Anglian *that* arose comes from an understanding of a well-known grammaticalisation process. The diachronic transformation of demonstratives into third-person pronouns is a very common phenomenon. Ishiyama (2008) shows that demonstratives are a crosslinguistically common source of third-person pronouns – because of the functional similarity between them, he says – and they are often morphologically related to each other or even indistinguishable.

Diessel (2000: 119) also says that demonstratives have very frequently become third-person pronouns in the languages of the world, and indeed provide a major source for such pronouns:

> There is one class of function words that provides an especially frequent source for the development of grammatical markers: demonstratives such as English *this* and *that*. . . [One] grammatical marker that is commonly based on a demonstrative is the third person pronoun (cf. Lehmann 1985; Givón 1984; Heine & Kuteva 2002). The development originates from an anaphoric demonstrative pronoun functioning as an argument of a verb or adposition. For instance, the French third person pronouns *il* and *elle* developed from the anaphoric use of the Latin demonstrative pronoun *ille*. (Diessel, 2000: 2)

The Latin demonstrative *ille illa illud* 'that' was "the source of nearly all third person pronouns in Romance" (Alkire & Rosen, 2010: 199), for example French *il* 'he, it', Spanish *el*.

Diessel (1999: 120) adds that "we find anaphoric pronominal demonstratives tracking emphatic, contrastive and unexpected discourse topics. Anaphoric demonstratives that develop into third person pronouns become de-stressed and their use is gradually extended to all persisting topics."

This is precisely, I suggest, what occurred in the case of East Anglian English *that* taking over the role of *it*.

4.7.5 Possessive pronouns

As we saw in 2.5.2, Viereck (1975) shows that the typical East Anglian possessive pronoun forms are *mine, yours, his, hers, ours, theirs* but that *yourn, hisn, hern, ourn, theirn* do occur in the immediately adjacent areas of Lincolnshire, Northamptonshire, Huntingdonshire, Bedfordshire, and Hertfordshire. David Britain (p.c) also reports some usage of these forms in the Fens of northern Cambridgeshire and far-western Norfolk. A Cambridgeshire example of *his'n* can be found in Text 13 in Chapter 7. And *ourn* and *yourn* are also cited by Gepp (1920) for western Essex, and by Vasko (2010).

The possessive pronouns *mine, yours, his, hers, ours, theirs* are generally used in East Anglian English to refer to a place where somebody lives:

Less go round mine. 'Let's go to my place.'

4.7.6 Reflexive pronouns

The East Anglian dialect typically has an entirely regular system of reflexive pronouns based on the possessive pronouns – *myself, yourself, hisself, herself, ourselves, yourselves, theirselves;*

He hurt hisself.

4.7.7 Relative pronouns

As in eastern England generally (see Britain, 2021), the East Anglian relative pronoun is *what* for both animates and inanimates:

He's the one what done it.
A book what I read.

4.8 Adjectives

Like most dialects, East Anglian dialects permit double comparatives of the type *That one's more nicer than th' other one.*

4.9 Temporal adverbials

The traditional dialects of northern East Anglia not only have forms such as *t'night* and *t'day* but also *t'year, t'mornen, t'week* 'this year, this morning, this week'.

Now
An East Anglian feature found at most social levels is the use of *now* rather than *just* in expressions such as *I'm now coming!.*

4.10 Intensifiers

Wholly, normally pronounced /hʊliː ~ hʊlə/, is widely used as an intensifier in[95] the traditional dialect:

That wholly poured.

Right can be used in a similar way:

You hatta be right careful. 'You have to be very careful.'

---

95 See also 5.6.3.

Rare can similarly be used:

That wus a rare ol'job.

And the older traditional dialect also had *master* as an intensifier:

That wus master strong.

4.11 Prepositions

As in nonstandard dialects generally, there are many differences of prepositional usage between the local dialects and Standard English (Vasko, 2005). Distinctively East Anglian usages include:

*I went **round** John's* (i.e. to John's [place])
*I went **down** the city.* (i.e. to Norwich from the suburbs)
*I'm went **up** the city.* (i.e. to Norwich from the country)

Unstressed *of* is usually [ə], often even before a following vowel (where it induces intrusive /r/):

a *pound of apples* /ə paund ər æplz/

When not reduced, it is very often realised as *on* (Peitsara, 2000):

What do you think on it?
There wus a couple on 'em.

Alonga, derived from *along with* or, more likely, *along of*, signifies 'together with':

Do you come alonga me!

4.12 Conjunctions

4.12.1 *Time*

It is very well known to older East Anglians that in the traditional dialects, *time* operates, or operated, in a way which is equivalent to the Standard English subordinating conjunction *while*, as the following examples show:

> *Go you and have a good wash and change, time I get tea ready.*[96]
> Go and have a good a wash and change while I get tea ready.

> *You remember what old Martha used to say, time she were alive.*
> You remember what old Martha used to say, while she was alive.

The *English Dialect Dictionary* lists *time* as a form meaning "whilst, while, during the time" and gives examples of this usage from two separate geographical areas: Yorkshire and north Lincolnshire; and Norfolk, Suffolk and Essex.

The three East Anglian examples cited in the Dictionary are:

time I do this = while I do this [which is labelled "East Anglia"]

Wait outside time I'm gone in. [which is quoted from Cozens-Hardy's 1893 work *Broad Norfolk*]

He come time I was gitten 'o' my wittles = he came while I was getting my victuals [labelled "Suffolk"].

The presence of this conjunction in North Lincolnshire and Yorkshire, on the one hand, and Norfolk, Suffolk and Essex, on the other, could represent the results of two independent episodes of grammaticalisation, given that even at their closest, Norfolk and North Lincolnshire are about 90 miles/150 kilometres apart: the parallel with the grammaticalisation of the general English noun *while* as a conjunction shows that this kind of development is not an unexpected one. Alternatively, it might be simply that the EDD lacks data for the intervening areas, or that the form has died out in the intervening area, dividing an initially unified area into two.

---

96 The examples in this section are taken from local dialect literature. They all tally very well with my own experience over many decades of the forms used by local dialect speakers.

4.12.2 *Do*

A remarkable example of East Anglian conjunction-formation involves the use of the originally verbal from *do* as a conjunction equivalent to general English 'or, otherwise'. The *English Dialect Dictionary* give examples of this usage of *do* from Norfolk, Suffolk, Essex and Cambridgeshire. The Dictionary's gloss is "used elliptically for *if you do* etc.", but this is not entirely correct, as can be seen from Norfolk dialect literature examples such as:

> *You lot must have moved it, do I wouldn't have fell in.*
> You lot must have moved it, or I wouldn't have fallen in.

The EDD itself cites a number of examples, including the following.
From Cambridgeshire:

> *Don't go anigh that ditch, do you'll fall in.*
> Don't go near that ditch, or you'll fall in.

From Norfolk:

> *Don't you leave that old hare lying there, do the old crows will joll her.*
> Don't leave that old hare lying there, or the old crows will peck at her.

From Norfolk/Suffolk:

> *Don't keep on a-dewin o' that, dew you'll get inter' a mess.*
> Don't keep on doing that, or you'll get into a mess.

From East Suffolk:

> *Don't come here again; du, I'll throsh yow.*
> Don't come here again or I'll thrash you.

From Essex:

> *Don't you sleep 'ithin that plaice, do to-night you'll be a-larfin on the wrong side o' yer faice.*
> Don't sleep in that place or tonight you'll be laughing on the wrong side of your face.

> *I have to put it close agin m' eyes, do I can't see at all.*
> I have to put it close against my eyes or I can't see at all.

Do is functioning in these examples as a non-verbal form with no semantic content connected to "doing" anything, and is equivalent to Standard English *otherwise, or*.

I hypothesise that this grammaticalisation as a conjunction is ultimately due to phonological developments involving the loss of phonetic material in this strongly stress-timed dialect, as discussed in 3.1 (Trudgill, 2018). This hypothesis is strengthened by the fact that less advanced, less completely grammaticalised forms can still be found in the dialect, such as the example *Don't come here again; du, I'll throsh yow* cited in the *English Dialect Dictionary*, where the comma in the second clause strongly suggests that *du* (do) is a truncated form of "if you do".

We can reconstruct three crucial stages in the diachronic development of *do* as a conjunction which are all exemplified in dialect literature texts. Phonetic erosion is involved during the first stage.

Stage 1

Don't you take yours off, do you'll get rheumatism.
Don't take yours off, or you'll get rheumatism.

Don't you tell your Aunt Agatha about the coupons, do she'll mob me.
Don't tell your Aunt Agatha about the coupons, or she'll tell me off.

Don't you walk upstairs yet, do you'll whitewash the whole stair carpet.
Don't walk upstairs yet, or you'll whitewash the whole stair carpet

Don't you put her proper name in, do she'll pull both on us for libel.
Don't put her proper name in, or she'll sue both of us for libel.

Compare these with examples where *don't* appears rather than *do*:

Put that there antimacassar over her face, don't she'll give me nightmares.
Put that antimacassar over her face, or she'll give me nightmares.

You'd better turn that broom the other way up, don't you'll be breaking someone's neck.
You'd better turn that broom the other way up, otherwise you'll be breaking someone's neck.

Shet that gaate, don't yar old sow'll girr out.
Shut that gate, or your old sow will get out. (EDD: Cozens-Hardy, 1893)

These forms represent the earliest stage in the grammaticalisation process, where phonetic erosion has led to the complete loss of lexical material. In each of the above examples, the re-insertion of material such as . . . *if you* . . . would convert these back into the pre-grammaticalisation form of the construction, as with:

Don't you take yours off; [if you] do you'll get rheumatism

or

Don't you take yours off; [you] do, you'll get rheumatism

or

> *Don't you take yours off; do [and] you'll get rheumatism*

and

> *You'd better turn that broom the other way up;[if you] don't you'll be breaking someone's neck.*

Here, at stage 1, a verbal-type negative/positive distinction between *do* and *don't* is still maintained, together with the grammatical link of tense between the verb in the first clause and the quasi-auxiliary verb form in the second.

Stage 2
At stage 2, as grammaticalisation progresses, tense agreement is broken and *do* and *don't* begin to occur in non-present-tense contexts:

> *Have the fox left?- No that in't, do Bailey would've let them went.*
> Has the fox left? – No, it hasn't or Bailey would've let them [the hounds] go.

> *He pinned ahold of her other leg, don't she'd have been in.*
> He pinned hold of her other leg, otherwise she would have been in.

> *She say that wouldn't have done to have done nothing to the boy, do I might have gone round for nothing, not knowing.*
> She said that it wouldn't have done to do anything to the boy, or I might have gone round for nothing, not knowing.

The distinction between positive and negative quasi-verbal forms is still maintained here, since the positive form *do* in the second clause corresponds to a negative form in the first clause, and vice versa. But the originally present-tense forms *do* and *don't* are now being applied in past-tense contexts, as is illustrated by the fact that expansion to sentences with fully verbal *do* and *don't* is no longer possible: we would expect instead *had* and *hadn't*:

> *Have the fox left?- No that in't, [because if it had]* ~~do~~ *Bailey would've let them went.*

Stage 3
The final stage in the grammaticalisation process can be seen in the following examples:

> *Sing out, do we shall be drownded!*
> Call out, or we shall be drowned!

Where's the ladder?- That stand in the stackyard, do that did do.
Where's the ladder? – It's standing in the stackyard, or at least it was.

Keep you them elephants still, do we shan't half be in a mess.
Keep those elephants still, or we won't half be in a mess.

In these examples, as it happens, there still appears to be grammatical agreement between present-tense forms in both clauses, but we see that the originally verbal negative/positive distinction has now been entirely lost, with *do* appearing where in earlier stages *don't* would have been expected: the *do/don't* distinction has been neutralised in favour of *do*.

Our final examples, however, show clearly that the process has gone to completion, because there is no quasi-verbal grammatical link either to the tense or to the negative/positive polarity of the preceding clause:

That's a good job we come out of that there field, do he'd've had us!
It's a good job we came out of that field, or he would have had us!

That was up to him to do his job proper, do there wouldn't be nothing yet nobody to start things off again.
It was up to him to do his job properly, otherwise there wouldn't have been anything or anybody to start things off again.

We stabled them elephants right in the middle, do we should've capsized.
We stabled those elephants right in the middle, or we would've capsized
Things must be wonderful bad, do master would never have broke.
Things must be extremely bad, or master would never have gone bust.

The complete life-history of East Anglian conjunction *do* is thus:
I. phonological erosion and reduction, and loss of lexical material of the type *... if you ...*
II. loss of tense marking with *do* and *don't* occurring rather than *did, didn't*.
III. loss of negative/positive polarity, with loss of *don't* and neutralisation in favour of *do*.

4.12.3 (nor) yet

The form *yet* may function as a conjunction equivalent to *nor* in constructions such as:

There weren't no laburnum, yet no lilac.
There wouldn't be nothen nor yet nobody to start things off again.

4.12.4 *(no) more*

The form *(no) more* can function as a conjunction equivalent to *nor* or *neither*:

> *The fruit and vegetables weren't as big as last year, more weren't the taters and onions.*

The development of these new conjunctions in East Anglian English represents an endogenous innovation in the dialect, as does the change from *it > that*. These contrast with the retention in the dialect of conservative forms which have been lost elsewhere, such as imperative forms of the type *Sit you down!*; and plural forms like *housen*.

5 East Anglian lexis and discourse features

'East Anglian lexis' is not an entirely unproblematic notion for a number of reasons. First, it is not easy to identify lexical items which are found in all of East Anglia and nowhere else: the *Word Geography of England* [WGE](Orton & Wright, 1974), which is derived from the *Survey of English Dialects* materials, has very few maps with lexical isoglosses coinciding precisely with the boundaries of East Anglia, though I do mention some instances below.[97]

Then there are also, unsurprisingly, many lexical differences within the East Anglian region: splinters are called *shivers* in Norfolk and *slivers* in Suffolk; a mould-board on a plough is called a *plat* in northern Norfolk but a *breast* in the south. 'Snail' tends to be *dodman*[98] in Norfolk, but *hodmandod* in Suffolk.

In several cases there are also isoglosses which run across East Anglia, and then continue way beyond the region. The SED materials show that a *swingletree* – the loose horizontal bar which goes between a cart-horse and the cart – is known as a *horse-tree/hoss-tree* in central and western Norfolk, but also in southern Lincolnshire; in eastern Norfolk the word is *hampletree;* and southern Norfolk is part of a larger area which includes Suffolk and Essex, but also the whole of southeastern England as far as Hampshire, where it is *whippletree.* An *aftermath* – a second crop of hay – is called *eddish* in northwest Norfolk (as in Cambridge and Huntingdon, as well as Lincolnshire, Leicestershire, Rutland and beyond); but in the rest of the county the term is *second-crop*, as it also is in Suffolk and northern Essex, with much of the rest of Essex having *second-cut*. According to the WGE, *gorse* is called *furze* all along the south coast of England and up into Buckinghamshire, eastern Essex, most of Suffolk, and the south of Norfolk; it is known as *gorse* from south Yorkshire and Lincolnshire down to Cambridgeshire and western Essex; and, rather remarkably, it goes by the Norse name of *whin* not only in Scotland and the far north of England but also in western Norfolk[99] as well as in Orford, east Suffolk: *whin* is from Old Danish *hvine*, and *furze* comes from Old English *fyrs*.

---

97 In this discussion of the lexis of the dialects of East Anglia, I will be making frequent reference to the *English Dialect Dictionary* (EDD); the *Oxford English Dictionary* (OED); and *A Word Geography of England* (Orton & Wright, 1974) (WGE).

98 The OED suggests a possible connection with *dod* 'bare, rounded hill-top' from ME *dodden*, 'to make the top of something bare'.

99 In the SED localities of Docking, Great Snoring, Grimston, N. Elmham, Gooderstone, and Shipdham.

Then there are other words which are found only in East Anglia – but not in the whole of the region. The word for an orphaned bottle-fed lamb is *cosset* in the far south of Norfolk, northern Suffolk and the northwestern corner of Essex; but elsewhere in the region it is *pet-lamb*. *Sunk* 'ill-cooked food' is listed by the EDD as being found only in Norfolk; and the same is true of *troll* 'to tire with walking; to walk too far'.

Another issue concerns the fact that lists of local words compiled by enthusiasts often cite words which they consider to be 'dialectal' but which are in fact simply words which are known only to people who have worked in or are close to the older agricultural world, and are therefore unknown to townspeople and the younger generations. *Pightle* 'small field or enclosure' is a good example of this phenomenon: the EDD gives it as being found in the North Country, the South Country, East Anglia, Rutland, Huntingdon, Northamptonshire, Bedfordshire, Hampshire, and Berkshire – which would seem to be almost everywhere in England except the West Country! Also, some words which are thought by many East Anglians to be local are not actually local at all: *squit* 'nonsense' may not be known to Londoners, but it is known and used in the dialect of Herefordshire, which is a very long way from eastern England.

Other apparently dialectal words might more accurately be described as archaisms: they are simply retentions of usages which have died out in General English but happen to have survived, for the time being, in East Anglia, such as *to allow* 'admit', *nigh* 'near', *forenoon* 'morning', *howsomever* 'however', *happed* 'happened', *vexed* 'distressed'. *To squat,* given in the EDD as an East Anglian word meaning 'to quiet, compose; to put to silence' as in *squat the child!*, appears as a non-regional word in the OED, where it is labelled 'obsolete'. The East Anglian dialect word *tempest* 'storm' was formerly known all over England; and so was *harnser* 'heron', in the form *heronshaw* 'young heron'. The noun *gay* 'picture (especially in a book)' is described by the *Oxford English Dictionary* as "now rare (*British regional* in later use)".

Yet other so-called dialect words are in fact simply General English words with distinctively local pronunciations. *Troshen* and *troshel* are not East Anglian dialect words as such but the General English words *threshing* and *threshold* with an East Anglian pronunciation. *Blar* 'cry' is a local form of *blare;* the word *duzzy* 'foolish' is the East Anglian variant of *dizzy* (from Old English *dysig* 'foolish'); and *brotch* or *brawtch* 'to open' are regional forms of *broach*. The EDD entry for Norfolk *sarnter* /saːntə/ makes it clear that this is simply a local form of *saunter,* although Suffolk *sarnick* is a more genuinely local derivation. Similarly, *darb* /daːb/ is a variant of *daub;* and *garp* /gaːp/ 'stare' is probably a variant of *gape*. *To dudder* 'to shiver' is a local form of *dither*, which originally meant 'to tremble'.[100]

Finally, there are also words which are widely enough known in the anglophone world generally but tend to be used more frequently in East Anglia than in many other areas, such as *hull (hurl)* 'to throw', *reckon* 'to think, believe', and *rum* 'strange'.

5.1 Origins

In spite of these caveats, there are still a rather large number of vocabulary items which can legitimately be characterised as being distinctively or predominantly East Anglian. A number of these are widely used by people who are not necessarily otherwise very dialectal speakers, such as *linen* 'washing, laundry' – and so also *linen-line, linen-peg* etc.; *sowpig* 'woodlouse'; *to find up* 'to look for and find' (see 5.1.3); and *troughings* 'guttering': Kontic's SED data-based map for *troughings* (1990: 112) indicates that the form occurs throughout Suffolk, in all of Norfolk except the Fens, in all of Essex except the southwest. and in central Hertfordshire.[101]

Some East Anglian lexical items are of uncertain origin. The word *shud* 'shed', for example, is not a variant of *shed* but goes back to Late Middle English *schudde* which, according to the OED, is of "of obscure origin" but apparently reflects a Germanic root **skeud-: *skaud-: *skud-* 'to cover' cf. Low German *schode*. The EDD shows it as occurring in Yorkshire, Derbyshire and Herefordshire as well as Norfolk and Suffolk. (*Shed* itself is probably a variant of *shade*, according to the OED.) And *moise*, sometimes *moize, moys*, is a Norfolk and Suffolk verb meaning 'to thrive, to do well'. Forby (1830) has it as 'to mend, improve, increase'; and the OED acknowledges the form as being from East Anglia but has no etymology for it.

Much East Anglian vocabulary, however, is easier to account for and can be thought of as comprising historical strata stacked one on top of the other, reflecting the different waves of invaders and settlers who have crossed the English Channel and the North Sea to Essex, Suffolk, Norfolk and Cambridgeshire over the centuries, as described in 1.1.

---

100 The old northern East Anglian dialect had a number of forms in which medial /ð/ had become /d/, e.g. *further* <fudder>, *Southery* <Suddery> – see below on *later dental hardening* (5.1.3).
101 *Guttering* is from Old French *gutiere*.

5.1.1 Brittonic

The lowest, i.e. the earliest, stratum of vocabulary consists of words which were brought into Britain by the first linguistically identifiable arrivals, the speakers of Brittonic Celtic. However, this layer consists almost entirely of the toponyms and hydronyms listed in 1.1, such as *Lynn*: there are no other distinctively East Anglian vocabulary items which can be identified with any degree of assurance as being of Brittonic origin. This is of course hardly surprising, given that Norfolk and Suffolk were amongst those areas of Britain which Brittonic first disappeared from, as we saw in 1.2.

There is, it is true, the word *dene,* which the OED defines as "a bare sandy tract by the sea; a low sand-hill; as in the *Denes* north and south of Yarmouth". This may be related to *dune,* in which case it is an old Germanic word which, according to the OED, was probably originally borrowed from the same Celtic root which gave modern English *dune* and *down* (as in the South Downs). But then the borrowing from Celtic would have taken place on the Continent rather than in Britain. Briggs argues that *dene* as an English word, whatever its ultimate origin, "seems very likely to have originated in or near Great Yarmouth and spread to the north Suffolk coast. The word 'dune' is certainly a later reborrowing of Dutch *duin*" (Briggs, 2020c).

A slightly better possibility for a truly East Anglian survival from Brittonic is provided by the word *cockey* which, in the *English Dialect Dictionary,* has citations only from East Anglia. *Cockey* means, or meant, 'stream'. There were several cockeys in Norwich: London Street in the city centre was formerly known as Cockey Lane. These urban cockeys came to be used mostly for carrying off sewage, and after they had been covered over the word came to be interpreted as 'sewer, drain'. Philologists are agreed that the *-ey* element probably comes from Old English *ea* 'river' – the same word which appears as the final element in the names of the East Anglian rivers Waveney and Wissey. The *cock-* element is much more difficult to account for. Sandred & Lindström (1989) tell us that origins in Old English *cocc* 'gully' and Old Norse *kók* 'gullet' have been proposed; but they also consider the possibility that it comes from Brittonic *kok* 'water channel'.

A final possibility concerns the word *quant* 'a long pole for propelling a punt or a wherry', *to quant* 'to push a boat along using a quant'. The EDD shows *quant* as occurring only in East Anglia, Kent and Sussex. It gives a number of quotations, including one from the 1895 book *Birds, Beasts and Fishes of the Norfolk Broadland* by Peter Henry Emerson, who was an author and photographer specialising in marsh and fen scenes: "If a good quanter goes in after the pike, he will soon 'muddle' him up". The etymology of *quant* is difficult, but

Walter Skeat (1835–1912), Professor of Anglo-Saxon at Cambridge and President of the English Dialect Society, suggested that *quant* could go back to Ancient Celtic *quonto*, which was related to Latin *contos* and Ancient Greek *kontos* 'punting-pole'.

5.1.2 Old English

It is naturally much easier to identify the layer of East Anglian vocabulary which is of Anglo-Saxon origin. The logical possibilities are that these lexical items may have always been confined to East Anglia; or that they may once have been found in all (or at least all Anglian) varieties of Old English but have now become confined to East Anglia; or that they may over the centuries have developed particular meanings or usages within the region.

The noun *blee* 'resemblance', for example, comes from Old English *bleo* 'colour, hue'. In General English this had become a poetic word with the meaning 'complexion, visage' by the Middle English period, though it survived until the 19th century in the dialects of Northumberland, Yorkshire, Derbyshire and Lincolnshire where, however, it was by then 'obsolete' or 'obsolescent' according to the EDD. The semantic extension to 'resemblance' is not noted by the EDD, but must be an East Anglian innovation. Forby (1830: 28) illustrates it with the example "The boy has a strong blee to his father".

The usage of *boke* 'bulk' can be seen in *The Boy John Letters* (see Chapter 7), where the Boy John writes that the straw stacks are not so big this year because the straw is rather short and "there earnt a lot a boke ter year". According to the OED, the origin lies in Old English *búc* 'belly' (cf. German *Bauch*).

Broad, as in the Norfolk Broads – the area of rivers and shallow reedy lakes well known as a destination for people enjoying boating and walking holidays – is a Norfolk dialect form which dates from at least the mid 17th-century. The word signifies a place where one of the main rivers of the region broadens out into more extensive lake-like waterways – so "broad waters", as opposed to "narrow waters" or rivers. In 1651, Sir Thomas Browne wrote of "lakes and broades".

A *caddow*, most often pronounced /kædə/, is a jackdaw. The *-dow* element is possibly to be identified with the *-daw* part of *jackdaw*, with *daw* meaning 'a small bird of the crow type', although it is not actually attested in Old English. The *ca-* element is possibly from an old word meaning 'jackdaw'. The EDD also gives examples from Northumberland, Yorkshire, and Lincolnshire.

Dickey 'donkey' is a relatively recent East Anglian lexical item, with the OED having no examples before 1781. The original English word for donkey was *ass*, but this became embarrassing for some speakers when rhoticity-loss made *ass* a possible homonym of *arse* (Trudgill, 2016). This led to the development of a number of euphemisms derived from male personal names: *donkey* from *Duncan*, *cuddy* from *Cuthbert*, *neddy* from *Edward*, and *dickey* from *Richard*. According to the OED, *dickey* is found only in Norfolk, Suffolk and Essex.

Dwainy 'weak, sickly' may be from Old English *dwinan* 'to waste away', Middle English *dwine*, which still survives in General English in the originally diminutive form *dwindle*. Alternatively, it could be from early Modern Dutch *dwijnen* 'to vanish'.

To fang 'catch hold of, seize' is a common Germanic verb: modern German *fangen* means 'to catch', and so do Dutch *vangen* and Danish *fange*. In English, however, by the time of the compilation of the EDD, the word in this meaning had become regionally confined to the geographical periphery: Lowland Scotland, Northumberland, Cumberland, Westmoreland, and Yorkshire in the north; Shropshire, Worcestershire, Somerset, Devon and Cornwall in the west; and East Anglia in the east. Sir Thomas Browne (1683) cites the word *fangast* as meaning 'marriageable' (see Ruano-García, 2016). The EDD says of this word that it "is not now known".

To fare 'to seem' is from Old English *faran* and is basically the same word as general English *fare*, as in *he didn't fare very well*, but has acquired a particular meaning in the region. The OED glosses the item as having the dialectal meaning of 'to seem likely, bid fair' and adds that "with *infinitive* it is often little more than a periphrasis for the finite vb." citing, from Dickens's *David Copperfield*, "How do you fare to feel about it, Mas'r Davy?"[102] The EDD gives the meaning 'to behave; to appear, seem', locating this usage in north Yorkshire and Lincolnshire as well as East Anglia, and provides examples such as 'He fared so downhearted' (Essex).The EDD also shows that this meaning has led to the development of the innovative East Anglian noun *faring* 'appearance', as in "I did not like his farings, for his colour went and came" (Suffolk).

To find is obviously a General English word, but *to find up*, as in *I'll find that up for you*, is an East Anglian locution which means 'to look for and find'. It is employed by East Anglians whose speech is otherwise not particularly dialectal. The EDD gives examples from Norfolk and Suffolk and glosses it as 'to discover by search'.

Fit is a General English adjective, but the OED describes the word in the particular meaning of 'in a suitable condition for doing or undergoing something; prepared, ready' as "obsolete". It still survives in this sense in East Anglia, however, as in *Are ya fit?* 'Are you ready?' (e.g. to go out).

---

102 *David Copperfield* (1850) is partly set in Yarmouth (Norfolk) and neighbouring areas.

Hackle is an Essex (but according to the EDD apparently not Norfolk or Suffolk) word meaning 'clothing' (Gepp, 1920). The OED has it as a word of Germanic origin, cognate with Old Saxon *hakul* 'cloak'.

To hain 'to raise, heighten' is probably an East Anglian innovation. It appears in the EDD as being found only in Norfolk and Suffolk – the dictionary cites a 1465 example from the Paston Letters (see 2.3): "he shuld heyne the price of the mershe". The OED supposes that the etymology of the form lies in HIGH + -EN. It cites ten examples, from 1440 to 1898, five of which are explicitly labelled as being from Norfolk or Suffolk. The others include two from the *Promptorium parvulorum*, which is usually attributed to a friar from Lynn, Norfolk; the Paston example; and a quotation from *Lenten Stuffe* by Thomas Nashe, who was born in Lowestoft, Suffolk, in 1567.[103]

A *holl* is a 'hollow, dip in the ground'. This is Old English *hol* (which could also mean 'cave'), Middle English *holl*, related to *hole* and *hollow*.

According to the OED, *loke* 'lane, blind alley, narrow grass path' is a peculiarly East Anglian word (Norfolk and east Suffolk) which is probably from Old English *loca* 'an enclosed place', which may be related to *lock*.

Mardle 'talk, gossip, chat', both a noun and verb (Spurdens, 1858), can be seen from the EDD to be very much an East Anglian word, something which is also confirmed by the OED. There have been hesitant attempts to suggest an etymology in the word *mardle* 'pond' (from French *mardelle*), presumably on the grounds that this was the sort of chat people would indulge in by the village pond, but this is highly doubtful. A very much more likely source is to be found in Old English *maþelian/maðelian* 'to speak, declare', Middle English *mathelen*. The change from to /ð/ to /d/ indicated by the orthographic change from <th> to <d> is said by Lass & Laing (2009) to be a rather common change in varieties of Middle English, which they have termed *later dental hardening*. There is, however, a problem in accounting for the orthographic <r>. The obvious explanation is that the current spelling arose after the loss of rhoticity in East Anglia – whereupon /aː/ could be rendered as <ar> – and that there was never any actual /r/ in the pronunciation. Indeed, the EDD has one East Anglian example which reads "Several narbors stood maudling together in the road".

Another item which almost certainly has its roots in Old English nevertheless does not have an entirely agreed etymology. This is *mawther* (or *mauther*) 'young woman, girl', which the OED characterises as "chiefly East Anglian". It must have been East Anglian for many centuries, since Ihalainen (1994: 202) quotes Ray's 1674 work *A collection of words not generally used* as identifying

---

[103] The tenth example is a 1635 citation from *Shepheards Holy-day* by Joseph Rutter.

mawther as an Eastern England word: Ray locates it to Cambridgeshire, Norfolk, Suffolk, and Essex. And Sir Thomas Browne's 1683 publication *Of Languages and Particularly the Saxon Tongue* cites *mawther* as a word "of no general reception in England but of common use in Norfolk, or peculiar to the East Angle Countries" (1683: VIII; VI). It was also listed by Forby (1831), as well as by Edward Moor in his *Suffolk words and phrases* (1823). It was cited to Ellis's mid-19th-century fieldworkers as being the normal word for 'girl' throughout Norfolk and Suffolk – but by this time only in those counties (Map 5.1). The neutral meaning of 'young woman' has in more recent times been at least partly replaced by the less favourable meaning of 'large, awkward girl'. Etymologically, experts have considered a connection with *mother*. It may also be derived from Old English *mægð* 'girl' and so be related to *maid(en)*: *maid* is still used in the meaning of 'girl' in certain traditional West Country dialects. Interestingly, Keith Briggs has suggested that the word *girl* itself, whose etymology is widely considered to be unknown, may actually have its origins in northeastern Suffolk, perhaps with some etymological connection to the name of the town of Gorleston: "there is support for the claim that the word *girl* arrived in Standard English from East Anglian speech, whatever its ultimate origin", with the possibility that the word has a connection to Middle Low German via east coast seaports such as Gorleston (Briggs, 2020b: 201; 2020d).

Milches /mɪlʃəz/ is a form of *milts*, where *milt* means 'the soft roe of a male fish, notably herring'. Fried *milches and roes* is, or was, a common light meal.

Ought 'nil, zero', as in *Lowestoft Town won five-ought*, is from Old English *oht* 'anything'.

Pent, which is probably a variant of *penned*, has the particular East Anglian meaning of 'hard pressed for time', especially, according to the EDD, 'hard pressed to finish a piece of work within a limited period'.

Pit 'pond' is the same word as General English *pit*, but has a closer connection to the original meaning of Old English *pytt* 'well'. The meaning of 'hole in the ground for water' has become obsolete in many areas but has survived in northern East Anglia: the WGE (Map 38) shows this only for Norfolk and southeast Lincolnshire. Many East Anglian ponds are the result of marl-digging where the resulting pits have become filled with water (Prince, 1962).

According to Moor (1823), *rudle* was a drink made of warm beer, gin and sugar with a slice of lemon peel. Insofar as the word is still used, it now normally refers to weak tea, no doubt originally a jocular reference to the pale colour of tea which is not strong enough. The OED supposes an origin related to *ruddy* 'red', and cites only Moor's Suffolk example, but the word certainly occurs also in Norfolk.

124 — 5 East Anglian lexis and discourse features

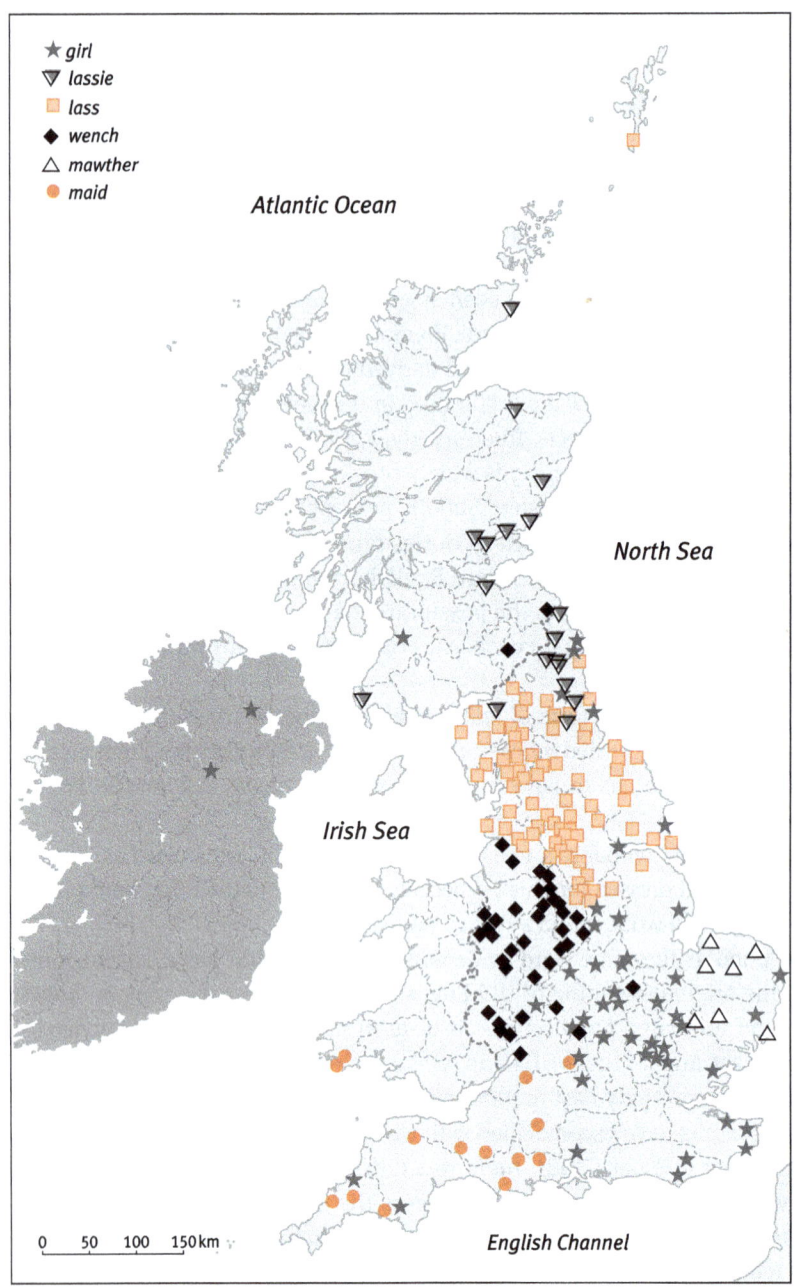

Map 5.1: Mawther.

Sosh most often occurs in the phrase *on the sosh* 'not straight, sloping, slanting'. *Soshways*, according to Cozens-Hardy (1893), means 'diagonally'. The EDD gives examples from Norfolk and Suffolk, as well as from Northamptonshire. In the writing of the Northamptonshire poet John Clare (1793–1864), who came from Helpston (now in Cambridgeshire), *sosh* occurs as a verb: flying crows are said to "sosh askew". The form comes from an original *a-swash*, but according to the OED the etymology of this is obscure. The word has been used in East Anglia for at least some centuries. John Palsgrave was a priest at the court of Henry VIII and a brilliant lexicographer. In 1530 he published a book called *Lesclarcissement de la langue francoyse* 'Elucidation of the French language', in which he demonstrated the usage of the French *à guinguois* 'askew' with the example "A-sosshe as one weareth his bonnet". Palsgrave came from North Barningham, in North Norfolk. Another East Anglian way of expressing the same thing is *on the huh* (/hə/).

Stam 'to amaze' is from an old form *stam* 'state of bewilderment', related to Old English verb *stamerian* 'to stutter'. It appears in the EDD as being a form found in Northamptonshire as well as East Anglia, with examples such as "He was stammed that she should be so careless".

Stingy /stɪndʒi/ 'cruel, malicious' is a General English word which most usually signifies 'mean, ungenerous'; but the East Anglian dialect preserves the probably original meaning which shows a historical relationship to *sting*.

According to the EDD, *thape* is an East Anglian (but also Yorkshire and Cheshire) word meaning 'gooseberry'. The OED suggests that the origin possibly lies in *theve-berry*, with *theve* being derived from *theve-thorn*, an older English word for 'thornbush'. *Theveberry* was shortened to *theaberry* and then to *thebes*, hence later *thapes*. Sir Thomas Browne has the word as *thepes*. Outside of East Anglia, the initial consonant was most often changed to /f/, so *feaberry, fayberry, fabes*. Forby (1830), too, gives an alternate Norfolk form *fapes*: "Fapes s. pl. gooseberries. Variously called also feaps, feabs, fabes and thapes; all abbreviations of feaberries". The headword in the OED is *feaberry*.

Swad is what people elsewhere call *brawn* or *pork cheese*. It consists of pieces of meat from the head and other parts of a pig, set in aspic with onion, pepper and other spices; it is traditionally eaten cold with vinegar and mustard. The word is pronounced with the distinctive local /ɐ/ vowel discussed in 3.2.1.1, and appears in the *English Dialect Dictionary* as <sward>. The EDD shows the word itself as being used all over the North and Midlands of England. The Norfolk variant is cited as *swerd, swad, schwad*, meaning 'the hard, outer rind of bacon'. But there are two additional meanings from Norfolk, from Sydney Cozens-Hardy's 1893 book *Broad Norfolk*: 'a Norfolk dish composed of the rind of pork, seasoned, rolled up tight, boiled and eaten in slices' and – the meaning I am familiar with – 'a kind of brawn, pork-cheese'. It comes from Old English *sweard*, 'bacon rind': the corresponding German word is *Schwarte* and the Dutch *zwoerd*. In the West Frisian language of northern Holland, the word is *swaard*. The *sward* part of the poetic English word *greensward*, meaning 'grass-covered ground, turf', has the same origin as *swad*: just as bacon rind is a covering layer of skin, so *greensward* is a covering layer of grass.

The word *wem* or *wame* refers to an imperfection, such as a stain on a piece of clothing. It comes from Old English *wam* 'spot, blemish', which became Middle English *wem* 'defect (including moral defect), injury, stain'. The word has been obsolete in General English for centuries, but was alive and well in East Anglian English within living memory.

5.1.3 Old Danish

On top of the layer of Old English-origin vocabulary, we find the later lexical stratum derived from Old Norse – predominantly Old Danish – which arrived with the Vikings. As is well known, very many General English words are of Scandinavian origin. Items which entered English as a result of the Viking invasions include: *call, dirt, disk, droop, egg, ill, kid, kindle, loft, odd, root, scold, skirt, sky, ugly, weak*. And there are scores of others, including the grammatical borrowings *they, them* and *their* (see 4.7.4).

But in the parts of Britain where Danish or Norwegian influence was especially strong, there are even more Scandinavian words in local speech. This is particularly true of parts of Scotland, the Lake District, and Yorkshire, where words such as *nieve* 'fist' and *lake* 'to play' occur. But as a result of their Danish heritage, the dialects of East Anglia, too, have a number of words of Old Danish origin which, while most of them are not confined to East Anglia, are not part of the general vocabulary of English either. Because of Viking settlement patterns, this is particularly true of Norfolk and Suffolk, as opposed to Essex and Cambridgeshire.

To addle is not a verb which is known to many East Anglians today, but it is cited by Forby (1830) as an East Anglian word meaning 'to thrive, grow'. It is listed in the EDD as being found in Norfolk, Suffolk and Essex as well as the North Country. It is said by the OED to derive from Old Norse *óðla* 'to acquire property for oneself' from *óðal* 'property'. The modern Danish word *odel* means 'freehold property'.

Bairn 'child' – the modern Danish word is *barn* – is today most usually associated with Northumberland, Scotland and Northern Ireland, but Lowman (see 2.5) recorded it as still in use in Norfolk in the 1930s. Map 77 in WGE shows *bairn* as extending south to the Lincolnshire-Norfolk border but not beyond.

Beck 'brook' is very clearly of Danish origin: the modern Danish word is *bæk*. In its EED entry, *beck* is shown as occurring in Norfolk and Suffolk, as well as in Durham, Cumberland, Westmorland, Yorkshire, Lancashire, Nottinghamshire and Lincolnshire, but it is absent from Cambridgeshire and Essex. Half a century later, it is shown in WGE (Map 39) as surviving in Norfolk, and the word is certainly still alive and well today in Norfolk even amongst children.

Carr 'bog overgrown with brushwood', a word which occurs frequently in the region of the Norfolk Broads, comes from Old Norse *kjarr*. It often occurs in the form of *alder carr* or *osier* (traditionally /ʊʃɪ/) *carr*, depending on the trees involved.

The word *deen* 'noise, sound' is usually found in negative sentences: *He never made a deen*. It might be a form of *din*, from Old English *dynn*, but the long vowel suggests rather an origin in Old Norse *dynr*, compare the modern Faroese *dynur* 'noise, din'.

Grup 'small trench, often at the side of the road' – mostly *groop* in areas other than East Anglia, according to the EDD – is probably the same word as Norwegian *grop* 'pothole'. Forby (1830) has "*grup*, *groop*, a trench, not amounting in breadth to a ditch. If narrower still it is a *grip*; if extremely narrow, a *gripple*".[104]

The General English word *hook* derives from Old English *hōc* 'hook', but the East Anglian form *hake* 'hook over a cooking fire, pothook' probably comes from the related Old Norse word *haki*.

Hulver 'holly', a word which according to the EDD is found only in Norfolk and Suffolk, seems to come from Old Norse *hulfr*.

And while East Anglia does not have the Scandinavian-origin north-country word *lig* 'to lie', the word *ligger* 'plank laid across a dyke as a bridge' does occur.

Marram 'sea grass' is identical to modern Danish *marehalm*, literally 'sea reed': *marram* is given in the EDD as being found in Lincolnshire as well as in East Anglia.

The word *paddock* (the EDD has this from Suffolk and Essex) or *pudd* 'toad' is related to Scandinavian *padde* 'toad'.

In the WGE (Map 165A), *ranny* 'shrew' is shown as occurring throughout Norfolk; in all of Suffolk except the far southeast; in the eight easternmost Essex localities; and in northern Cambridgeshire – making it a good candidate for the status of a "truly East Anglian word". One suggested etymology is Latin *mus araneus* 'spider mouse', but there is no obvious explanation as to how this could have turned into an eastern English dialect word. The OED suggests a much more likely link to Old Norse (and indeed Modern Icelandic) *rani* 'snout'.

---

[104] David Britain reports the form *grupple* from the Norfolk Fens.

A *snack* 'snib, latch of a door' is more usually *sneck* in the north of England and Scotland. The etymology is uncertain, but the OED suggests a possible connection to "Norwegian dialect *snaka* 'to snatch (of animals)'".

As we saw earlier (1.4), the word *staithe* 'landing stage' has an Old Norse origin (it is also found in Scotland, Northumberland, Yorkshire and Lincolnshire).

And *stroop* 'throat, gullet', reported in the EDD for Northumberland as well as East Anglia, comes from Old Norse *strúpe* (modern Norwegian *strupe* 'throat').

5.1.4 French

As is well known, French vocabulary has had an enormous impact on English, but there are nevertheless some items of French origin which can probably be said to belong to the lexis of East Anglia rather than to General English. One possible source would be the refugee "Stranger" Protestant Walloon communities of Colchester and Norwich who established themselves in the region in the second half of the 16th century. Many of these immigrants from the Low Countries worked as weavers, and one word they seem to have brought to Norfolk, Suffolk and Essex is *lucam* 'attic window', which is very probably from French *lucarne* 'skylight'. The word was most often used to refer to the upper windows where weavers used to sit and work to get the best light.

Other East Anglian French-origin words, however, predate the arrival of the Strangers, and are generally Anglo-Norman forms that survived in East Anglia after they had died out elsewhere. One such is the word *duller/dullor* 'noise, to make a noise' as in *Do you stop that dulleren!* It is probably the same as *dolour* 'pain, grief, anguish', first recorded from around 1320. This was originally from Latin *dolere* 'to grieve' via French: modern French has *douleur*. The EED lists it only from Norfolk, Suffolk and Essex. The OED tells us that there was one meaning of *dolour* 'the outward expression of grief; lamentation, mourning; to make dolour, to lament, mourn', which is now obsolete and was last recorded in 1634.

The EDD cites *carnser* as a Norfolk and Suffolk word, also spelt *caunsey, cansey, carnsey*, which refers to 'a causeway, a raised footpath or area over or by a marsh'. The origins of the word are to be found in Anglo-Norman *caucie*, corresponding to modern French *chaussée* 'roadway'.

Another dialect word of probable French origin is *couch* 'left-handed', also *left-couch, couch-handed*. According to the EDD this also occurs in the form of *cooch, coochy* in Devon and Cornwall, but *couch* is the form reported for East Anglia. A probable etymology for this is French *gauche* 'left'.

Culch 'rubbish' is known from Norfolk, Suffolk and Essex and is thought by the OED to be from Anglo-Norman *culche* 'couch, bed, layer, stratum', modern French *couche*.

Perk 'perch, as of a bird' is also of Anglo-Norman origin, from Norman *perque*. The corresponding and more widespread form *perch* is from Old French. Both forms come from Latin *pertica* 'rod'.

A *relly* is a 'narrow ledge or shelf built into a wall'. Moor lists the word as *rilly* 'the dado of a room', as do Forby (1830) and Nall (1866), who both seem to have copied their entries from Moor. Skipper (1996) has it as *rally*. The OED does not know the word.[105] It may be related to *rail*, and so originally from Old French *reille* 'bar'.

A *biffin* or *biffen* is a type of cooking apple particularly associated with Norfolk. This local name represents a dialectal pronunciation of *beefing*, itself an East Anglian word referring to a 'bullock fit for slaughter', from *beef* (from Old French *boef* 'ox'). These apples are so called because they are deep red in colour. It is of course only the derived forms *biffen* and *beefing* which are dialectal. Norfolk Biffins are mentioned by Charles Dickens in his novels *A Christmas Carol*, *Martin Chuzzlewit*, and *Dombey and Son*.

According to the EDD, *million* 'pumpkin' occurs in Norfolk and eastern Suffolk.[106] A good assumption would be that this usage of *million* represents a folk-etymological modification of *melon*. Both *melon* and *million* are words which came into English from French.

5.1.5 Dutch

Although the lexical contribution of Dutch to Standard English is nothing like that of French, it is well established as being of some importance. The loanwords involved tend to fall into a limited number of distinct semantic fields. It is not surprising, given the maritime trading connections between the Low Countries and Britain, that there are numerous words of nautical origin: *bluff, boom, buoy, cruise, deck, dock, drill, freebooter, iceberg, keelhaul, leak, morass, pump, skipper, sloop, smack, smelt, smuggle, yacht*. Other borrowings are probably or possibly trade related: *to bluff, brandy, bundle*. There are a few, later words having to do with painting: *etch, easel, landscape, sketch*; and some others of no particular provenance: *cackle, frolic, grab, offal, roster, skate, slurp*.

---

[105] It was certainly known and used in my North Norfolk family.
[106] From time to time my North Norfolk grandmother would make a *million pie*.

The issue of the Dutch/Flemish contribution to East Anglian lexis, however, is more difficult to determine. Dutch and English are closely related West Germanic languages, and resemblances between Dutch and forms of English are therefore most often due not to the influence of Dutch on English, but to their common origin. Nevertheless, when we find English words that resemble Dutch and which are found *only or mainly* in East Anglia, then it is worth considering whether or not they derive from close contact across the North Sea; or from the Flemish speakers who arrived with the Norman conquest; or from the Flemish weavers who arrived in the 14th century; or from the massive numbers of Dutch-speaking Strangers who arrived in the 16th century, as outlined in 1.6. In this latter scenario, the geolinguistic assumption would be that Dutch words which first arrived in Norwich and Colchester then diffused to the rest of East Anglia, in the familiar pattern of the diffusion of linguistic innovations outwards from urban central places.

According to Markus (2021), the highest proportion of dialect words of Dutch origin in the EDD are found in Durham; Kent and Sussex; and Norfolk, Suffolk and Cambridgeshire. With more recent data, Pettersson's study of the SED materials (1994) has shown that there are more words of Dutch and/or Low German origin in English dialects than in General English, and that the areas of England with the largest number of such dialect words are in Lincolnshire, Norfolk and Essex. She suggests that "this is natural since the Dutch came across the North Sea and primarily settled in the areas in which they first landed".

One phenomenon which is widely accepted as being the result of language contact between northern East Anglian English and the Dutch of the Strangers is the presence in Norwich and other Norfolk towns of open areas which are not called *squares*, as they would be elsewhere, but *plains*. This seems rather uncontroversially to be a borrowing of Dutch *plein*: in Norwich there is a Bank Plain, St Andrew's Plain, St George's Plain, St Giles's Plain and several more. Yarmouth has Priory Plain, St Peter's Plain, Theatre Plain and Whitehorse Plain. Cromer has Lifeboat Plain. And this naming tradition is continued to the present day, albeit somewhat self-consciously, in new-build areas.

Other East Anglian dialect words which have been suggested as being of Dutch origin (Trudgill, 2003) include *push* 'boil, pimple', which is another truly East Anglian word: the WGE (Map 107) shows it as occurring in all the Cambridgeshire, Norfolk and Suffolk SED localities, plus in northeastern Essex and northern Hertfordshire. The most obvious derivation is from Dutch *puist*, Low German *pust* 'pimple', as suggested by the OED; but the first examples in the OED come from the 1400s, so this is clearly not an item that arrived with the 16th-century refugees.

On the other hand, *dwile* 'floorcloth, dishcloth' is not recorded until the late 1700s and so it can well have arrived with the Strangers: Forby (1830: 101) defines it as "a refuse lock of wool" or "a mop made of them" or "any coarse rubbing rug". The EDD shows this word as being confined to the dialects of Norfolk and Suffolk, apart from one example from Cambridgeshire. The OED suggests a derivation from Dutch *dweil* 'mop, floorcloth', which is clearly correct.

A *hutkin* or *hudkin* is a covering for a sore finger – a fingerstall. The EDD has examples from Norfolk, Suffolk and Cambridgeshire: "That there cut on your finger's rare and angry – you'd better put a hutkin on." *Hoedekin* in medieval Dutch meant 'little hat'. The suffix *-kin* is an old Germanic diminutive morpheme which is related to German *-chen,* as in *Mädchen* 'girl', and survives most frequently in modern English in surnames such as Wilkin(s) and Watkin(s). According to the OED, the suffix was unknown in Old English, and many English words with this suffix are borrowed from Dutch.

To crowd is defined by the EDD as 'to push, move, shove, especially to push a wheelbarrow', with examples only from Norfolk and Suffolk. The word may well, then, come from Dutch *kruien,* earlier *kruyden,* 'to push a wheelbarrow'. It is true that Old English did have a verb *crúdan* 'to push', so the case for an origin in the Low Countries cannot be entirely certain. But the fact that the meaning is very precisely 'push a wheelbarrow'[107] in both the Low Countries and in East Anglia, and that the English word is restricted to Norfolk and Suffolk, just across the North Sea from Holland and Belgium, does point in that direction.

Dannocks 'thick leather gloves used by hedgers' is shown by the EDD to be East Anglian; and the OED claims that the etymology lies in the name of the Belgian town of Tournai, which in Flemish is called Doornik.

Other East Anglian words (Trudgill, 2003) which have been suggested as being due to Dutch are less certain. *Deek* 'dyke/dike, ditch' could be from Dutch *dijk*: it is shown in the EDD as a variant of *dike*, but is given as occurring with the FLEECE vowel in East Anglia as well as in the other southern East Coast counties of Lincolnshire and Kent, which could make it a trans-North Sea word.

Fye out 'to scour, clean up' is also purely East Anglian, according to the EDD, but the dictionary lists, too, the similar form *fay/fey/feigh* as occurring very widely with a similar meaning in 19th-century dialects in many parts of northern England. The northern form with the FACE vowel is supposed by the OED to be from Old Norse *fǽgja* 'to cleanse, polish'. But this does leave open the possibility that the Norfolk/Suffolk form with the PRICE vowel is a borrowing of Dutch *vegen,* earlier *vagen* 'to sweep'.

---

107 Also, in 20th-century East Anglia, 'to pedal a bicycle vigorously'.

Mouse-hunt 'weasel', cf. *mouse-hunter* in Text 4 in Chapter 7, comes from Middle Dutch *muushont* 'weasel' according to the OED, and is labelled "East Anglian" in the EDD.

5.1.6 Other languages

Cooshie, a noun defined by the EDD as a 'sweet, lollipop', occurs only in Norfolk and Suffolk. One possibility is that this has the same origin as General English *cushy* 'soft, easy, as of a job', which comes from Hindi-Urdu, according to the OED. Many such words were brought back from India by British soldiers, but the geographical restriction of this term to Norfolk and Suffolk renders this unlikely, and favours instead an origin in Romany, the language of the Romani or Gypsies which is a close relative of Hindi/Urdu, where *kushti* means 'good': for the last several centuries there has been a relatively high proportion of British Romani in East Anglia (see 1.7).

This may account, too, for the frequent occurrence of the adjective *rum* 'strange' in East Anglian English, as particularly in the expression *'Ass a rum'n* 'That's a strange thing'. *Rum* 'strange' is, significantly, an especially British word – Americans often do not know what it means; and the best etymological account of its origin is that it comes from the Romany word *rom* 'man'. The English meaning was originally 'exceptionally good', later 'exceptional', and subsequently 'odd'.

To mob 'scold, nag, complain' derives from the word *mob* 'unruly crowd', which is an abbreviation of Latin *mobile vulgus* 'excitable crowd'. In most of the English-speaking world, it requires a large group of people to 'mob' somebody, but in East Anglia you can do it all by yourself. The EDD gives examples of this usage from Essex, Suffolk, Norfolk, and Northamptonshire.

5.2 East Anglian Fishing vocabulary

East Anglia has a west coast, a north coast and east coast, with many ports and fishing harbours including (King's) Lynn, Wells, Sheringham, Cromer, and (Great) Yarmouth in Norfolk; Lowestoft, Southwold, Aldeburgh, and Felixstowe in Suffolk; and Harwich, West Mersea, and Leigh (-on-Sea) in Essex. It is not surprising, therefore, that the area has developed an extensive and to some extent distinctive maritime and fishing vocabulary.

This has been intensively researched by David Butcher, a Lowestoft man, whose 2014 book *Fishing Talk* is a rich source of information about coastal lexis. It is unsurprising that quite a number of the maritime words he cites have a trans-North-Sea Dutch or Scandinavian origin. The following examples are all taken from Butcher (2014).

A *cran* is 'a measure of capacity for fresh herrings', officially 37.5 gallons (about 750 fish). Like a number of other East Anglian fishing terms – because of the British East Coast fishing connections – this item is of Scottish origin but it comes not from Scots, but from Scottish Gaelic, where *cran* is 'a measure for fresh herring'.

Another even longer-distance connection is signalled by *digby*, which is a particular type of dried or cured herring, named for Digby, a seaport in Nova Scotia, Canada.

A *fantail* is a 'Northern squid'.

A *heft* is anything a rope could catch or snag on, causing it to foul.

A *lop* means a heavy swell on the sea. The OED has *lop* as 'a state of the sea in which the waves are short and lumpy', and suggests that the word is onomatopoeic in origin.

Love is an East Anglian word referring to one of the transverse beams that supported the spits in a smokehouse for curing herring: the OED has no etymology for this, but the EDD has the form *louver/louvre* 'an opening in the roof of a building to let out the smoke', which *love* might be connected to, as Butcher suggests. The related and today more familiar meaning of *louvre* is 'an arrangement of sloping boards, laths or slips of glass overlapping each other, so as to admit air, but exclude rain'.[108]

A *mand* /ma:nd/ is a 'wicker basket holding about two-and-a-half stone[109] of herring' (p. 83): an obvious source for this is Dutch *mand* 'basket'.

Mash means 'mesh', as in a net, and seems rather obviously to derive from medieval Dutch *masche* with the same meaning.

Ped is an East of England word, of uncertain origin, meaning a 'tall wicker basket' as used by the fishermen.

To scud is 'to shake herrings from the meshes of a drift-net'.

Shannock means 'to go longshore fishing': people from Sheringham on the North Norfolk coast are popularly known as Shannocks, and many Sheringham men were involved in this kind of fishing. *Shannock* derives from the fact that the local pronunciation of the place-name *Sheringham* is often /ʃæɹɲəm/.

A *tusk* is a particular type of cod. The word is of Scandinavian origin: the Danish word for *cod* is *torsk*.

Yoll is the East Anglian variant of *yawl* 'a small kind of fishing boat' and is probably simply the Dutch word for the same kind of boat, *jol*.

---

[108] As the OED points out, *louvre* in these senses has no connection with the Louvre in Paris.
[109] 35 lbs = c.16 kgs.

Other interesting terminology includes *down* and *up*, which mean respectively 'northwards' and 'southwards' with reference to the North Sea, because the ebb tide flows in a northerly direction. According to Butcher, when fishermen left Suffolk for Shetland, they "went down to Shetland" (2014: 44).

5.3 Agricultural terms

Barringer's *A History of Norfolk* (2017) contains a section on East Anglian agricultural terms which cites words and usages, some of which have a good claim to be peculiarly or especially East Anglian. The term *breck*, for instance, is particularly associated with the Breckland[110] area of southwestern Norfolk and the adjacent area of northwestern Suffolk, which is characterised by poor sandy soil with heathland-type vegetation, small meres with variable water levels, and more recent tree plantations. The name *Breckland* was first applied to the region in 1894 by the Thetford-born journalist and naturalist W.G. Clarke, with reference to the medieval system of the farming of this infertile region by rotation. Each section of land was ploughed in turn every tenth year, with 90% of the land thus lying fallow at any one time, producing a series of "breaks" or *brecks* across the landscape.

Assart, originally a loan from French, signifies a piece of forest or pastureland converted into arable land.

Foldcourse is most usually employed to refer to a sheepwalk, i.e. a relatively small tract of land for the grazing of sheep.

Shack is glossed by Forby as 'the shaken grain remaining on the ground when harvest and gleaning are over; or, in woodland countries, the acorns, or mast under the trees'. Animals turned into the stubble after harvest were said to be *at shack*. The word appears to have the same origin as *shake*.

A *terrier* was a catalogue or register of land, from Latin *terrarium* via French *terrier*.

5.4 Archaic East Anglian vocabulary

One of the earliest reports we have on specifically East Anglian lexis comes from Sir Thomas Browne (1683) who, as we saw (5.1.3), complied a list of 17th-century words "peculiar to the East Angle Countries". Browne was born in

---

110 Not to be confused with the modern Norfolk local government area of the same name.

London in 1605, but moved to Norwich in 1637 and lived there until he died in 1682. Among the words he mentions are the following items which are for the most part no longer known to most East Anglians.

Cothish 'unwell, weakly' is derived from the Old English-origin word *cothe* or *coath* 'disease', characterised by the OED as "obsolete". It occurs in the form of *cothy* in Text 2 in Chapter 7.

Kedge or *kidge* 'brisk, active, lively' is recognised by the EDD as being mainly East Anglian, with examples from Cambridgeshire, Norfolk and Suffolk. The OED labels it as "East Anglian dialect", but has no etymology for it. In more recent times, Skipper (1996) reports the word as *kedgy* and specifies that it typically signifies 'agility in the elderly'.

Sibrit 'banns of marriage' is reported in the EDD under the headword *sibberidge* as occurring in Norfolk and Suffolk in forms such as *sibberet(s), sibbits, sibbret, siberet, sibrets, sibright*. Skipper (1996) has it as *sibbits* or *sibrits*. The OED gives the origin of its corresponding headword *sibred* 'kinship, consanguinity' as lying in Old English *sib* 'kin'. It cites as East Anglian dialect the use of *sibred* in the meaning of 'banns of marriage', and explains that this usage probably stems from the mention in the banns of "sibred" (consanguinity) as an impediment to marriage.

Browne's *thurck* also appears in the EDD, where it is located to East Anglia and the South Country, under the headword *thark* 'dark'. The headword is given as *therk* in the OED, which states that this obsolete form is apparently a variant of Middle English *derk* 'dark', but that the change from /d/ to /θ/ or /ð/ is "abnormal and unexplained".

Another source of older terms comes from the work of Joshua Larwood (1748–1808), who was Rector of Swanton Morley in Norfolk. At the very beginning of the 19th century, Larwood published a book (Larwood, 1800) which contained, amongst much else, a "Norfolk Dialogue". This was republished by Professor Walter William Skeat in his *English Dialects from the Eighth Century to the Present Day* (Skeat, 1912), and is reproduced in this book as Text 2 in Chapter 7. This dialogue is of great interest for its antiquity, and it contains a number of lexical items which are labelled by the EDD as "obsolete", as well as others which are not in the EDD at all, probably because they were no longer known by the very end of the 19th century.

Two of these forms can be seen in Larwood's phrase *she's ollas in dibles wi' the knacker and thackster* 'she's always in trouble with the collar-maker and thatcher". *Dibles* has an entry in the EDD, which cites it as coming from Norfolk and Suffolk, and glosses it as 'difficulties, embarrassments, scrapes', as in *I ha' bin in the dibles this mornin'*. The word does not appear in the OED, though some writers assume that there is some etymological connection with French *diable* 'devil'.

Nacker or *knacker* is shown by the EDD to occur in Lincolnshire, Huntingdonshire and Northamptonshire as well as in the core East Anglian zone. The dictionary glosses it as 'a saddle or harness maker'. Ray (1691) has it as 'one that makes collars and other furniture for cart-horses'. The etymology is uncertain. *Thackster* is the East Anglian form which corresponds to Northern *thacker* and southern *thatcher*.

Beergood 'yeast' has references in the EDD only from East Anglia. Other sources (for example Ray, 1673) cite another word for yeast as being typical of East Anglia and Kent: *gosgood*. The OED gives the etymology of this form as being from *God's good*, also used of 'something considered to be without human owner'.

Another of Larwood's words is *snasty*, which appears in Skipper (1996) as 'bad-tempered'. The EDD has it as *snaisty* 'cross, peevish, angry, annoyed' and locates it to Yorkshire as well as to Cambridgeshire, Norfolk, Suffolk and Essex – it is also cited in Charnock's 1880 *Glossary of the Essex Dialect* and in Gepp's 1920 *A Contribution to an Essex Dialect Dictionary*.

Paryard 'enclosed yard for livestock' is also a typically Suffolk and Norfolk form: it occurs in the writings of Norfolk-born George Borrow (1803–1881). The *par-* element appears to come from an old verb meaning 'to enclose', but I have found no further etymological information for it.

Pur is 'a poker, to poke (a fire)'. According to the EDD, it occurred in Scotland and the North of England as well as in East Anglia. The OED has tentative Dutch and Scandinavian etymologies under the heading of *purr*.

5.5 Discourse features

5.5.1 Terms of address and greetings

The famous but now obsolescent East Anglian general term of address, *bor* is thought to come from Old English (*ge*)*bur* 'dweller, farmer'. This is the same element which is found in *neighbour*, Old English *neah bur* 'near-dweller'; and in modern Dutch *buur* 'neighbour'. The EDD has it only from Cambridgeshire, Norfolk, Suffolk and Essex; so while the origin is certainly common West Germanic, the usage as a term of address is probably an East Anglian innovation. According to Forby (1830), the term "is applied indiscriminately to persons of both sexes and all ages", but in modern times it has been almost exclusively used to males. There is also a specifically female form of address in the traditional dialect, namely *maw*, which is an abbreviated form of the word *mawther* 'girl, young woman' which we mentioned above (5.1.3).

Both of these forms are singular only. As a form of address to two or more people, the quasi-pronominal second-person plural form *together* (as discussed in 4.7.1) can be used, as in "Good afternoon, together!"

Boy and *girl* (typically /gʌl/) can also be used as terms of address for people of all ages: *Are y'alright, gal? Come you on, boy!* These forms are also conjoined to personal names and used as terms of reference for adults: *Here come the Boy Harbert; That look like the Gal Mary*. One of best of all pieces of Norfolk Dialect writing can be found in a book which goes by the title of *The Boy John Letters*: the pieces in it were written by an author who signed his name as "The Boy John" (see Text 3 in Chapter 7).

Another traditional term of address is *ol' partner,* used in addressing males. The vowel in *partner* is often short /ʌ/ rather than long /a:/ (see 3.2.1.3): [ʌʊl pʌʔnə].

A typical greeting is *Are y'alright?* which, rather like General English *How do you do?*, is grammatically a question but does not necessarily require an answer. Typical leave-taking formulae include *Mind how y'go!* and *See you later!* (which does not necessarily imply seeing someone later). A traditional Norwich form of 'goodbye' is /hɛ: gu:/ *Here go!*

In the older dialect, one response to a greeting or a toast wishing someone a good day or good health, according to Sir Thomas Browne, was *sammodithee,* apparently derived from 'the same unto thee'. The EDD labels this expression "obsolete East Anglian" and quotes the following dialogue: "'A health to you, Peter,' said I. 'Sammodithee,' replied he."

5.5.2 Answer particles

Yes – often /jɪs/[111] – and *no* are the most usual affirmative and negative answer particles in East Anglia. In the northern part of the area where /ʌu/ and /u:/ remain distinct, as in *mown* and *moan* (see 3.2.1.2), *no* is normally /nʌu/ as the negative particle but can be /nu:/ when emphatic.

There is also, however, an alternative East Anglian affirmative particle, namely *ah!* This appears to be the East Anglian equivalent of the much more widespread *aye* 'yes'.[112] East Anglian *ah* is perhaps more often used to express agreement rather than to answer yes-no questions directly (Trudgill, 2016). So:

---

[111] See "yis" in the Margaret Paston letter, Chapter 7, Text 1).
[112] The origins of *aye* are unknown: according to the OED, it is not known to be an Old English word, and was first recorded as late as the 16th century.

Is that cold outside? – Yes.
Thass cold!   – Ah, that is.

Interestingly, both *yes* and *no* also have East Anglian variants which are used specifically in very emphatic contexts. These variants are most usually spelt *jearse* and *dow*, and are pronounced so as to rhyme with *pierce*[113] and *cow* respectively. These special answer particles have been extensively studied by Howe (2018). *Jearse* occurs as in *Are you goen' out Saturday night? – Jearse!* (= Yes, of course, obviously, naturally, you needn't have bothered to ask!). *Dow* occurs as in *Have you done your homework yet? – Dow!*[114] (= No, don't be daft, of course I haven't!). Howe suggests that *jearse* could be derived from *dear, yes!* in the sense of 'oh dear me, yes!'. Similarly, *dow* might be derived from *dear, no!* His extensive research shows that these forms are still widely used today, including by young people, in Cambridgeshire, Huntingdonshire, Norfolk, Suffolk, and northeastern Essex, as well as in parts of Lincolnshire.

5.5.3 Intensifiers and interjections

Traditional dialect intensifiers, as already briefly noted (4.10), include the relatively archaic *master*, together with *rare* and *wholly* (which in the basilect rhymes with *fully*). For *master*, the EDD gives examples from Norfolk, Suffolk, Essex and Hertfordshire, including *That fared a master long time to me* and *That's a master fine hoss you a* [have] *got* . For *rare*, the EDD cites the Suffolk example *A rare great old sow*. And for *wholly*, we find *That snew wholly; That fared wholly warm;* and *You may me believe I was wholly vexed*. Lowestoft fishermen also employed *funny* as an intensifier, as in *That come over funny dark* (Butcher, 2014: 54).

There is also probably a greater tendency than in most other regions to use the adjective *old* to indicate familiarity or disparagement: *Thass oony an ol' sparra* 'It's only an old sparrow'; *Thass a load a old squit* 'It's a lot of nonsense'.

A frequent interjection is *blast!* /blaːst ~blɐst/ or *cor blast!*

---

113 Note that no /r/ is involved.
114 This example is recalled from my own Norwich schooldays.

5.5.4 Truce terms

Iona & Peter Pie's book *The Lore and Language of Schoolchildren* (1959) has a fascinating section on the truce terms which are called out by children wanting time out from a game. In different parts of the country, terms include *fainites, barley, kings, keys,* and *crosses*. The Opies reported that in East Anglia the term used was connected to the form *crosses*, namely *exes*. My own recollection, confirmed by colleagues from Ipswich, is that the usual East Anglian form in the 1940s, 1950s and 1960s was *exies*, accompanied by the crossing of fingers.

5.6 Conversational style

Dialects differ in their conversational styles as well as in their accents, grammars and vocabularies. Some urban dialect areas, for instance, are known for the ability of their speakers to conduct conversations containing quick-fire wit and repartee. In other areas, such as East Anglia, slower speech styles and more sardonic wit is appreciated. This is part of a much wider pattern in the world's languages whereby different communities have different norms for the use of language. These norms can involve various parameters: how much people say, how quickly they speak, how loudly they talk, and the degree to which they talk to strangers.

In England, differences involving norms of this type often emerge from informal anecdotes and tales about different parts of the country. In his 1927 book *In Search of England*, H.V. Morton recounts the story of a car trip he took around the country in the 1920s. He wrote that, after he had travelled from Lincolnshire into Norfolk: "I was lost in a Norfolk lane, so I stopped a man and said to him: 'Good morning! Can you tell me if I am right for Norwich?' The Norfolkman replied: 'What d'ye want to know for?'."

Most East Anglians even today would understand that that was a joke, albeit an anti-outsider joke: the old Norfolkman was teasing Morton, as is very common in the British Isles. But Henry Canova Vollam Morton did not understand it as such, and attributed it to a distrust of outsiders, not realising that as an upper-class outsider – driving a car in the 1920s was not a privilege available to the average rural person – he was simply the victim of East Anglian humour. The sense of humour, and conversational style generally, which tend to go along with the traditional East Anglian dialect are by no means confined to this region, but the style is typically slow, deadpan, sardonic, understated, and ironic.

6 East Anglian English in the world

During the 1600s, the period of our history when the English language first started leaving the British Isles and travelling across the Atlantic (Trudgill, 2017), Norwich was the second largest city in England, Ipswich was the seventh, Yarmouth the eighth, Cambridge the tenth, and Colchester the twelfth (Hoskins, 1984). It would therefore not be at all surprising to find that East Anglian English initially played an important role in the formation of the new Colonial Englishes which were soon to start developing in the Americas, and then subsequently in the Southern Hemisphere. In this chapter we examine some of the evidence that this was the case by investigating both phonological and grammatical features.

6.1 Bermuda and the Caribbean

The first location where any sizeable group of native speakers of English became successfully established outside the British Isles was the Jamestown settlement in Virginia, in what is now the United States of America. It was founded in 1607 by the London Company, with apparently very little East Anglian participation. The second such episode followed very soon after, however, on the hitherto uninhabited island of Bermuda (Ayres, 1933). Here the first English speakers to arrive, in 1609, were en route for Jamestown when they were shipwrecked on the island – Bermuda is about 550 miles/900 km east of the North American mainland.

Modern Bermudian English does show some signs of some possible East Anglian input in its formation. For instance, the LOT vowel in Bermudian English (see Trudgill, 2019) is typically unrounded [ɑ], as in northern East Anglia (see 3.2.1.1), though that is, of course, a feature of most North American Englishes. More intriguingly, the consonants /w/ and /v/ are merged in Bermudian English. Because of the phonotactics of /w/ in English, this merger can only manifest itself in syllable-initial position, giving homonyms such as *wine* and *vine*, *Wales* and *veils*. The actual phonetic quality of the single merged consonant is [β] or [β̞] – a voiced bilabial fricative or approximant. Ayres writes of an "apparent interchange of [v] and [w]" (1933: 9) in Bermuda but, as discussed in Trudgill et al. (2003), this is a typical misperception on the part of listeners who have the distinction in their own speech: there is no interchange, in fact, but rather a merger on an intermediate articulation, as Ayres also finally concludes. Fascinatingly, the merger is also a feature of the traditional dialect of Charleston, South Carolina: Primer (1888) wrote that the Charleston dialect of his period was characterised by "coalescence of /v / and /w/, with resulting homonymy of *wail* and *veil*, etc." (McDavid, 1955: 37).

As we saw in 3.2.2, this merger was very much a feature of southeast of England dialects in the 1700s and 1800s, particularly in East Anglia: Wright (1905: 227) states that "initial and medial v has become w in mid-Buckinghamshire, Norfolk, Suffolk, Essex, Kent, east Sussex". However, according to Jordan (1974) there is evidence of a loss of contrast between /w/ and /v/ going back to the late 14th century, so it is perfectly possible that the merger was actually transplanted directly from England to Bermuda at the time of the first settlement.

The *v-w merger* also occurs today in Montserrat, which was settled by English speakers in the 1630s; the Bay Islands of Honduras, which were occupied by English-speaking buccaneers in 1642 (Davidson, 1974); the Bahamas, which saw settlement by dissident Bermudian anglophones, also in the 1640s, as well as colonists from England; and in several other extra-territorial Englishes (Trudgill et al., 2003).

6.2 New England

The third anglophone settlement outside the British Isles occurred in 1610, in Newfoundland (Clarke, 2010). This was organised by the Bristol Society of Merchant Venturers, which had been given a charter by King James I for establishing a colony on the island; it seems to have had no East Anglian involvement. However, the next episode of English-speaking colonisation beyond the British Isles chronologically was the well-known Puritan New England settlement by the so-called Pilgrim Fathers, in Plymouth, Massachusetts, which began in 1620. Here it is rather well established that there was, by contrast, considerable East Anglian involvement.

The New England area of the northeastern United States – the modern states of Maine, New Hampshire, Vermont, Massachusetts, Rhode Island and Connecticut – today contains very many place-names which are also East Anglian toponyms: Ipswich, Massachusetts dates from the 1630s; and both Norwich and Colchester, Vermont were settled in 1763. Just a few of the additional Norfolk-origin names in New England include Attleboro [Attleborough], Burnham, Hingham, Lynn, Newmarket, Norfolk, Norwich, Rockland, Thetford, Walpole, Wayland, Windham [Wymondham], Wolcott [Walcott], and Yarmouth. Suffolk names include Brandon, Haverhill, Holbrook and Wenham; from Essex we find, amongst others, Braintree and Dedham; and from Cambridgeshire there are Cambridge and Ely.

Of course, this is only suggestive of heavy East Anglian settlement, but we do know that the Pilgrim Fathers who founded the eastern New England Massachusetts colony were predominantly from the radical Puritan eastern counties of England, and a high proportion of the adult pilgrims on the *Mayflower* who settled the Plymouth Colony came from Norfolk and Essex (Johnson, 2006).

It would be surprising if this had not had some linguistic consequences, and there is in fact good evidence that it did. For instance, the typical East Anglian pronunciation of *room* and *broom* with the FOOT vowel is also typical of New England (Francis, 1961). More importantly, the phonological phenomenon of the 'East Anglian short *o*', which involves the usage of the FOOT vowel in GOAT words, as in *boat* /bʊt/, *home* /hʊm/, also occurs in New England, as we briefly noted in 3.2.1.1. It is in fact a very well-known characteristic of New England English: the 'New England short *o*' has been discussed a number of times in the literature on American dialects, e.g. in Avis (1961) and in Kurath & McDavid (1961: 12). Avis tells us that the heartland of the New England phenomenon lies in eastern Vermont, New Hampshire, northeastern Massachusetts, and Maine, as well as in southwestern New Brunswick, Canada. Kurath (1964: 150) writes:

> Only New England [in the USA] preserves the original [Middle English] distinction [of ǭ and *ou*], though to a limited extent. Here the old monophthong survives in checked position as a short and fronted mid-back vowel /ɵ/ as in *stone, road, coat* /stɵn, rɵd, kɵt/, contrasting with upgliding /o/, as in *know, grown*.

Kurath (1965) asks the question: "Is the survival of contrasting vowels in New England to be attributed to English folk speech?" and answers: "New England usage in this matter probably derives from English folk speech or from a regional type of Standard British English reflecting folk usage." In an earlier publication (1928) he gives a more geographically detailed answer to the question: "The population of the seaboard of New England had come for the most part from southeastern counties of England"; and "the shortened vowel of *coat, whole*, and *home* is recorded for East Anglia".

However, there is an important difference between the East Anglian and the New England phenomena: the 'New England short *o*' contrasts with the FOOT vowel as central [ɵ] versus back [ʊ], while in northern East Anglia the vowels are identical: *road* and *hood* are perfect rhymes and have been at least since the late 1700s, as reported by Forby (1830: 90): "The long o ... has also in some words the common short sound of the diphthong *oo* (in *foot*), or that of the vowel *u* in *pull*", citing the examples of *bone, stone, whole* (see 3.2.1.1).

Another interesting point is that items listed by Avis (1961) as occurring with the 'New England short *o*' include the following, which also demonstrate 'short *o*' in East Anglia: *boat, bone, broke, coat, goat, home, most, oats, post, road, stone, toad, toast, suppose, whole*. Avis, however, also cites a number of words which do not have 'short *o*' in New England but which do have it in East Anglia: *coast, drove, froze, over, rode, yolk*. This can perhaps be explained in terms of the loss of this recessive feature in New England in these lexical items. We can suppose that these words formerly had 'short *o*' in New England but had lost them by the time the research on which Avis's paper was based was carried out in the 1930s – or, more prosaically, that the field worker simply failed to elicit this (stigmatised) pronunciation.

However, there are also two further issues which are problematic if we wish to establish any connection. First is the fact that, while in neither dialect can shortening occur in open syllables, for obvious phonotactic reasons, East Anglia retains a distinction in open syllables between the two original ME lexical sets, while New England does not, as Kurath acknowledges in his phrase "to a limited extent":

	hood	road	go	low
East Anglia	/ʊ/	/ʊ/	/uː/	/ou/
New England	/ʊ/	/ə/	/ou/	/ou/

The number of problematical words involved here is rather small. GOAT items which have stressed syllable-final /uː/ in northern East Anglian English are rather few: *Coe, foe, go, Joe, no, roe, so, toe, woe*.[115] Again, we can therefore argue that this difference between East Anglia and New England can be accounted for by dedialectalisation in New England. We could hypothesise that New England English formerly had a distinct vowel also in open syllables, but that it has lost it under the influence of more mainstream forms of English.

To turn now to a different phonological feature, it is also possible to argue that East Anglian English was involved in the development of the *yod-dropping* feature which is widespread in North America. Unlike in most of the British Isles and the Southern Hemisphere, varieties of English in the USA and Canada outside the American South have yod-dropping after /t/ and /d/ as well as after /n/, as in words such as *tune, duke, new*. As we saw earlier (3.2.2), modern northern East Anglia has taken the long historical process of the loss of /j/ before /uː/ to its logical conclusion and now does not even have /j/ in *cue, huge, music* or *view*. A reasonable view, however, would be that at the time of the settlement of New England by East Anglians, yod-dropping had already progressed from the

---

115 *Hoe* has /ou/ rather than /uː/: it had *ou* in Middle English and was originally spelt <howe> etc. The current spelling, which dates only from the 18th-century, is unetymological.

post-/r/ and post-/l/ contexts, as in *rule* and *lute*, to include all post-alveolar consonantal environments, as in *suit, nude, student, due*, and it was this stage which became established as English spread westwards across the American continent. The spread of yod-dropping to post-velar, post-glottal and post-labial environments then proceeded to occur back in East Anglia after the New England settlers had departed.

6.3 The American South and African American English

6.3.1 The 'Southern drawl'

According to Wells (1982: 529), "the best-known characteristic of southern pronunciation [in the United States] is the so-called southern drawl" which "involves relatively greater length in unstressed, accented syllables as compared to unstressed" with "a wider weakening of unstressed syllables than in other accents". McDavid (1968) agrees: the 'Southern drawl' involves "prolongation of the most heavily stressed syllables, with the corresponding weakening of the less stressed ones".

It will be recalled that this is precisely the way in which the rhythmic phonology of East Anglian English was characterised in 3.1. We saw there that stressed syllables tend to be longer and more heavily stressed in East Anglian English than in most other accents, and that unstressed syllables are correspondingly shorter. We also saw there that Ferragne & Pellegrino (2007) showed that East Anglian English was the most stress-timed of all the fourteen British Isles dialects which they investigated, with comparatively great durational differences between stressed and unstressed vowels. Figure 3.1, from Ferragne & Pellegrino, demonstrated that the East Anglian dialect had the largest ratio of the length of stressed to unstressed syllables of all the 14 accents investigated. It is possible, then, to see a role here for East Anglian dialects in leading to the development of the 'Southern drawl', although this is of course conjectural.

6.3.2 Conjuction *do*

However, there is one characteristic which almost certainly made its way from East Anglia to the American South, perhaps strengthening the hypothesis about the 'Southern drawl'. This is the grammatical feature discussed at some length in 4.12.2 in which, in the older traditional dialects of East Anglia, the obviously originally verbal form *do* functions as a conjunction that is approximately semantically equivalent to the conjunction *otherwise*. The *English Dialect Dictionary* shows that this usage was once found in the rural dialects of Norfolk, Suffolk, Cambridgeshire and northern Essex. It is not found anywhere in the British Isles outside East Anglia; nor, as far as I know, does it occur anywhere else in the English-speaking world at all – with one exception: the southeastern United States.

The *Dictionary of American Regional English* (DARE) cites a number of examples of conjunction *do* in the African American English as portrayed in works written by the novelist Zora Neal Hurston, which are set in northern Florida. Hurston was born in 1903 in Eatonville, Florida, the first incorporated Black town in the United States. She was a folklorist as well as a novelist, and she studied under the famous linguist and anthropologist Franz Boas (1858–1942). There is every reason to believe that her renderings of her native Black Florida dialect are authentic. The examples given in *Dictionary of American Regional English* are as follows:

1. Dat's a thing dat's got to be handled just so, do it'll kill you (*Mules and Men*, 1935).
2. Don't you change too many words wid me dis mawnin', Janie, do Ah'll take and change ends wid yuh! (*Mules and Men*, 1935).
3. You got to have a subjick tuh talk from, do you can't talk (*Mules and Men*, 1935).
4. Yuh can't live on de muck 'thout yuh take uh bath every da – Do dat muck'll itch yuh lak ants (*Their Eyes*, 1937).
5. Git this spoon betwixt her teeth do she's liable to bite her tongue off (*Seraph*, 1948).

The DARE editors conjecture that the origins of this conjunctional *do* probably lay in an "abbreviation of *do you* (= *if you do*) etc. following negative statements or commands" (p. 94). But, as can be seen, while this explanation works for example 2, it does not for the others, which show progress towards the fully completed grammaticalisation also typical of East Anglia in that *do* is employed where *don't* might have been expected.

Interestingly, we also have conclusive evidence that conjunction *do* is used elsewhere in the American southeast, and that it remains current, or did until recently. In the 1994 field recordings made by Milton Tynch (see Tynch 1994), we find the following example from a Black speaker from the area of Edenton, Chowan County, in northeastern coastal North Carolina:

> And she come pull the covers back off that baby's face, don't that baby would have been dead.

Here we have the not fully grammaticalised negative form *don't*, but considerable grammaticalisation has nevertheless occurred, since *don't* is being used here in a past-tense context and is equivalent in meaning to *and if she hadn't*, as in some of the East Anglian examples. But Tynch, who is a native of the area, further points out (p.c.) that not only does conjunctional *do* occur as well as *don't* in contexts similar to those in which it occurs in East Anglia, but that it also occurs in the speech of Whites in Chowan County. This is further confirmed by one of the informants for the *Dictionary of American Regional English*, who writes (p. 94) that in eastern North Carolina, during the period approximately 1915–1930, "I remember hearing White people, speakers with moderate education, saying things like 'Shut the door tight, do it'll blow open before morning' and 'Leave the note in the middle of the table, do she won't see it'."

It is of course perfectly possible that East Anglian and southeastern US conjunction *do* represent independent developments. After all, if grammaticalisation can happen once, it can happen again. In section 4.12.2, I hypothesised that the grammaticalisation of *do* as a conjunction was ultimately due to phonological developments involving the loss of phonetic material. In Trudgill (2018) I further argued that this loss of phonetic material – and hence the rather extensive grammaticalisation of new conjunctions – was initiated by the extreme stress-timed nature of East Anglian dialects. In 3.1 we saw that East Anglian hyper-stress-timedness is relevant because, as Schiering (2010) argued, the extent to which phonetic erosion occurs in linguistic change has to do with a rhythm-based typology, in which languages are grouped into mora-based, syllable-based and stress-based languages; and in which it is stress-based languages which show a significantly higher degree of phonetic erosion than the others. "Stress-based phonologies show a strong erosive force in reducing and deleting unstressed syllables" (Schiering, 2006: 5). English is clearly a stress-based language as far as most of its mother-tongue varieties are concerned; and East Anglian dialects of English show greater stress-effects than most others. But, as our discussion of the 'Southern drawl' above showed, certain dialects from the American South show equally great stress effects, and would therefore be equally prone to grammaticalisation initiated by phonetic erosion.

However, a more likely scenario is that this feature, which has never been available in any form of Standard English, was brought to the American South by settlers who were speakers of East Anglian dialects. In (at least some parts of) the southeastern United States it was then not only retained in White nonstandard dialects of English but also acquired by speakers of African American English.

6.3.3 Third-person singular present-tense zero

A final East Anglian grammatical feature which has to be mentioned in connection with the American South and African American English is third-person present-tense singular zero, as in *she like, he go*, which as we saw in 4.1.1 and elswhere, is a characteristic of East Anglian English.

East Anglian dialects played a prominent role in discussions in the sociolinguistic literature in the 1960s and 1970s, when one of the major sociolinguistic issues was the historical origins of African American English (Fasold, 1972). Creolists tended to argue that, to the extent that African American Vernacular English was linguistically different from White varieties, this was due to the fact that African American English dialects had their origins in an earlier creole similar to Gullah and other English-based Atlantic creoles (Bailey 1965). Dialectologists, on the other hand, were instead more likely to argue that differences were due to differential loss and retention of original features of British Isles English, together with subsequent independent developments (Dillard 1970; Burling 1973).

A number of features of African American English were advanced as evidence. One of these was the absence of third-person singular *-s* (Fasold 1972). The creolists pointed out that loss of *-s* represented a typical case of simplification of the sort which often happens in language contact situations, and that the Caribbean and other Atlantic English-based creoles also demonstrated this feature. The dialectologists' view (see Kurath 1928) was that third-person singular present-tense zero was a feature of certain British Isles dialects, and the obvious explanation was that Black varieties had acquired and retained this original British Isles feature, while White dialects for the most part had not. The British Isles dialects in question were, of course, those of East Anglia.

6.4 Australasia

The Southern Hemisphere Englishes have a much later origin than the Atlantic Ocean Englishes; but here, too, it is possible to suggest that there may have been East Anglian influence, at least insofar as phonology is concerned.

There is no doubt that East Anglian dialects did arrive in the Southern Hemisphere as part of the colonisation process, because we have direct evidence of this. In Trudgill (2004) I cite data from one particular speaker who was analysed as part of the Origins of New Zealand English project, led by Professor Elizabeth Gordon and carried out from the University of Canterbury, Christchurch, New Zealand (see Gordon et al., 2004). This speaker is a Mrs German, who was born in 1867 in Clinton in the South Island of New Zealand and lived in nearby Balclutha. Her parents were middle-class people who had come from Bury St. Edmunds in Suffolk.

Mrs German preserves a number of obviously East Anglian features in her speech. She lived her entire life in New Zealand, so these features can only have been acquired from her parents, which can provide us with important information about how East Anglian English was spoken by middle-class people born in the 1840s.

Her vowel in the lexical set of LOT is unrounded [ɑ]. As we saw in 3.2.1.1, this remains a feature of older northern East Anglian speech today. Suffolk these days has the rounded vowel [ɒ], but Mrs German's pronunciation is a very good indication that the rounded vowel is a relatively recent newcomer into southern East Anglia, and that it has over the past several decades been gradually moving its way northwards.

The word *was* is pronounced /wuz/ rather than /wɒz/ (see 4.1.7). It is interesting to find that this must have been general even in middle-class East Anglian speech during the 19th century. Mrs German also pronounces the words *home* and *homestead* with the FOOT vowel /ʊ/ rather than /ou/: she retains the 'East Anglian short *o*' (3.2.1.1). She also has distinct vowels in *no* and *snow*, and in *place* and *play*. As we saw in 3.2.1.2, the speech of Norfolk – but not contemporary Suffolk – preserves the former distinction, as /u:/ versus /ʌu/, while *place* and *play* were until quite recently distinguished as /e:/ versus /æi/.

In addition, Mrs German has the vowel of *church* etc. as short [ɜ] rather than long [ɜ:]. This is not the short [ɐ] vowel described in 3.2.1.1 as being typically East Anglian, but her pronunciation suggests that she has an apparently partially dedialectalised vowel, with the newer London-based closer quality [ɜ] but the older East Anglian lack of length.

In Mrs German's speech, word-final /t/ is quite often realised as [ʔ] (see 3.2.2), which is of considerable interest since, although it is often assumed that t-glottaling was an urban innovation, it is equally possible that it had its origins in East Anglia: the only area of England to have considerable amounts of glottalling in the records of the *Survey of English Dialects* is East Anglia (see 8.3). The fact that Mrs. German has this suggests that it has probably been a feature of East Anglian English at least from the 1850s.

As far as the actual origins of Southern Hemisphere Englishes generally are concerned, Hammarström (1980) argued that Australian English was simply transplanted Cockney. But an examination of Australian phonology makes it clear that if Australian English was originally a transplanted dialect from somewhere in England, then it certainly would not have been from London. It is true that London English and Australian English both agree in being non-rhotic, in having the FOOT-STRUT split, and in having Diphthong Shift (Wells, 1982) i.e.

wide diphthongs in GOAT and FACE. But they differ significantly in two important respects. First, Cockney typically has a back vowel, around [ɑː], in the lexical sets of START, BATH, PALM, START whereas Australian and New Zealand English have a very front vowel, around [aː]. Secondly, unlike London English, Australasian English has the Weak Vowel Merger. As we saw in 2.6, this term, from Wells (1982), refers to the phenomenon which occurs in those accents of English which have schwa rather than the KIT vowel in unstressed syllables in words such as *wanted, village, horses, naked, David,* so that *abbot* and *rabbit* rhyme. London, on the other hand, does not have the merger, and has the unstressed KIT vowel in *village* and *horses.*

It turns out that if we search the SED materials for areas of England which have schwa in *wanted*, wide diphthongs in GOAT, non-rhoticity, a front vowel in START, and the FOOT-STRUT split, then there is precisely one. This constellation of phonological features can be found only in the traditional dialects of parts of central and eastern Essex (Trudgill, 1986: Map 4.3, p. 137). If there *was* a single location in Britain from which Australian English was transplanted around the world, then it would have had to be not London but rural Essex, as the only area of England which has this group of features.

It would of course be ludicrous to suppose that rural Essex did in fact provide the sole input for a transplanted Australian English, and it is therefore safe to assume that this particular combination of features must have arisen as a result of dialect mixture, as I argued in Trudgill (2004). But there is also good evidence that East Anglia, including Essex, was *one* of the sources of the regional British Isles dialect input into Australasian English. For example, I argue in Trudgill (2004) that the presence of the Weak Vowel Merger in Australian English is due to the fact that this feature – rather than the Cockney absence of the merger – was the majority variant in the original dialect mixture that developed out of dialect contact in the new colonies, with Cockney being out-influenced with respect to the merger as a result of the combined inputs of Irish English (Trudgill, 1985; Corrigan, 2021), East Anglian English, the English West Country, and the far north of England, which all have this merger.

There is evidence, then, of an East Anglian contribution to the formation of Southern Hemisphere English, but it is indirect and less conclusive than the data from North America. This no doubt indicative of the diminished relative demographic significance of East Anglia between the 17th and 19th centuries, and of the smaller role played by East Anglians in the settlement of Australasia.

7 East Anglian texts

This chapter consists of twelve annotated texts illustrative of dialectal East Anglian English, three each from the counties of Norfolk, Suffolk, Essex and Cambridgeshire, with one text from each county – two in the case of Essex – being transcriptions of recordings which are available on the British Library Sounds website using the links cited. These twelve texts are preceded by a 15th-century text from the Paston Letters, written in Norfolk by Margaret Paston.

NORFOLK

7.1 Mautby, Norfolk, 1448

Margaret Paston
Students of East Anglian English are very fortunate to have available to them the famous Paston Letters collection, which consists of correspondence amounting to a thousand or so letters written by and to members of the Paston family in the 15th and 16th centuries. The family were landed gentry who took their name from the village of Paston, which is situated between North Walsham, Mundesley and Bacton, close to the northeast coast of Norfolk. The early letters provide the best evidence we have from anywhere for what vernacular Late Middle English and Early Modern English were like.[116]

The following text is the postscript to a letter that was sent in 1448 by Margaret Paston (1423–1484) to her husband, John Paston. Margaret was originally from Mautby, on the (former) island of Flegg (see 1.4) in eastern Norfolk. Although the Pastons were generally literate, this text, like most of the letters, was dictated to a scribe. It is nevertheless actually unmistakably written in the East Anglian English of the 15th century. In the letter, Margaret tells her husband about the aftermath of a dispute which took place between the Paston's family chaplain, James Gloys, and a member of a rival family, John Wymdam (or Wymondham – the name of the Norfolk town of Wymondham is still pronounced /wɪndəm/ – see also 1.7).

Qwhan Wymdam seyd that Jamys xuld dy I seyd to hym that I soposyd that he xuld repent hym if he schlow hym or dede to hym any bodyly harm; and he seyd nay, he xuld never repent hym ner have a ferdyng wurth of harm thow

---

[116] More excellent information is available at www.thisispaston.co.uk.

he kelyd you and hym bothe. And I seyd, ȝys, and he sclow the lest chylde that longyth to ȝour kechyn, and if he dede he were lyke, I sopose, to dy for hym. It is told me that he xall kom to London in hast. I pray ȝou be ware how ȝe walkyn if he be there, for he is ful cursyd-hertyd and loumysch. I wot wel he wyl not set upon ȝou manly, but I beleve he wyl styrt upn ȝou or on sum of ȝour men leke a thef. I pray ȝou hertyly that ȝe late not Jamys kom hom aȝen in non wyse tyl ȝe kom home, for myn hertys ese; for be my truth I wold not that he were hurt, ner non man that longyth to ȝou jn ȝour absens for xx pound. And in gode feyth he is sore hatyd both of Wymdam and sum of hys men, and of other that Wymdam tellyth to his tale as hym lyst, for ther as Wymdam tellyth hys tale he makyth hem belevyn that Jamys is gylty and he no thyng gylty. I pray ȝou hertyly here masse and other servys that arn boun to here wyth a devout hert, and I hope veryly that ȝe xal spede ryth wele in all ȝour materys, be the grase of God. Trust veryly in God and leve hym and serve hym, and he wyl not deseve ȝou. Of all other materys I xall sent ȝou wurd in hast.

Middle English Forms

The letter "yogh" <ȝ> represented [j] in prevocalic position and [x] in postvocalic position. In this text, word-inital yogh mostly corresponds to <y>, as in *ȝe* = *ye*, *ȝys* = *yis* 'yes'.

The word *loumish* appears in Middle English dictionaries with the meaning of 'meddlesome, contentious'. *Schlow/sclow* is the preterite of *to slay* (see below). *To speed* signified 'to succeed, go well'. To *stirt upon* is 'to rush at with hostile intent'. *Wot* means 'know' and *longyth* is 'belongs'. *Boun* here means 'available'. *As hym lyst* is 'as he pleases'.

East Anglian forms

The text uses one specifically East Anglian orthographical convention of the period. This is seen in the spelling of the forms *xuld* 'should', *xall* 'shall' where <x> is used rather than <sh> or <sch>. This apparently had no phonetic or phonological significance.

As far as actual East Anglian phonology is concerned, we saw in 2.2 that words such as *what, where, wheel, whale, white* were spelt with initial <hw> in Old English but that the spelling changed to <wh> under the Normans. Then in the 1200s, scribes in western Norfolk started writing these words with <qu>, as in *quat* 'what', which seems likely to have reflected a phonological change /hw/ > /kw/ (Lass & Laing, 2016). By the end of the 15th century, this new pronunciation, or at least spelling, had spread to the rest of Norfolk and down into Suffolk as far as the border with Essex. In this Margaret Paston text, the first word is *qwhan* 'when', which illustrates the point very nicely.

We also saw in 2.2 that the loss of the voiceless velar fricative /x/ through the change /-xt/ > /-t/, as in *taught, right, night,* happened earlier in Norfolk and Suffolk than anywhere else (Beadle, 1977). I hypothesised that this might have been connected to contact with Old Danish. We can see this change in this Paston letter from the spelling of *right* as <ryth>. We can also see other examples of the typically East Anglian loss of the velar fricative generally in *schlow/sclow*, the past-tense form of *slay* 'slew', which was *sloʒe, slogh* in many other Middle English dialects; and in *thow* 'though' rather than *thoʒ, thogh*.

We noted, too, in 2.2 that Seymour (1968) says that the lowering of *i* to *e* was typical of the Late Middle English of East Anglia. We can see this illustrated here in *kechyn* 'kitchen', *kelyd* 'killed' and *dede* 'did'. A further East Anglian feature cited by Seymour was the stopping of /ð/ to /d/, which is evident here in *ferding* 'farthing'.

As far as grammatical features are concerned, the third-person plural object pronoun here is the original southern *hem* rather than the incoming northern *them* (see 4.7.4). The present-tense plural form of BE used in this text is *aren*, here spelt <arn>. This was an originally Midland form which was at this period replacing the Southern *ben* (Lass, 1992) – a form which does make an appearance elsewhere in Margaret Paston's correspondence.

7.2 Swanton Morley, Norfolk, c. 1799

Joshua Larwood: a Norfolk dialogue

The following dialogue, as noted in 5.4, was written by the Rev. Joshua Larwood (1748–1808), who was Rector of Swanton Morley in central Norfolk. It was originally published in his book *Erratics: by a sailor; containing rambles in Norfolk, and elsewhere,* first published in London in 1800. (The subtitle is explained by the fact that Larwood had previously been a Royal Navy chaplain.) The dialogue is rather obviously artificial, and is clearly designed to allow for the inclusion of as many East Anglian dialect words as possible, but Larwood's knowledge of the dialect seems to be extensive and accurate. Larwood provided a 'translation' which is reproduced here, with some revision, alongside the dialogue.

Narbor Rabbin: D'ye know how the knacker's mawther Nutty du?	*Neighbour Robin*: Do you know how the horse-collar-maker's girl Ursula is doing?
Narbor Tibby: Why, i' facks, Rabbin, she's nation cothy; by Goms, she is so snasty that I think she is will-led.	*Neighbour Tibby/Stephen*: Why in fact, Robin, she's extremely ill. My word, she's so bad-tempered that I think she's out of her mind.
R. She's a fate mawther, but ollas in dibles wi' the knacker and thackster; she is ollas a-ating o' thapes and dodmans. The fogger sa, she ha the black sap; but the grosher sa, she have an ill dent.	*R*. She's a clever girl, but always in trouble with the collar-maker and thatcher; she's always eating gooseberries and snails. The chandler says she has consumption: but the grocer says she's out of her senses.
T. Why, ah ! tother da she fared stounded: she pluck'd the pur from the back-stock, and copped it agin the balk of the douw-pollar, and barnt it; and then she hulled it at the thackster, and hart his weeson and huckle-bone. There was northing but cadders in the douw-pollar, and no douws: and so, arter she had barnt the balk, and the door-stall, and the plancher, she run into the paryard, thru the pytle, and then swounded behinn'd a sight o' gotches o' beergood.	*T*. Why, yes! The other day she seemed to be struck mad: she snatched the poker from the back of the stove, and flung it against the beam in the dovecote and burnt it; and then she threw it at the thatcher, and hurt his throat and hipbone. There was nothing but jackdaws in the pigeon-house and no pigeons; and so, after she had burned the beam, and the door-frame, and the floor, she ran into the cow-yard, through the small field, and swooned behind several pitchers of yeast.

R. Ah, the shummaker told me o' that rum rig; and his nevvey[117] sa that the beergood was fystey; and that Nutty was so swelter'd, that she ha got a pain in the spade-bones and jott. The thacker would ha' gin har some doctor's geer in a beaker, but he sa she'll niver moize agin.	*R.* Yes, the shoemaker told me about that comical trick; and his nephew says that the yeast was musty; and that Ursula was so suffocated that she has got a pain in her shoulder-blades and bottom. The thatcher would have given her some doctor's medicine in a tumbler; but he says she will never thrive again.

East Anglian Lexis

Ah! 'yes', as we saw in section 5.6.2, is particularly but not exclusively used in East Anglian English to express agreement, rather than to answer yes-no questions directly.

Beaker is clearly thought by Larwood to be a Norfolk word because he employs it in this text and translates it as 'tumbler'. Forby (1830) also lists *beaker* as an East Anglian word meaning 'drinking-glass', and Moor (1823) includes it as a Suffolk word meaning 'glass, drinking vessel'. The problem here is that, because the word *beaker* is familiar to most people in Britain today, it is not immediately clear what was East Anglian about it. The OED defines *beaker* (except in archaeological and scientific usages) as 'a large drinking vessel with a wide mouth' but characterises it as being "now chiefly in literary use". Contemporary informants, on the other hand, mostly say that it refers to a vessel without a handle which is typically used for cold drinks, often given to small children, usually made of plastic, and which might be employed in the bathroom to hold toothbrushes.

So what was East Anglian about this word in the 18th and 19th centuries? The OED defines *tumbler* as referring to 'a tapering cylindrical glass cup without a handle or foot, having a heavy flat bottom'. The answer seems to be, then, that *beaker* was the East Anglian dialect word for the sort of drinking glass which would have been called a *tumbler* elsewhere. Larwood was clearly referring to a drinking glass – after all, there was no plastic available in his time – and this is confirmed by the definitions of Moor and Forby.[118] *Beaker* was not an East Anglian word as such; it was simply this particular meaning which was especially associated with East Anglia. The etymology of the word is not entirely clear, but it seems to have come into English from Old Norse *bikarr*.

---

[117] A common general colloquial pronunciation of *nephew* (from French *neveu*) at the time.

[118] In the 1940s and 1950s there were, in my Norfolk childhood home, rather substantial drinking glasses called *beakers*, which were what we normally drank water out of. *Glasses* were lighter and made of thinner glass.

Beergood 'yeast', *cadder* = *caddow* 'jackdaw', *cothy/cothish* 'unwell', and *dibles* 'trouble' are all discussed 5.4.

Dodman 'snail' is discussed briefly in 5.0.

Douw, more usually *dow* 'pigeon', is a dialectal variant of *dove*.

Fate (adj.), translated by Larwood as 'clever', is a form of *feat* 'fitting, suitable, proper, adroit, smart' which occurs (or occurred) in the dialects of Northumberland, Yorkshire, Lincolnshire and East Anglia, and is derived from Old French *fait*, from Latin *factus* 'made'.

To fare 'to seem' – see 5.1.3.

Fogger is translated by Larwood as 'man in the chandler's shop' but is cited in the EDD as 'a petty chapman carrying small wares from village to village'. According to the OED, it is an Eastern dialect word signifying 'pedlar, hawker, merchant, shopkeeper' which probably came from *Fogger* or *Fugger*, the surname of a family of German bankers and venture capitalists.

Fystey, more usually *foisty* or *fowsty* 'mouldy, musty', may be from Dutch *fust* 'cask' and/or Old French *fust* 'barrel'.

Gotch is a Norfolk, Suffolk and Essex word for a large rounded jug. The OED lists the word but has no etymology for it.

Grosher is a variant of *grocer*, formerly also *grosser*, from Old French *grossier* 'one who buys and sells in the gross i.e. in large quantities, a wholesaler'.

Huckle is a dialect word for 'hip (bone)' derived from dialectal *huck* 'hip', which may be related to *hook*.

Knacker 'harness maker' – see 5.4.

Mawther 'girl' – see 5.1.3.

Moize or *moise* 'thrive' – see 5.1.

Narbor: this variant of *neighbour* is listed in the EDD as occurring in Norfolk and Suffolk only. Supposing that the first <r> of the spelling is unetymological, it is not inconceivable that this East Anglian form with /aː/ in the first syllable was influenced by the Medieval Dutch form *nabuer* cited in the OED, and/or by Old Danish *nábúi*.

Paryard 'cowyard' – see 5.4.

Plancher is a formerly general but now East Anglian word meaning 'floor of planks or boards', from Anglo-Norman French *planche* 'board'.

Pytle = *pightle* 'small field' – see 5.0.

Pur 'poker' – see 5.4.

Rum 'strange' – see 5.1.7.

Sight is being used here in the meaning, as explained by the OED, of "a show or display of something" and " hence, a great number or quantity; a multitude; a 'deal' or 'lot'" (see also Text 7).

Shummaker /ʃʌməkə/ was the local pronunciation of 'shoemaker'.

Snasty or *snaisty* 'bad-tempered', *thackster* 'thatcher', and *thapes* 'gooseberry' are discussed in 5.4.

Tother is derived from forms such as *that other* and first appeared in Middle English. According to the OED, it is 'now dialectal'. The EDD has citations from most parts of Britain.

Weeson appears in the OED as *weasand* meaning 'throat, gullet, windpipe'. The dictionary describes the status of the word as being "now chiefly dialect". It is of Old English origin.

East Anglian Grammar

1. Present-tense forms are infrequent in the past-tense narrative of this dialogue, but third-person singular zero (see 4.1.1) is entirely consistently used in the forms that do occur:

*D'ye know how the knacker's mawther Nutty **du**?*
*She **ha** [have] the black sap; but the grosher **sa** [say], she have an ill dent.*
*His nevvey **sa** [say].*

2. Notice also that *D'ye know how . . . Nutty du?* corresponds to "Do you know how Nutty **is doing**?" in contemporary English. In 4.1.3 it was mentioned that older East Anglian dialect speakers often employ simple (non-progressive) verb forms where other dialects would use continuous (progressive) forms with *-ing* participles.
3. We also saw in 4.1.2 that *a*-verbing is usual with the present participles of continuous verb forms in the traditional dialects of East Anglia, and that transitive verbs normally insert *of*, often in the form of *on*, before the object of the verb. We can see this in the Dialogue in *she is ollas **a-ating** o' thapes* 'she is always a-eating of gooseberries'.
4. The preterite form of *to run* in this text is *run* (see 4.1.4).
5. We noted in 4.1.8 that *have* is most often pronounced without the final /v/, unless the next word begins with a vowel. There are many examples in this dialogue of *have* written as <ha>.

East Anglian Phonology

1. We saw in 3.2.1.1 that the traditional dialects of East Anglia did not have the nurse vowel /ɜː/. Instead, /ʌ/, a short open vowel, slightly front of central, tends to occur in the lexical set of *church, first,* i.e. in words which had Middle English *ir, ur* in closed syllables; in open syllables /aː/ occurs, as in *fur* /faː/, *sir* /saː/. As we also saw, however, things can be a little more complicated

than that, with some variability in the occurrence of /ʌ/ and /aː/. We see that illustrated here, with *hulled* 'hurled' indicating the pronunciation /hʌld/, while the spellings *barnt* 'burnt' and *hart* 'hurt' indicate /aː/.

2. We also noted in 3.2.1.2 that, in the older dialect, a number of words descended from ME /ɛː/, such as *beans, creature,* had the /eː~ɛː/ vowel of FACE rather than the expected more modern /iː/. This feature is represented in this text in the form *ating* 'eating'.
3. We also see the words *say* and *day* spelt here as <sa, da>. As reported in 3.2.1.3, this represents the pronunciations /sæ, dæ/, with the TRAP vowel occurring in open syllables – unusually amongst varieties of English.
4. We saw in 3.2.1.1 that Ihalainen (1994: 226) wrote about the 'Norwich *a*', referring to the unrounding of the vowel in words like *top*, noting that "it is one of the features exploited by Larwood in his Norfolk dialogue", which we can see here in the form *Rabbin* = *Robin*.
5. The *arter* spelling of *after* represents the pronunciation /aːtə/. The EDD shows that pronunciations of *after* without /f/ are found right across southern England, in Cornwall, Devon, Somerset, Dorset, Hampshire, Sussex, Kent, Middlesex, Essex, Suffolk, Norfolk, Cambridgeshire, Northamptonshire, Warwickshire, Staffordshire, Oxfordshire, and Berkshire.

7.3 Potter Heigham, Norfolk, 1946

Sidney Grapes: *the Boy John Letters*

The Boy John Letters represent a body of East Anglian dialect literature of not a little genius. The letters were written to and published in the Norwich *Eastern Daily Press* newspaper, between 1946 and 1958. Sidney Grapes (1887–1958) was the proprietor of a bicycle shop, later a garage and motor business, in Potter Heigham, located in Broadland, Norfolk. In the years before the Second World War, he acquired a reputation as a Norfolk dialect comedian, performing at social functions in many parts of the county and on the radio. The letters appeared in the newspaper at irregular intervals – Grapes would simply write them when he felt like it – and were always signed "The Boy John" (on this name, see 5.6.1). They purported to be reports of events in the Boy John's village and, in addition to the Boy John himself – a farm worker – they featured as their main characters his Aunt Agatha, Granfar, and old Mrs. W, their neighbour. Most of the letters ended with a PS containing one of Aunt Agatha's aphorisms, which became famous throughout the county, such as "Aunt Agatha she say: all husbands are alike, only they have different faces so you can tell 'em apart".

Aunt Agatha's Dickey Ride
December 24th, 1946

Dear Sar – Well, the time a' cum round agin for me and Arnt Agatha and Granfar, to rite an wish yow, and yar starf an orl, a werry Happy Christmas. Arnt Agatha, she say, specially to that there gentleman wot go about a taken them photos o' pretty plearces in Norfolk, he must a' got a bike, to git about like he dew.

Oh! I must tell you about Arnt Agatha, last summer. We had a garden fate at the Wickerage, an weeks afore-hand you could buy shillin tickets, then save em all up, then spend em on anything at the fate. Well Arnt Agatha, she was wery busy and dint git there till ever so late, an then ewerything wus sold. She had six shillin tickets wot she'd saved, an orl she could spend em on wus on six shilling rides round the field on the Wicar's owld dicker, wot he'd lent for the purpus. Well bor she cum home orl o' a muckwash – she looked a job.

Granfar, he mobbed har, and he called har a silly old fule. He fear to ha been a pearkin tru a hole in the fence and see har. He say, "There she wus a bobbin up and down on that old dicker's back, a' holden har hat on wi one hand, an har teeth in wi the tother, she look disgustin."

Poor Granfar, he mob about everything nowadays. He go down to the pub every nite, he come back a-mobbin about the beer, he say he's right glad when he a' had enuf on it. Arnt Agatha say, "Well yow put em in," he say, "I never put *them* in, I votted Learbor."

Well fare you well together, a Happy Xmas to all you wot read this – Yours obediently,

THE BOY JOHN

P.S. – Arnt Agatha she say, If you dorn't git orl you want, think of the things yow dorn't want – an *dorn't* git.

East Anglian Lexis

Afore is found in dialects in many parts of Britain. According to the OED, in Modern English the word is "archaic, regional, or nautical". It is not a variant of *before* but derives from early Middle English *on-fore*, while *before* comes ultimately from the archaic form *by-fore*.

Bor is an East Anglian address form noted in 5.6.1.

Dickey, dicker /dɪkə/ 'donkey' is discussed in 5.1.3.

Fear = *fare* 'seem' (5.1.3). We saw in 3.2.1.3 that northern East Anglian English has merged the vowels of NEAR and SQUARE.

Granfar 'grandfather': in the traditional dialect of Norfolk, *father* is typically *far* /faː/. The *Survey of English Dialects* records this *far* pronunciation for all of its thirteen Norfolk localities, except Outwell in the Fens, which is no surprise, and Ludham in the Broads, which is. It is not recorded for any of the other East Anglian or neighbouring counties. *Granfar* was not infrequently /grænfə/. It is tempting to see a role for Danish *far* 'father' in this peculiarly Norfolk form.

Mob 'scold, nag, complain' was discussed in 5.1.7.

Peak: the spelling *pearkin* of the present participle of this verb indicates the pronunciation /pɛːk/. This spelling works because the East Anglian dialect is non-rhotic: no /r/ is to be inferred from the use of <r>, and because in northern East Anglia the lexical sets of NEAR and SQUARE have merged on /ɛː/. According to the OED, *peak* is a Midlands and East Anglian form corresponding to General English *peek*, meaning 'to look through a narrow opening'. The pronunciation with /ɛː/ is an instance of the phenomenon whereby, as noted in 3.2.1.2 and in the notes to Text 2, a number of words descended from ME $ẹː$, such as *beans, creature*, preserve the earlier vowel instead of the shifted form with /iː/.

Tother – see under Text 2.

East Anglian Grammar
1. The form *wus* 'was' indicates the pronunciation /wʊz/, as noted in 4.1.7.
2. *Fare you well* is an illustration of the typical East Anglian imperative with the explicit second-person pronoun (see 4.1.5).
3. *Fare you well together* is an example of the East Anglian second-person plural pronominal form *you . . . together*.
4. Almost all the many citations of *yow* 'you' in the EDD come from Norfolk, Suffolk and Essex, though there are a few from Lincolnshire, Yorkshire and the West Country. The pronunciation of *you* with the MOUTH vowel is also well-known to occur in the contemporary West Midlands. This pronunciation is the expected outcome of the Great Vowel Shift, and was general in the Midlands and the South of England until the second half of the 17th century, by which time, according to the OED, it "had come to be regarded as a vulgarism" which however "survives in a number of modern regional English varieties". The current General English form with the GOOSE vowel is the result of a lengthening of the medieval weak form which, because short, was not subjected to the diphthongisation of the vowel shift.

    Almost all the very many instances of the possessive form *yar* 'your' cited in the EDD come from Cambridgeshire, Norfolk, Suffolk and Essex – there are just a very few from Lincolnshire and Yorkshire.
5. The plural demonstrative *them* as in *them photos* corresponds to Standard English *those*. Note also the form *that there* in *that there gentleman*: as we saw in 4.6, *here* and *there* are often used as reinforcers with demonstratives as in *this here, that there*.
6. As noted in 4.7.7, the usual relative pronoun in East Anglian English is *what*, as in *that there gentleman wot go about*.
7. *On*, as we saw in 4.1.1, often appears rather than *of*: e.g. *he a' had enuf on it*.

The Boy John Letters also contain a number of other East Anglian grammatical features which have already been mentioned:
- third-person present-tense singular zero is the norm: *he say, he mob, he go, she say, he dew*. Grapes is able to write *do* as <dew> because East Anglian yod-dropping makes homophones of *do* and *dew*.
- *a*-verbing, as in *a taken, a bobbin, a' holden, a-mobbin*. The spelling <holden> accurately represents the pronunciation of the *-ing* suffix as /ən, ~n/.
- as already noted, *have* is most often pronounced without the final /v/, as in *the time a' cum* 'the time have come'; *he fear to ha been*; *he a' had enuf*.

East Anglian Phonology

1. The NURSE vowel appears here as /aː/ in *sar* 'sir', *har* 'her', as described in 3.2.1.3.
2. The traditional East Anglian English merger of /w/ and /v/ is indicated in this *Boy John* letter in *Wickerage, Wicar, ewerything, werry*.
3. The forms *agin, git* demonstrate a frequent feature of southeast of England dialects, namely the raising of /ɛ/ to /ɪ/ before alveolar consonants, as very frequently in *git* 'get' (see also Text 11).
4. The Middle English distinction between monophthongal *ā* and diphthongal *ai* as in *daze* /dɛːz/ vs. *days* /dæiz/ is indicated in the spellings <plearces, Learbour> contrasting with spellings such as <say>. These spellings work for Norfolk readers because the dialect is non-rhotic and the lexical sets of NEAR and SQUARE have merged on /ɛː/. It is significant that in this text Grapes gives this phonological distinction of *ā* and *ai* to Granfar, who is generally portrayed in these pieces as speaking in a more conservative way than the other characters.
5. The form *dicker* represents the pronunciation of *dickey* 'donkey' as /dɪkə/. It will be recalled from 3.2.1.1 that schwa is the only unstressed vowel phonotactically permitted in traditional East Anglian dialects.
6. We saw in 3.2.2 that the cluster /θr-/ has become /tr-/, which can be seen here in the form *tru* 'through'.
7. The spelling *fule* 'fool' requires some explanation. The English of northern East Anglia, as we saw in 3.2.1.2, has two close rounded vowels: the central vowel /ʉː/ occurs in *beautiful, rude*, while the back vowel /uː/ occurs *nose, road* (but not in *know, rowed*). Items such as *boot, rood, fool* can have either the more dialectal /ʉː/ or the less dialectal /uː/. Sidney Grapes uses spellings for the *rude* set such as <sewt> *suit*, <trew> *through*. This enables him to represent dialectal pronunciations of words from the *boot* set by using spellings such as <fule> *fool*, <muve> *move*. These spellings are only possible because of the presence of yod-dropping in the dialect, so that <tew> is understood to begin with /t-/ and not /tj-/. But they convey totally unambiguously to a local audience that the pronunciation is dialectal /fʉːl, mʉːv/ rather than dedialectalised /fuːl, muːv/, which is what would be understood from the standard spellings <fool, move>.
8. The form *dorn't* 'don't' is also of interest. The most common contemporary pronunciation of *don't* northern East Anglia is /duːnt/ or /dʊnt/; but <dorn't> occurs in older East Anglian dialect texts and clearly indicates the pronunciation /dɔːnt/. Skeat (1912) has *I dorn't think I cud clime it now* from a 1839 piece, also cited in the EDD, written by Charles Clark from Great Totham, Essex, which is about 10 miles/16 kilometres southwest of Colchester.

7.4 North Elmham, Norfolk, 1957

Edward J Dawson (b.1873, retired gamekeeper and a smallholder)

https://sounds.bl.uk/Accents-and-dialects/Survey-of-English-dialects/021M-C0908X0060XX-0300V1
North Elmham is about 5 miles north of Dereham and about the same distance southwest of Fakenham. Elmham is one of the toponyms which occurs in both Norfolk and Suffolk – see 2.1.

> **Edward:** Well, that's what we call a mouse-hunter about here, I believe they're practically extinct now. And they, they, there's, was some in Hampshire, what about to say, but they didn't call them the same name. Well, stoat, he's a long fella, white throat, belly dark, chestnut back, with a darker streak down the middle and a long, black tail, and chocolate marks on his muzzle. And often they turn white in the wintertime. I a catched five or six in various stages of white and brown.
>
> **Q.** What is the colour underneath, then?
>
> **Edward:** Yellowish-white, creamy white under the throat; and fight like the very devil, they do. But mister mouse-hunter, he's as long as a weasel. Well they, they in't much thicker 'n your finger. And they, he got a little black tail. But the other customers a', well a chocolate tail, but the other customers a' got a tail the same colour as the other part. And the other one, he's chocolate colour and the face just like a weasel or a stoat only a little bit darker. Then there's another blook I just saw down on some middows there one day not, what, about a couple of year ago. In't I told you about 'm?
>
> **Q.** Who was that?
>
> **Edward:** I told [?] about it. I'd never seen one before. Funny thing, I was reading in a, in a book about some animals and I come across of it. That is a, a black vole. Oh, the loveliest little customer as you ever see and I think he's about, between five and six inches long. With no hair from his hocks, or his knees you might say, to the feet. And they were pink. Pink nose and a pink tail. And the other part as black as coal. The loveliest fellow you ever saw in your life. He, I, his, I was putting a snare down again the edge of the dyke. Well, I set a foot on it, he come out the hole, ooh, and sat looking at me. Well obviously 'I never seen a bloke like you afore. I don't know what you are', but then I made out when I was reading this book . . .
>
> They used to pay the women a halfpenny a bushel, picking the stones off the new leys. And they all used to pu-, a bushel skep with the bottom out. They'd fill that for 'em and lift the skep up and leave them in little heaps . . .

East Anglian Lexis

Afore – see Text 3.

Skep is a predominantly East of England word referring to particular type of large basket. It comes from Old Norse *skeppa* 'basket, bushel'.

Ley, lea, lay is 'land laid down for pasture, grassland' and is, according to the EDD, in general dialectal use.

Mouse-hunter clearly refers here to some kind of mustelid,[119] though it is not clear which. The OED glosses *mouse-hunt* as 'weasel, small stoat', and the term is identified there as coming from Middle Dutch *muushont* (5.1.6).

East Anglian Grammar
1. *In't* is the typical present-tense negative form of *have* and *be*, as we saw in 4.2.2. Of the examples here, in *they in't much thicker* it is *be* that is being negated, whereas in *in't I told you about 'm?* it is *have*.
2. As noted earlier, *have* is most often pronounced without the final /v/, and this appears here in the forms *I a catched; the other customers a' got a tail*.
3. A number of verbs have nonstandard preterites in this passage: *catched, come, seen*.

East Anglian Phonology
1. The 'East Anglian short *o*' can be heard on this recording in the pronunciation of *bloke* as /blʊk/, transcribed here as <blook>.
2. The distinction between Middle English monophthongal *ā* and diphthongal *ai* is clearly preserved, with words such as *stage* having a quality around [eː~ eᵛⁱ]. *Tail*, on the other hand, has [æi].
3. As we have already seen, in the older dialect some words descended from ME /ɛː/ had the /ɛː/ vowel of FACE rather than the expected more modern /iː/. This can be heard here in the first occurrence of the word *weasel*. The other occurrences all have /iː/.
4. *Here* is clearly diphthongal, with a schwa offglide, unlike the more modern monophthongal pronunciation with /ɛː/.
5. The word *half* here, as noted in 3.2.1.3, has /æː/ as opposed to the /aː/ that occurs in *dark*.
6. The spelling *fella* 'fellow' indicates the pronunciation with word-final schwa which is common in very many varieties of English. In a more particularly East Anglian fashion, *belly* also occurs here with word-final schwa, illustrating

---

119 British mustelids include weasels, stoats, pine martens, polecats and ferrets.

the point that schwa is the only vowel which can occur in unstressed syllables in the traditional dialects of East Anglia.
7. As described in 3.2.2, /l/ is often 'clear', i.e. not velarised, in syllable-final position after high front vowels. This can be heard here in the pronunciation of the word *well*.
8. The pronunciation of *meadow* with the KIT vowel is a further illustration of the raising of /ɛ/ to /ɪ/ before alveolar consonants.
9. The pronunciation of *under* as "onder", as mentioned in 3.2.1.1, can be heard in *underneath* "onderneath".
10. The typical East Anglian glottalised pronunciation of intervocalic /p,t,k/ can be heard here, for example in *hunter, darker* /daːkʔə/.

Suffolk

7.5 Southwold, Suffolk, c.1930

Ernest R. Cooper *Mardles from Suffolk*

The local pronunciation of Southwold is, or was, "Sowle" /sʌʊl/, hence Sole Bay, the area of the North Sea off the coast from Southwold. The Battle of Solebay (1672) was the first naval battle of the Third Anglo-Dutch War.

The following text is an extract from Chapter 10 of Cooper's book, *The 'Half and Halfer' on a blowing night.* (The "Half and Halfer" was the name of a harbour-side pub.)

I dunno why but to-night fare to make me think o' that night we went after the *Decima*, what was a-torchin orf the town. About twenty-five year ago that was, but I was one of 'em that time, and when we got to her she was a proper wreck, topmast and spreet gone, and every stich o' canvas blown clean out on her, and dew you think them fallers would come out on her? Not they.

We went right alongside to get 'em, and a sea took us, and lumped our bote right on top o' the lee-board, smashed our pad to shatters, and started the deck planks, so we hollared to them to look sharp, for the seas were a-goin right acrost her amidships, but she worn't so bad aither ind; the skipper stood in the hoodway aft and sung out she wornt makin no water, and he thought if he let goo his anchor she'd ride it all right till we could get a tug.

We were then about three or four mile from the shore, and settin orf like all that, but they won't come out, and so we left'em ridin there in the open sea and made for Lowestoft; we went in there about three in the mornin, and got the *Dispatch* as soon as we could. She took us in tow and away we went agin, right in the teeth on it, to go out o' the Stanford [Channel of Lowestoft harbour].

Goin through the Gat we took a full grown sea that broke the towrope like a bit o' spun yarn, but the tug sune picked us up agin, and by and by we browt the wind more aft, and most on us got underneath the foresail, and went along a little bit more comfortable.

Howsever, when we got to where we left the wassel, she worn't nowhere to be seen, and we cruised up and down for an hour or more, till at last we found her ridin a good nine mile from the land, and drivin orf into the sea like billy-oh; once we got to her that din't take us long to pass the rope, and some of our chaps, what we put aboard, slipped the cable, and we hung on astarn; I rackon that was about nine o'clock afore we got her into Lowestoft, and my heart we put away a funny brakfast when we got ashore.

That was wery nigh a twenty-four hour job afore we got home agin, and though the weather was jest as bad as what that is to-night, we only got £50 for it.

East Anglian Lexis

Acrost is described in the OED as a variant of *across* with excrescent *-t*, as also in the case of *against* from earlier *agains, amidst, amongst, betwixt*. It is also said by the OED to be a widespread regional feature, so it is by no means only East Anglian. Unlike *against* etc., however, it is also said by the dictionary to be nonstandard. According to the OED, the development of the excrescent *-t* was probably reinforced by the fact that the word was frequently followed by *te*, as a variant of *the*, and perhaps also by association with superlatives in *-st*.

Afore 'before' – see Text 3.

Fare 'seem' – see 5.1.3.

A *gat* is a nautical term referring to an opening or channel between sandbanks. It is related to English *gate* but comes from Old Danish *gat*, as in the name of the Kattegat, the strait between Danish Jutland and the West coast of Sweden. According to the EDD, *gat* is particularly associated with Norfolk and Suffolk.

Howsever 'however' is a form of *howsomever*, which is particularly associated with Suffolk. *Howsomever* has the same origin as *howsoever*, but has Old Danish *-som-* 'as' rather than Old English *-so-*.

Nigh 'near', as was noted in 5.0, is a word which is more archaic than regional.

Spreet is a nautical term corresponding to the more general term *sprit*, as in *bowsprit*, defined by the OED as 'a spar running out from a ship's bow to which the forestays are fastened'. *Sprit* is from Middle English *spritte*; the form *spreet* as used by these Suffolk mariners may have been influenced by Middle Dutch *spriet*.

East Anglian Grammar

1. In *that din't take us long*, and *that was about nine o'clock*, we see how, as described in Chapter 4.7.4, *that* rather than *it* occurs as the third-person singular neuter pronoun.
2. I wrote in 4.1.7 that East Anglian *weren't*, the typical negative preterite form for all persons, can be pronounced in a number of different ways: /wɜːnt/, /waːnt/, /wɔːnt/, /wɒnt/. The spelling used in this Suffolk text, <wornt>, indicates /wɔːnt/.

3. The spellings <won't> and <din't> indicate pronunciations of *wouldn't* and *didn't* with /d/ assimilated to the following /n/.

The text also contains a number of other East Anglian grammatical features that we have already commented on in this Chapter:
- *a*-verbing, as in *a-torchin, a-goin*
- demonstrative *them* as in *them fallers* 'those fellows'
- relative pronoun *what*, as in *chaps what we put aboard*
- *on* corresponding to *of*: e.g. *out on her, most on us*.

East Anglian Phonology
1. The NURSE vowel appears here as /aː/ in *astarn*.
2. The East Anglian preservation of the distinction between ME ǭː and ME *ou* is signalled in *goo* /guː/ 'go' and *bote* /buːt/ 'boat' versus *blown* /blʌun/ and *grown* /grʌun/. *Brought* is represented as *browt*, indicating a pronunciation, as discussed in 3.2.1.2, with "the same vowel as *mown, know*", so /brʌut/.
3. As noted in 3.2.2, traditional East Anglian English has a merger of /w/ and /v/. This is illustrated here in *wassel* 'vessel', and *wery* 'very'.
4. *Orf* indicates /ɔːf/, as described in 3.2.1.1, where it was observed that /ɔː/ is found before front voiceless fricatives, as in *off, cloth, lost,* particularly in the word *off*.
5. *Ind* 'end' and *agin* 'again(st)' demonstrate the raising of /ɛ/ to /ɪ/ before alveolar consonants.
6. *Jest* represents a common East Anglian pronunciation of *just*.
7. On the spelling <sune> *soon*, see the phonological comments to Text 3 on the spelling *fule* 'fool'.

7.6 Pakefield, Suffolk, 1980

David Butcher (2014) *Fishing Talk* **(Poppyland Publishing)**
The following is part of "The sinking of the *Eta*" in which David Butcher reproduces a verbatim transcript of a tape-recording of a story as told to him by a Pakefield man, Ned Mallender (1896–1981).[120] Mr Mallender was the skipper of the trawler *Eta* when it sank during World War II, but he was not on board at the time because he was at home in bed ill. Butcher's tapes are lodged with the Suffolk Record Office.

I wuz in the *Eta*. She blew up. I wuz skipper o' the *Eta*, fishin' out here. This was the Christmas trip in thirty-nine, an' I went out an' got pneumonia. An', o'course, I went an' see the doctor when I come hoom, an' he ordered me straight t'bed, with kylon [kaolin] poulticees an'all that sort o' stuff. Yeah. Poultices. They used t'put 'em on the chest. Now, the boat went t'sea agin on the Thursday. An' the Friday night I had this dream. I wuz in bed up here. Now, all of a sudden, I wuz blew up. In the bed! I laid in my bed, but I think I'm on my ship. She was blew up, see. Now then, in the meantime, I said t'the boys, 'Now, look. She ent sinkin' fast. We're got time t'do everything. We larnched the boat, an' she leaked, an' we pulled her back agin and wrapped a sail round her – the mizzen sail. 'Now,' I said, 'where are the oars?' The oars were blown out o' the boat, see, so we went an' got two shovels out o' the pound. An' I said t'the cook – his nairme wuz Hood – 'Git my torch out o' my berth'. An' I hetta lower him down inta the cabin 'cause the steps were gone. All the port side stuff wuz down. That wuz a mine in the trawl, so they told me. We got inta the little boat, an' we pulled away from her, an' I woke up. Wi' fright, see. An my wife come inta the room an' say, 'Whatever is wrong wi' you?'. She say, 'You're bin a-shoutin' an' gorn ahid'. I say 'I've hed a rotten dream, ol' dear'. She say, 'What about?'. I say, 'My ship's blew up!'.

Well, o'course, about half-past nine in the mornin, up come my brother-in-law. An' he say, 'How's the ol' boy? Is he fit t'hear the news?' She say, 'What news?' He say, 'His boat wuz blew up last night'. 'Well,' she say, 'He wuz a-dreamin' that last night, an' shoutin' all the odds.' She say, 'The crew are saved, 'cause he said so. They were in the little boat, paddlin' away wi' shovels.' 'Yeah,' he say. 'Thass what they say'.

© 2014 David Butcher

---

[120] The story is very well worth reading in its entirety.

East Anglian Lexis
Little boat is a technical East Coast fishing term, defined by David Butcher in *Fishing Talk*, as "a drifter or trawler's lifeboat – always mounted on the afterdeck on steam or diesel vessels, but placed amidships on a smack" (2014: 76).

East Anglian Grammar
1. The form *wuz* indicates the pronunciation /wʊz/ of the preterite of the verb *to be,* as noted in 4.1.7.
2. The text has the preterites *come* and *say*, which are identical with present-tense forms. Because of the absence of third-person singular *-s*, even third-person singular preterite forms such as *my wife come* and *she say* are homophonous with present-tense forms, but it is clear from the context that preterites are involved.
3. *Laid* is the preterite of *lay* = Standard English *lie*: we saw in 4.1.10 that a number of causative/non-causative pairs have been merged in the dialect.
4. From *I wuz blew up*, it is clear that in the dialect *blew* functions as the past-participle as well as the preterite of *to blow*.
5. In this text, the present-tense negative of BE is *en't*, one of the variants cited in 4.2.2.
6. *That wuz* again illustrates how *that* rather than *it* occurs as the third-person singular neuter pronoun. The form *thass* /ðæs/ is usual in East Anglia as the pronunciation of *that's*,
7. The forms *we're got* and *we're bin* are to be interpreted as *we have got, we have been*. As already noted (3.4.2), *have* is normally pronounced without a final /v/, so the weak unstressed form of *have* is /ə/, making it identical with the weak form of *are*, such that *we have* and *we are* are homophonous and can both be written <we're>.
8. As we saw above, *a*-verbing is usual with the present participles of continuous verb forms in the traditional dialects of East Anglia, so that in this text we find *a-shoutin'* and *a-dreamin'*.

East Anglian Phonology
1. The word *home* appears here as *hoom*, indicating the typical 'East Anglian short o' pronunciation /hʊm/.
2. *Agin* 'again', *git* 'get', and *ahid* 'ahead' are further instances of the typical dialectal raising of DRESS to KIT in pre-alveolar environments.
3. *Nairme* 'name' = /nɛːm/ indicates the preservation of the Middle English distinction between monophthongal *ā* and diphthongal *ai* as in *daze* /deːz~dɛːz/ vs. *days* /dæiz/. On the spelling with <air>, see the notes to Text 3.

4. *Gorn* /gɔːn/ 'going' illustrates *smoothing* as analysed in 3.2.1.3, the process whereby vowel sequences ending in schwa, in this case /uː/+/ə/, are "smoothed" into long monophthongs, in this case /ɔː/.
5. *Larnched* /laːnʃt/ 'launched' shows the retention in the dialect of an older and once very widespread pronunciations with /aː/ which also occurred in, for example, *laundry, saunter. Launch* is etymologically related to *lance*.

7.7 Tuddenham, Suffolk, 1957

Mr Bill Scott (b.1877, retired shepherd)

https://sounds.bl.uk/Accents-and-dialects/Survey-of-English-dialects
/021M-C0908X0061XX-0300V1
Mr Scott talks about sheep farming during WWI 1914–18. The interviewer is the much admired Stanley Ellis (1926–2009), the senior and, by common consent, best of all the SED fieldworkers and transcribers (see 2.6).[121] Tuddenham is another of the village names which occurs in both Norfolk and Suffolk (see 2.1). The Suffolk village lies about 7 miles northeast of Newmarket and about 10 miles northwest of Bury St Edmunds.

>**Bill**: Oh, I was up there a month, up there a month a-shearen.
>
>**Q**: How many sheep could you shear in that time?
>
>**Bill**: Well, we sheared 450, two of us. . . . Oh ah, I used to hev a thousand down 'ere. I a'clipped a thousand in the clippen season, for him, plenty o' times. Oh yeah. I a'had, what, 6 or 7 weeks o'clippen right straight off. Yeah, I used to do about 40, used to do about 40 a day and I had nobody wi' me only, like, myself was there, I hadn't no help nor nothen – well, the shepherds when they come and brought'em up and brought 'em back . . . . I used to draw'em and clip'em and tie up the wool and carry it away.
>
>**Q**: How did you learn to do it?
>
>**Bill**: Well, had to learn when, I learnt, my first sheep I clipped when I was about 14 years old. And then I went and clipped some up a gang where they go 13 and 14 in a gang; and then when I got alonga the sheep of my own, like, I clipped my own sheep. So they din't come so I had all the sheep. When we first done'em they didn't – that weren't only about 7/6d a score. You gotta clip 20 sheep for 7/6d, and now you'll get over 30 shillings for a score. . . . Oh, of course there's more wages now than there was then. Well, there's a certain time of the year, you see, to clip 'em. You clip the hoggets, you see, in June or May, and then you clip the ewes in June. When it git a little warmer, see, we clip in the month of June, that's supposed to be all done in the month of June, all about where there is to be clipped.
>
>**Q**: When was lambing time?
>
>**Bill**: January I used to – January, and sometimes I had some lambed in January, and sometime in March. Yes I used to hatta – I had a man along wi' me in the daytime to help me, but I was all alone at night. I used to – he used to come at seven o'clock in the

---

121 https://en.wikipedia.org/wiki/Stanley_Ellis_(linguist)

morning, and go away at 5 in the evening, like, that was his time. And then the rest of the day and that, an' night I used to hatta see a'ter myself.
[Comment about hurricane lamps.]

Bill: Till the war that's made a mess on it. When the war was running you worn't allowed a light. You had to feel about for 'em in the dark. And there was one night that was really dark, that was, and I laid on my bench in the hut, and to tell you the truth I was having a doze, and all of a sudden I heard my old dog growl. And I thought to myself, well, there's something on. And I laid there, and I kept listening, and I got a damn good stick if anybody should come, and presently I hear something rattling. And I thought to myself: I don't know, that must be the davil about here, a-rattling chains. But when I got up off my rack like this, I got my stick and opened the door, and when I got that – there was some soldiers' horses had got away, and they'd got these here clogs on, you know, chains, and them there chains was a-rattling. Well, that put the wind up me. I thought that was the devil about there when that . . . and old dog then, when I went out, of course he set a-barking. And then the next night, I got my guvnor, young guvnor, to come up have a night 'long with me. And of course they catched the horses, see, got them back agin. So he had a night up there, and he brought some whiskey, and he just had a night or so up there to see what shepherding life was. And didn't that snow:!

East Anglian Lexis

Ah 'yes', as noted in Text 2 and 5.6.2.
Clip 'shear'.
Draw 'to pick out sheep from a flock'.
Hogget 'yearling sheep'.
Guvnor = governor 'boss'. This is not specifically East Anglian but general colloquial British English.

East Anglian Grammar

1. *I hadn't no help nor nothen* 'I hadn't any help or anything' is a very nice example of the negative concord (agreement) or multiple negation (see 4.2.1) which is typical of the vast majority of dialects of English, but in this particular case it is notable that we have quadruple negation. Note also the negation of *have* without *do*-support – *I hadn't* rather than *I didn't have* – something still preserved in Scottish and Irish English but now mostly lost in East Anglia. Multiple negation with *only* can be seen in *That weren't only about 7/6d a score*.
2. In Text 4 we saw the negative preterite of BE spelt as <wornt>, indicating /wɔːnt/. This pronunciation can be heard in this Text in *you worn't allowed a light*.
3. I have transcribed *have* /hɛv/ here as <hev>.

Text 7 also contains a number of other East Anglian grammatical features which have already been commented on in this chapter:
- *that* rather than *it* as the third-person singular neuter pronoun: *that was*
- the verb-form *was* as /wʊz/
- *come* as the preterite of *come*, and *catched* as the preterite of *catch*: *when they come and brought them; they catched the horses*
- *a-*verbing, as in *a-shearen* 'shearing', *a-barken* 'barking'
- *on* corresponding to *of*: *made a mess on it*
- *laid* as the preterite of *lay*: *I laid on my bench*.
- third-person singular zero *it git* = 'it gets'
- plural demonstrative *them (there)* as in *them there chains*, cf. also *these here clogs*.

East Anglian Phonology
1. 'East Anglian short *o*' occurs here in *supposed*: /spʊzd/.
2. This text is notable for its obvious rhoticity on the NURSE vowel, as in *first*, *learnt*. Also, unlike one of the younger people on the recording who can be heard pronouncing *drawing* as /drɔːrən/, Mr Scott has neither intrusive /r/ nor linking /r/: he has *draw'em* as /drɔːəm/ and *for'em* as /fɔːəm/.
3. The vowel in *here* is very diphthongal /iə/, in contrast to the monophthongal /ɛː/ of more modern northern East Anglian speech. This NEAR vowel also occurs in *heard*. NEAR and SQUARE have not been merged, as they have been further east and north in East Anglia.
4. The vowel of *score* is also strikingly diphthongal /ɔːə/, but this is a characteristic of the vowel in word-final position only.
5. The MOUTH vowel is noticeably different from the corresponding [æʉ] or [œʉ]-type vowel of eastern Norfolk and Suffolk and also from the [ɛʊ]-type vowel found in parts of Essex (see 3.2.1.2). Mr Scott's vowel is typically around [ɛʉ], as can be heard particularly in *thousands* and *growled*.
6. The Weak Vowel Merger is apparent here, for example in the pronunciation of *rattling* /rætlən/ and *horses* /hɔːsəz/, with schwa rather than the KIT vowel in unstressed syllables.
7. T-glottaling occurs in, for example, *rattling*; and glottalisation of /k/ occurs in *back again*.
8. *Agin* 'again' is an instance of the dialectal raising of DRESS to KIT in pre-alveolar environments, as discussed above.
9. *After* written as <a'ter> indicates /aːtə/, as in Text 2 above.

10. *Devil* is transcribed here as <davil>, showing the lowering of the DRESS vowel to the TRAP vowel before front voiced fricatives, as described in 3.2.1.1.
11. *Something* occurs as /sʌfən/.

Essex

7.8 Colchester, Essex, c.1894

Charles Benham: the Essex Ballads

Charles Benham JP (1860–1929) was a journalist who came from Colchester. His *Essex Ballads,* written in the dialect of the Colchester area, were published in 1895. The following is one of the ballads:

Miss Julia: the Parson's Daughter – A Ballad of Love

I loike to watch har in the Parson's pew,
A Sundays, me a-settin' in the choir;
She look jest wholly be'utiful, she do.
That fairly sim to set my heart a-fire.

Her gowden hair, a-glist'rin in the sun,
Them bright blew eyes – good lor, I see em now!
I carn abear it when the sarmon's done,
That fare to make me feel I dunner how.

Las' Saddy, I was 'long o' Tom and Bill,
Down on th' allotment, back o' Thompson's Farm,
When she come past us, walkin' tard the hill,
A basket of them paigles on her arm.

"Nice evenin', John," she say, as she goo by,
An' smiled – goodstruth, you mighter knock' me down.
"That is indeed, Miss", I was go'n to say,
But there, I couldn't, give me 'arf-a-crown.

Says Bill, a-larfin', as she turned the lane,
"She's waiting for yer, roun' the corner, bor,"
I give 'ee sich a look, he larft again,
An' made me feel that mad I could a swore.

I carnt abide it when these bits o' chaps
Talk of Miss Julia, saime as if they might
If she was some bloke's gal, but lor, prehaps
I think too much o' har, a jolly sight.

That sim ridic'lous nons'nse this, I doubt,
A-tellin' on yer how she make me feel,

But who's to help it when she walk about
More like a angel than a gal a deal?

That made me wild to see that Lunnon chap,
What come down to the Hall las' Mon'ay week,
A-coaxin' o' the dawg there in har lap,
She settin' in the garden – dang his cheek.

But there, Miss Julia! Lawk a mussy me,
I didn't oughter think of har n' more.
That aint as if she knaow I care for she,
And do I reckon she'd give me what for.

East Anglian Lexis

Abear is said by the EDD to be "widely diffused through the dialects", with examples from Yorkshire and Lancashire. It is equivalent to General English *bear* meaning 'endure, tolerate' and, as the EDD says, it usually occurs together "with the verb *can* and a negative", as here in *I carn [can't] abear it*.

Bor, as we saw 5.6.1, is an East Anglian address term, probably derived from the same root as the second element of *neighbour*.

Doubt here signifies 'fear' or 'suspect', a meaning which according to the EDD is in 'widespread dialectal use'.

Fare 'seem' was discussed in 5.1.3.

Paigle 'cowslip' is a dialect word which is recorded by the EDD from eastern England (Yorkshire, Lincolnshire, Northamptonshire, Hertfordshire, Huntingdonshire, Cambridgeshire, Norfolk, Suffolk, Essex, and Kent), as well as Dorset and Pembrokeshire. The more recent Survey of English Dialects records the word only from Hertfordshire, Cambridgeshire, Suffolk and Essex. The etymology is not known.

Sight 'a lot' – see Text 2.

Reckon is being used here, as cited in the EDD, in the sense of *think, suppose, conjecture, imagine*. It is in widespread dialectal use in Britain.

Wholly, as we saw in 5.6.3, is a traditional East Anglian dialect intensifier.

East Anglian Grammar

1. Third-person present-tense singular zero is the norm in this text: *she look, she do, that sim [seem], she make, she say, she goo, she walk*. The narrative present-tense form *says Bill* is is not very usual in most of East Anglia, but does occur in a number of other dialects in the British Isles, where present-tense *-s* can occur for all persons in narratives.

2. *A*-verbing is also common in this poem, complete with the following *on* [*of*] which occurs before direct objects: *a-settin', a-glist'rin, a-larfin* [laughing], *a-coaxin', a-tellin' on yer* [*a-telling of you* = 'telling you'].
3. In *that Lunnon chap, what come down to the Hall las' Mon'ay week*, it is clear that *come* is a past-tense form, though of course it is formally identical to the East Anglian present-tense form with zero-marking. The typical East Anglian preterite of *give*, namely *give*, also occurs here.
4. We saw in 4.1.10 that basilectal East Anglian English has lost the distinction between *sit* and *set* as well as *lay* and *lie*, and in this ballad we have *me a-settin' in the choir* and *she settin' in the garden*.
5. As reported in 4.7.7, the usual East Anglian relative pronoun corresponding to Standard English *who* and *which* is *what*. This occurs here in *that Lunnon chap what come down to the Hall*.
6. In 4.6, we noted that the distal plural form of demonstrative *that* is not *those* but *them*, as in many other dialects. Here we have: *them bright blew* [blue] *eyes* and *them paigles*.
7. *I was 'long o' Tom* illustrates the point made in the section on prepositions (4.11) that *alonga*, derived from *along with* or more likely, *along of*, signifies 'together with'.
8. In traditional East Anglian dialects, *the* normally appears in the form *th'* if the next word begins with a vowel, as noted in 4.5. We have an example here in *th' allotment*.
9. Pronoun Exchange, as in *That aint as if she knaow I care for she*, and *I give 'ee sich a look* 'I gave he such a look', was discussed at some length in 4.7.2 as a feature of the dialects of some areas of Essex and adjacent parts of Cambridgeshire, with examples from the *Ballads*.

East Anglian Phonology
1. As in Text 2, the NURSE vowel appears as /a:/ in *har* 'her' and *sarmon* 'sermon' but also as short /A/ in *mussy* 'mercy'.
2. The East Anglian preservation of the distinction between ME ρ: and ME *ou* was clearly still alive and well in this part of Essex at the end of the 19th century since the text has *know* as *knaow* but *go* as *goo*. On the other hand, the Long Mid Merger of the two originally different FACE vowels does appear to have taken place, since we have the form *saime* 'same', indicating a diphthong rather than a monophthong.
3. The spelling *dawg* indicates the pronunciation of *dog* with the THOUGHT vowel, as noted in 3.2.1.3.

4. *Sich* represents a widespread dialectal pronunciation of *such*. In Old English *such* was *swelc, swilc, swylc,* and one Medieval English descendant of this was *swych*, a form which occurs in the letters of Margaret Paston.
5. *Jest* represents a common East Anglian pronunciation of *just* – see also Text 5.
6. *A Sundays* = 'on Sundays'.

7.9 Tillingham, Essex, c. 1917

Mr Alfred Cornwall (b. 1882)

Berliner Lautarchiv https://sounds.bl.uk/Accents-and-dialects/Berliner-Lautarchiv-British-and-Commonwealth-recordings/021M-C1315X0001XX-0676V0

Mr Alfred Cornwall went to school in Tillingham on the Dengie peninsula of eastern Essex. This is one of our oldest sound-recordings of East Anglian speech, though the speakers on the recordings of Texts 4 and 7 were older than Mr Cornwell, being born in the 1870s. The recording comes from the Berliner Lautarchiv [Sound Archive] which was held at the Humboldt University in Berlin. This is one of the recordings of British and colonial prisoners of war made by linguist Wilhelm Doegen in Germany between 1915 and 1918. It is a version of the biblical Parable of the Prodigal Son, and contains no dialectal vocabulary as such; but speakers were asked to accommodate the text to their own way of speaking, and there are therefore some features of grammatical interest. The main interest, however, lies in the phonology: this recording provides fascinating information on how English was pronounced in eastern Essex by speakers born in the last two decades of the 19th century.

There was a man who had two sons. The younger of them said to his father, 'give me the part of your things that belongs to me'. So the father give him his share. Not many days a'terwards, the younger man gathered all his stuff together and went away into a far country and he began to be in want. When he was stoney-broke, a great famine come over the country, and he began to be in want. Before long, he had to take any job he could get and was pleased. When he found a job with a man of that country, this man sent him into the field as a pigman – stockman. He had no kip to sleep in. Many a time he would be glad to fill his belly with the husks that he fed the pigs with but even such food his master grudged him. At last when the young man come to think over what he had done, he said: Ah, how many hired servants of my father have all the food they want and even more than they want, and here am I dying of hunger. High time is it that I should go back to my father. This very day I will start for home. And I will go to my father and say to him: "Father, I have sinned against heaven and against you. I am no longer worthy to be called your son; make me one of your hired servants". And he arose and come to his father. When he was a long way off, his father see him, and had pity and run to meet him and fell on his neck and kissed him. And the young man said to his father "Father, I have sinned against heaven and against you, and I am no longer worthy to be called your son". But the father said to his servants "Bring forth the best clothes and put them on him and put a ring on his hand and shoes on his feet and bring here the fatted calf and kill it and lets eat and be merry for I thought my son was dead and he is alive again. He was lost and he is found."

East Anglian Lexis
Ah 'yes' was discussed in 5.6.2 and in the notes to Text 2.

East Anglian Grammar
There are some dialectal past-tense verb forms in this passage: *give, come, see* and *run.*

East Anglian Phonology
1. As we saw in 6.4, there are said to be some similarities between the accent of this part of Essex and Australian English. Features which might help to give this impression include the very front vowel of START, which is typical of the whole of East Anglia, but also a rather front realisation of STRUT, which is not (see 3.2.1.1). Mr Cornwall's FLEECE vowel is also very different from that found in more northerly areas of East Anglia in that, like Australian English, it has a very central first-element [ɜɪ] rather than [ɪi], as can be heard in *the part of your things that belongs to me*. Another resemblance can be found in the close articulations of DRESS and TRAP, something which was mentioned for East Anglia generally in 3.2.1.1.
2. Other notable features include the rather distinctive MOUTH vowel [ɛu]; and the fact that the long-mid merger of ME *ǫ:* and ME *ou* has been carried through, with the single GOAT vowel being a wide diphthong of the type [ɐu].
3. The speaker also has HappY-tensing, with /iː/ in *country, pity, belly,* which was unusual further north in East Anglia at this period, where /ɪ/ or /ə/ would have been more common.
4. Once again we can hear *after* with no /f/, in *a'terwards*. And *off* has the THOUGHT vowel (see 3.2.1.3).
5. The intervocalic /t/ in *a'terwards* has the typical East Anglian glottalised pronunciation, as described in 3.2.2: [aːtʔəwədz].
6. The most remarkable feature, however, is that Mr Cornwall has some rhoticity on the NURSE vowel in e.g. *worthy*. In 3.2.2 we noted that Lowman and the SED both recorded rhoticity on the NURSE vowel in coastal eastern Essex.

7.10 Cornish Hall End, Essex, 1961

Mr Fred Martin (b.1888, retired farm labourer)

https://sounds.bl.uk/Accents-and-dialects/Survey-of-English-dialects/021M-C0908X0018XX-0400V1

Cornish Hall End is a west Essex village about 11 miles northwest of Braintree (Essex), 11 miles east of Saffron Walden (Essex), and 7 miles south of Haverhill (Suffolk).

M: Not now – used to have horses round here. Yeah, used to hev'em, but course they don't not now, ain't got one about here now. No horses around here for miles now, only hunt'n horses or a child's pony. That's all there is now. What we call horses, cart-horses now – hard to find. I don't know anybody round here for miles. The last time I see one what worked that was about three year ago over Black Notley, I see an old farmer got one there in the tumbril, going up the Notley town like. He'd got a load of hazelt on then, on his cart, the bloke hed. There in't one round here, no as I know on, not today. Yes, you couldn't go on a farm when I started to work first without there was haps eight, ten, dozen horse.

Q: Who looked after the horses?

M: The horseman. The horseman used to look after the horses and he was paid two or three shill'ns extra, and that used to be well worth it – he'd got to go an hour of a morning to feed 'em, an hour of a night to clean 'em down after other people had gone hoom. That was about two shill'n or three shill'ns outside extra to what they used to get, Sundays and all, had to go and do it for this three shillings. Course, wages werent only twelve shill'ns a week that time o' day, twelve shill'ns a week. They used to get fifteen – that was a lot o' money that time. What's how it was was according to the price of things you see. An' I used to be horseman that time o' day. I had to, I used to be allowed about six horses a piece to look after, to feed an' that. Perhaps there was two horsemen like in the stable to see after they, if they'd got eight; three if they'd got twelve. Haps they'd got one extra horse put in, two if that. I never had more than six to look after. Then haps they'd have a man, like, to go in a morning, to half hour, help brush two down. They reckoned, sort of, on average four horses for a horseman to see after. Then when they used to turn out to plough, you see, they didn't only have two. Two'd goo on a plough – they used to take two each. There was the horseman, like, and th'other man was a sort of help-plougher – ploughman, they used to call they. Yes, odd ploughman.

Yes, the horseman was in charge of the job, like, for mark'n the furrows out, you see, yes mark'n the field out, you see, and odd one used to have to go behind him, do the ploughing, like, and the head horseman, they used to do the mark'n out. So if that was wrong when – stetches was wrong when they used to go down driddling, the horsekeeper had the blame, you see.

East Anglian Lexis
Driddling 'drilling'. I have found no other instance anywhere of what I assume to be a variant of *drilling*.
Haps 'perhaps'.
Hazelt: according to Charnock (1880), *hazelt brick earth* is "a kind of loam found in some parts of Essex".
Stetch 'a ridge of ploughed land between two furrows'. The EDD has examples of this word from East Anglia, Northamptonshire and Leicestershire. The OED suggests that the word may have the same etymology as *stitch*.
Tumbril (also *tumbler* elsewhere in East Anglia) 'a cart that tilts backwards to allow for unloading'.

East Anglian Grammar
1. Typical of East Anglian dialects is the occurrence of multiple negation with *only* (see 4.2.1). Here we have: *wages werent only twelve shillings a week* 'wages were only twelve shillings a week', and *they didn't only have two* 'they only had two'.
2. Pronoun Exchange was discussed in 4.7.2 – and above in connection with Text 8 – as a feature of the dialects of some areas of Essex and adjacent parts of Cambridgeshire. It is clear from this text that these areas include Cornish Hall End since this feature can be observed here: *there was two horsemen in the stable to see after they;* and *ploughman, they used to call they.*
3. The archaic use of *horse* as the plural form of *horse*, as here in *eight, ten, dozen horse,* is discussed in 4.3.4.
4. The usual East Anglian preterite of *to see* occurs here in *the last time I see one.*
5. The typical relative pronoun *what* also occurs in *the last time I see one what worked.*
6. *On* once again functions as *of* here in *no as I know on.*
7. East Anglian *that* = 'it' occurs several times, as in *that was about three year agoo* and *that was about two shillen.*
8. The preterite of BE is *was* /wʊz/ for all persons, as in *if the stetches was wrong.*
9. I have once again transcribed *have* /hɛv/ as <hev>.

East Anglian Phonology
1. The East Anglian preservation of the distinction between ME ǭ: and ME *ou* has been partly lost (see the Map 3.1), but /uː/ can be heard in *go* and *ago* as differing clearly from the /ʌʊ/ in *know*. 'East Anglian short *o*' also occurs, as with the /ʊ/ in *home*. *Only*, on the other hand, has the LOT vowel.
2. /aː/ in *hard*, *mark'n* 'marking' and /æː/ in *half* are distinct, as discussed in Chapter 3 and in the notes to Text 4 above.
3. A number of NURSE items have the typical East Anglian short vowel [ɐ~ʌ] e.g. in *turn*, *worked*. There is also some slight retroflection in *worked*.
4. MOUTH and PRICE are very distinctively [eʉ] and [ɒɪ] respectively.
5. The NEAR and SQUARE vowels are distinct from one another and are both diphthongal.
6. The Weak-Vowel Merger can be noted in the usage of schwa rather than the KIT vowel in, for example, *minutes* /mɪnəts/, *marking* [maːkʔən]. I have transcribed *shilling* /ʃɪlən~ʃɪln̩/ etc. as <shill'n> etc.
7. The typical East Anglian glottalisation of intervocalic /p, t, k/ can be heard in e.g. *marking* [maːkʔən].
8. Unlike in East Anglian dialects from further north (though see Text 12), there are some instances of h-dropping on this recording, e.g *horses* occurs both with and without /h/.
9. Also unlike in most of the other East Anglian dialects, dark *l* is particularly dark, i.e. velarised, and has some lip-rounding, e.g. in *miles*.
10. Again atypically of the general East Anglian English of this period, Mr Martin has some TH-fronting, e.g. *three* /friː/. Today this is very common, particularly in the speech of younger people throughout at least urban East Anglia (see more on this in 8.2).
11. Once again we can hear *after* with no /f/.
12. *Off* is again /ɔːf/.

Cambridgeshire

7.11 Little Downham, Cambridgeshire, 1958

SED https://sounds.bl.uk/Accents-and-dialects/Survey-of-English-dialects
/021M-C0908X0015XX-0200V1>

Little Downham is situated in the Fens between Mepal and Welney to the north-west of Ely, which it is separated from by an area of low-lying flat land known as West Fen. The speaker, here labelled S, is unidentified but the fieldworker is once again Stanley Ellis.

Q: What about when the high tides came up?

S: Well, you see, they used to be, at that time of day they used to be a bit dangerous, you see. Then. You were liable getting a flood, you see, a bank – if it got extry high these banks, they used to watch 'em some nights. My father stood here two days and one night with a hoss roped ready to flit, like, see, if this bank had'a' blowed, you see, you'd a' had to a' flitted up onto the hills somewhere. And we . . . he had the hoss yoked to – in a stall w'all the gears on, band to put it in the cairt or anything, like. Of course that was a tidy family on'em, on us, you see, and you couldn't a' walked us away, you'd a' had to put us in the cairt and drive us up onto the hill or somewhere.

Q: Has it ever blowed in your time?

S: No, never blowed in my time.

Q: Which was the most dangerous stretch?

S: This way up here, yeah.

Q: They strengthened somewhere?

S: All the way along it. Right the way along from t'other side of Mepal right up there to Welney. And I think, and they a' gone behind Welney, some part of it. Oh, they've riz this bank a lot, two or three different times, this bank' riz a wonderful lot in the last twenty or thirty year, you see. There allus was two men regularly used to work on it, all the year round, levell'n on it up and fill'n cracks up, and watch'n, you know, and keep an eye on the bank for cracks or anything in it, you see. If that cracked anywhere, they used to dig it out and fill it up agin.

Q: And what about the washes?

S: We never troubled about them. 'Course what went that way, were alright. That didn't matter about that providing the in-end bank didn't blow. That didn't matter about that bank between this and the wash where we are, see, that didn't matter, 'cause that used to get flooded right over the top of that. You wouldn't see that, for a length of places, you know. Away from here to Mepal, I've seen it, you know, level water just running over, you can design the bank, like, only you could see the water over the top of it. So you know it used to be a long way up this one, well when a bank had a weak place or anything they used to watch it, you see, and 'course they couldn't have done no good, only watch it and advise people to git out of the way if it had a' blowed, of course, once that'd got a hole through that would a' soon a' swept about a hundred yards of it, perhaps. Well, this here'd a' all been flooded all around here, right round to Ely, barring that hill, you know, in Downham and different places, that'd a' run up this drain and round into what they call the West Fen, and all out there.

East Anglian Lexis
Allus 'always'.
Blow 'burst', of river banks.
Design 'to trace the outline of, discern' – an archaic usage of this word.
Flit '(re)move, transport (oneself)'. This is a word found in dialects in many parts of England; as well as in standard usage in Scotland in the sense of 'move house'. It is of Old Norse origin, cf. Danish *flytte* 'move'.
Gears 'harness'. The EED has this word as occurring in East Anglia and southern Lincolnshire.
Tidy 'good'. *A tidy family on'em* = 'a good [i.e. large] family of them'.
Wash 'low-lying area of land which is often flooded'.

East Anglian Grammar
1. *Blowed* functions here as both the past participle and preterite of *blow* 'burst'. Stanley Ellis empathetically uses this form himself.
2. *Have,* as is typical in East Anglia, occurs mostly without the final /v/, giving the unstressed weak form /ə/, here transcribed as <a'>.
3. *Riz* 'raised'. As we saw in 4.1.10, East Anglian dialects often do not distinguish between causative and non-causative verb forms, in this case *raise* as opposed to *rise*. In this text, *riz* is the dialectal preterite and past participle form of the verb *to rise*, which functions here as the equivalent to both Standard English *raise* and *rise*.
4. East Anglian *that* 'it' occurs in e.g. *if that cracked anywhere, once that'd got a hole though it.*
5. As usual in these texts, *on* can be equivalent to *of*.

6. *A*-verbing does not occur here, but we do have *on = of* in *levell'n on it up* 'levelling it up'.
7. As in the other Fenland texts, the preterite of BE is *were* – *what went that way were alright* – as opposed to the *was/wus* of other East Anglian dialects.
8. *t'other* 'the other'.
9. As is normal in most varieties of English, negative concord occurs: *they couldn't have done no good*.

East Anglian Phonology
1. *Cart* is pronounced /kɛːt/ – I have transcribed it as <cairt>. The /aː/ vowel in *father* and *last* is clearly different from the vowel of *cart*. The same /ɛː/ vowel is indicated by the spelling <dairk> 'dark' in Text 13 from Marshall's *Fenland Chronicle,* suggesting a common Fenland development of ME ar > /ɛː/, otherwise found in dialects in Scotland and Northumberland. The same spelling also occurs in Text 13 in <mairster> 'master', but this has a different historical source.
2. The word *people* occurs here with the FACE vowel, another instance of the phenomenon whereby, as noted in 3.2.1.2, a number of words descended from ME ę: preserve the earlier vowel instead of employing the shifted form with /iː/.
3. The speaker has the typical north East Anglian distinction between ME ǫ: and ME ou, as in *over* versus *blow*.
4. The speaker has a rhotic pronunciation of words involving the NURSE vowel, as in *thirty*.
5. An example of early *r*-loss before /s/ occurs, however, in *horse*, transcribed here as <hoss>.
6. The MOUTH vowel has the distinctive south and west East Anglian [ɛʉ] pronunciation.
7. The Weak-Vowel Merger is very apparent in the pronunciation of the *-ing* suffix as [ən~n̩] and in the pronunciation of unstressed *it* with schwa.
8. The TRAP vowel is phonetically somewhat more open than the variant heard in the Norfolk, Suffolk and Essex recordings.
9. Unlike in dialects from further east, some instances of h-dropping do occur here.
10. East Anglian glottalisation of intervocalic /p, t, k/ (3.2.2) can be heard in, for example, *Mepal, keep an, twenty*.
11. *Extra* occurs here as *extry*. This might be a hypercorrection derived from the pronunciation of *very, money* etc. with word-final schwa.

7.12 Over, Cambridgeshire, c.1950

Alan Bloom: *the Fens* (Robert Hall Ltd)
Over is a village to the east of the River Great Ouse, about 10 miles/16 km northwest of Cambridge. The village name, pronounced /ˈʌvə/ according to Alan Bloom, is from Old English *ōfer* 'river bank' cf. German *Ufer* 'bank, shore'. The following passage is from Alan Bloom's 1953 book *The Fens*. Bloom (1906–2005) was a native of Over. I have combined here extracts from dialogues between Bloom and a local man he calls Jack Cook, who worked with the drainage pumps. Over was one of the Cambridgeshire localities investigated by Vasko (2010).

Well, I'll goo to blazes. Who'd ever thought o' seein' you – and a nice ole pickle yore ketched me in, but blarst, I'm proper glad to see ye none the more for that. However are ye arter all these years? Them ole diesel fumes got settled on me chest and then I got wet through and here I am – kain't eat, kain't sleep, kain't smook, kain't do nothin' ony lay 'ere abed and corf. Blarst – I do 'ate bein' like this 'ere – ruther 'ev the sweat runnin' orf me from 'ard work, I would. I've bin a frettin layin' 'ere when there's most work to be done. I een't wuth tuppence. [Bloom says he will come back another time.] Ah, thas it, bor. There's a lot I want to ask ye and vullike I'll be able to then.

[On his next visit, Bloom asks about the 1947 floods.]

We shall none of us see the like o'that agin. You know me – if there's anywhere I kin git with a boat, I have to try it. I used to goo all over the fields, over hedges, fences and ditches, and there weren't a field I din't punt over, just to be able to say I'd done it in years to come. One day, two days after the bank bust, I went nosin' round Trinity farm. I found a bull tied up in a shed. Poor ole feller, he were half-crazy standin' in water up to his belly, so I shoved him some hay down and come back and reported it to the owner and then at ten o'clock the next morning he and the RSPCA man come and arst me if I'd take 'em down. And proper rough it were. You know thas over a mile to Trinity Farm from here and it were one of the roughest trips I ever did 'ev in a boat. That were four o'clock next mornin' afore I got 'um, and the missus jest made up 'er mind she'd got rid o' me at larst.

East Anglian Lexis
Abed /əbˈɛd/ 'in bed' is said by the EDD to be "widely diffused throughout the midland and southern counties".
Blarst = blast. In 5.6.3, we saw how *blast* is frequently used as an interjection in East Anglian English. We noted in 3.2.1.3 that it could be pronounced with a short vowel, /blʌst/. The <blarst> spelling employed here, however, indicates the long vowel, /blaːst/.

The form *vullike* 'probably' would appear to be an example of univerbation involving an original *very+like*. It is not known as such to the EDD, but it does also appear in James Brown's *Gamgy Talk*,[122] a glossary of terms used in Gamlingay, a village 14 miles/23 kms to the west of Cambridge. Brown's entry reads: "*Vullike* – 'in all probability' e.g. y*ear, vullike I shull*", which we can transcribe as 'yeah, very-like I shall'. I am not aware of it as occurring in Norfolk, Suffolk or Essex.

Other forms that have already been noted and discussed above include *afore* 'before' (Text 3), *ah!* 'yes' (Text 2), and the address term *bor* (Text 3).

East Anglian Grammar
1. Unlike the contemporary dialects of the core areas of linguistic East Anglia, this Cambridgeshire dialect has generalised *were* as well as *weren't* for all persons as the preterite of *be*, as here in *that were, he were, there weren't* (see 4.1.7).
2. We have in previous texts seen *in't* and *en't* as negative present-tense forms of *be*. Here we see a different form, *een't* /iːnt/, which was noted for Cambridgeshire in 4.2.2, and occurs in the EDD in entries from southern Nottinghamshire and Leicestershire, showing that in this respect this relatively westerly part of Cambridgeshire aligns with the East Midlands rather than East Anglia.
3. *Kain't* = *cain't* does not occur in the core East Anglian linguistic area, but there are frequent citations in the EDD from Leicestershire. Once again, this Cambridgeshire dialect aligns with the East Midlands rather than East Anglia.
4. Other grammatical features that have already been discussed earlier in this chapter are:
   – the preterite forms *ketched* 'caught' and *come* 'came' (see e.g. Text 4)
   – plural demonstrative *them* 'those' (Text 3)
   – pronominal *that* 'it' (Text 5) and *thas(s)* 'that's, it's' (Text 6)

---

122 http://www.gamlingayhistory.co.uk/wp-content/uploads/Gamgy-Talk-4.pdf.

- *lay* 'lie' (Text 8)
- *din't* 'didn't' (Text 5)
- *a*-verbing, as in *a-frettin* (Text 2).

East Anglian Phonology
1. A very striking phonological feature of this text is h-dropping, as in '*ate* 'hate', '*ard* 'hard', '*ere* 'here'. This is a feature which is not generally found in East Anglia, as was noted in 3.2.2, but it can be heard variably on the Little Downham recording.
2. *Goo* 'go' and *smook* 'smoke' indicate /guː/ and /smuːk/ and suggest an at least partial preservation of the distinction between ME *ǭ:* and ME *ou*. The pronunciation of *home* as '*um* /ʊm/ shows the geographical extension of the 'East Anglian short *o*' to the western edge of the region.
3. On *wuth* 'worth', and *bust* 'burst', see Text 2. *Ruther* 'rather' is an example of the phenomenon mentioned in Chapter 3 whereby a small number of words such as *blast* and *partner* which originally had /aː/ can occur with the specifically East Anglian short vowel /ʌ/.
4. The pronunciation of *only* without /l/ is a common feature of East Anglian English. Here we have *ony* /uːnɪ, ʊnɪ/.
5. On *corf, orf*, see Text 5.
6. On *arter*, see Text 2.
7. On *git, agin*, see Text 3.
8. On *jest*, see Text 5.

7.13 Ramsey Heights, Cambridgeshire, c. 1938

Sybil Marshall: *Fenland chronicle* **(CUP)**

Sybil Marshall's 1967 book consists of her renderings of stories told by her parents, who lived in the Fens in Ramsey Heights, formerly in Huntingdonshire. This particular passage, Sybil Marshall says, was actually written down by her father himself, William Henry Edwards (1860–1940). He had only started writing the book – the first four chapters were in his own hand – when he was 77. We can suppose, then, that this text dates from the period 1937–1940. William wrote, Sybil tells us, "in the same way as he talked". Ramsey Heights is situated in a transitional zone between core East Anglian and neighbouring dialects and therefore has a number of features not encountered in other texts.

When we got 'um, the mairster war about ten or twelve foot down the golt pit, a-digging golt wi' the other men. So I went and stood aside the pit. None on'em di'n't take no notice on me, so I said "I say, mairster, we're sold th'ole porny". But 'e never looked up, on'y said quicklike, like 'e allus did, "I don't understand your langwidge". Ah, I understood his'n well enough. But 'e still went on wukkin', and never looked up. So arter a little while I said "Well, mairster, we ain't done nothink as we cayn't roightle". "Yew'd better goo an'roightle it then", the mairster said. So I went off to find Joe, and when I'ad found 'im, I said "Joe, bor, we're got tew goo an' git th'ole porny agin". "What's 'e say", arst Joe. So I says "Yew'd better goo an'see fer yerself if yew want to know", I says. "Now then, Joe bor, yew better git orf towards Sawtry". So we went 'um and got ourselves a bit o'grub, and got ready ter goo, but fust we thought we'd call for a pint at the mairster's 'ouse. So we drunk our beer, an' away we went. When we got outside the noight were dark, an' I says to Joe, "Well bor, this is a tidy kettle o'fish", but I knowed as we'd got ter goo, an' it warn't no use a-thinking as we a'nt. It took us a tidy while, ter git roight acrorss t'Sawtry in the pitch dairk. When we did git there we went an' found the man what we selled the porny tew. We telled 'im what we'd come fer. 'E di'n't take a lot tew it, neither. "You're the rummest lot o'dealers I ever see in me loife", 'e said. Anyway, we did get th'ole porny back, on'y we 'ad t'pay 'im fifteen shillin's. I reckon as 'e could see as we 'ad got wrong wi' the mairster. We led the porny 'um, but coming along the road, I see a gate afront on us, and I said "Joe, bor, we're wrong 'ere. I never see a gate anend the high road afore. We may goo back".

© 1967 CUP

East Anglian Lexis

Ah 'yes' – see notes to Text 9.

Anend 'beside, against' is an archaic form which more usually occurs as *anent*.

Aside = *beside*. The OED describes this prepositional usage of *aside* as "archaic and dialectal". Compare *afore* in Texts 3 and 12.

Bor is the East Anglian address form noted a number of times above.

Golt: according to the OED, *gault* is "a provincial name in the east of England for a series of beds of clay and marl, the geological position of which is between the upper and the lower greensand".

Porny 'pony' – according to the OED, *pony* 'small horse' was originally a Scots word and could appear in Scots as *pawnie,* but I have no explanation as to why this Fenland dialect has this particular form.

Roightle, i.e. *rightle* 'to put right' is not known to the EDD from Cambridgeshire, but it does give citations from Lincolnshire, Rutland and Bedfordshire, which all border on Cambridgeshire.

Rummest: we saw in 5.1.7 that *rum* is a typically East Anglian lexical item meaning 'strange, peculiar'.

East Anglian Grammar

1. *His'n* is not a feature of core East Anglian dialects. We saw in 2.5.2 and 4.7.5 that there is clear regional differentiation between eastern areas, which have the possessive pronouns *yours, his, hers, ours, theirs*, and areas further west which have *yourn, hisn, hern, ourn, theirn*. The eastern *theirs*-type forms are found all over Norfolk and Suffolk, and in eastern Cambridgeshire. The *theirn*-type forms are found in Northamptonshire, Huntingdonshire, Bedfordshire, Hertfordshire, western Essex, and western Cambridgeshire.
2. We saw in 4.1.7 that in the older East Anglian dialect the past-tense form of *be* was *war* /waː/ for all persons in the positive. I wrote there that, since the mid-19th century, the past-tense form of *to be* has been *wus* /wʊz/ for all persons in the positive, but *weren't* for all persons in the negative. As we can see here, however, *war* survived in Ramsey Heights at least until the 1930s.
3. *A-digging* is another typical instance of East Anglian *a*-verbing.
4. *None on'em di'n't take no notice* 'None of them took any notice': this is a very fine example of negative concord or multiple (in this case, triple) negation.
5. *We're sold* = 'we have sold' – see notes to Text 6.
6. *Knowed, telled* are dialectal regular preterite forms of verbs which are irregular in many other dialects.

East Anglian Phonology
1. The form *'um* /ʊm/ 'home' shows that the 'East Anglian short *o*' extends, at least in some words, into this area of the Fens.
2. The form *'um* also demonstrates h-dropping, which is not a feature of core East Anglian dialects but which can be seen in this text also in *'e* 'he', *'ad* 'had'.
3. *Goo* 'go' – see notes to Text 12.
4. *Dairk* 'dark' – see notes to Text 11. Note also *mairster* 'master'
5. *Fust, wukkin* 'first, working' – see notes to Text 2.
6. *Git* 'get' – see notes to Text 6.

8 The dynamics of East Anglian English: past, present and future

8.1 The expansion and contraction of linguistic East Anglia

As we saw in Chapters 1 and 2, a distinctively East Anglian form of English has existed for as long as the language itself: East Anglian English has been a feature in the English-language landscape ever since West Germanic Anglian speakers first arrived on the eastern shores of the island of Britain from continental Europe 1,500 years ago. The areas of England which are now Norfolk and Suffolk were predominantly settled by Anglians, who came from southern Jutland and Schleswig-Holstein and lived alongside the Brittonic and/or British Latin speakers, eventually replacing or absorbing them, as described in 1.3. Neighbouring Cambridgeshire and Essex were settled by Saxons who came from the North Sea coastal areas of northern Germany in the Elbe-Weser region.

Topographically, the Anglian-speaking area of Eastern England was bounded to the east and the north by the North Sea; and to the northwest by the Wash Estuary and the mostly impassable Fens. The inland boundary of East Anglia originally consisted of the ethnolinguistic frontier which separated it, in the south, from Saxon-speaking Essex, along the line of the river Stour; and in the west from Saxon-speaking Cambridgeshire, along the lines of the rivers Ouse, Lark and Kennett. Even when the Old English Kingdom of East Anglia later expanded politically westwards, as far as the River Cam, Cambridgeshire seems to have remained linguistically Saxon.

For many centuries, the Fenland linguistic boundary between Lincolnshire and Norfolk remained rather stable, but this degree of stability was not replicated at the midwestern, southwestern and southern edges of modern East Anglia. In the Old English and Middle English periods, there were still important isoglosses between Norfolk and Cambridgeshire; but the writings of Forby (1830) indicate that by the 18th century this situation had changed. As we saw in 2.3, Forby came from Stoke Ferry in Norfolk, very close to the Cambridgeshire border, and spent much time at Cambridge University. He observed (1830: 66) that the dialects of Norfolk, Suffolk and Cambridgeshire are "varieties, and even slight ones, of the same species, and are therefore properly called by the same name, East Anglian". We can have confidence that Forby was correct in this assertion only with respect to eastern Cambridgeshire, but his remarks do indicate that, during the Early Modern English period, there had been a significant expansion of linguistic East Anglia in a westward direction. And if we are to look for explanatory factors for this expansion, the most obvious would be the growing importance of Norwich as the major urban centre in the eastern region – until the 18th century it had the largest population of any centre in Britain after London – and thus its growing role as a major focal point for the outward geographical diffusion of linguistic innovations.

In 2.4 we also noted that, as described by Ihalainen (1994), Halliwell (1881) analysed the dialects of core East Anglia, i.e. Norfolk and Suffolk, as having linguistic links not only with Cambridgeshire but also with Essex. This is an indication that, even if medieval linguistic East Anglia stopped at the Suffolk-Essex border, by the 19th century this had changed, with (much of) Essex now belonging to the East Anglian dialect area: in the period 1500–1800 it would seem that linguistic East Anglia also expanded geographically towards the south. We can again explain this in terms of the growth of the influence of Norwich as the major central place for the diffusion of linguistic innovations across the region.

Subsequently, however, even the nature of the Fenland boundary started changing: important developments concerning the extent of East Anglia as a geographical dialect area actually started taking place in the Fens in the 17th century, though it was events during the 18th and 19th centuries which were to have the greatest linguistic significance (see 3.2.1.2). The Fens have been more or less uninhabitable for most of recorded history (Britain, 1991):

> the area between Cambridge and the Wash was for the most part undrained marshland which was subject to very frequent flooding. Up until the 17th century the northern coastline lay up to 12 miles further south than at present. Most of the Fenland population at that time lived on a few islands of higher ground and in small communities on this northern coastline. The southern two-thirds of the Fenland consisted of undrained marshland which was subject to tidal flooding in summer, more continuous flooding in winter and was hence too unstable in most places for permanent settlement.
>
> (Britain & Trudgill, 2005: 190)

Because of the impassability of the area, and indeed its undesirability as a place of habitation,[123] the Fens made for a serious barrier to communication, and it is no accident, therefore, that one of the most important dialect boundaries in the English-speaking world – the bundle of isoglosses between East Anglia, on the one hand, and Lincolnshire and the East Midlands on the other – developed there and still remains in place to this day.

From the mid-1600s onwards, however, Dutch engineers were invited to carry out drainage work in the Fens – an initiative which continued on and off

---

[123] Samuel Pepys writes of his travels "over most sad fenns, all the way observing the sad life which the people of the place do live, sometimes rowing from one spot to another and then wading".

for over 250 years. There was considerable opposition on the part of local Fenland people whose fishing and wild-fowling life-style was being threatened, with rioting and sabotage continuing into the early 1800s. But two new major drainage channels, the Old Bedford River and the New Bedford River ("the Hundred Foot Drain"), were cut across the Cambridgeshire Fens, joining the River Great Ouse to the sea by King's Lynn. Increasingly sophisticated pumping techniques led gradually to the bogs and marshland of the Fens being converted into some of the richest arable farming land in the country.

This in turn led to large-scale in-migration, including into the hitherto remotest central Fenland areas. Much of the in-migration (see Britain, 1997) was from southern Lincolnshire and the Soke[124] of Peterborough, areas immediately to the west of the Fens – and therefore to the west of the original dialect boundary (see 3.2.1.2). The other major source of in-migration was from the area immediately to the east of the Fens – and therefore to the east of the original dialect boundary, namely Norfolk. Between 1563 and 1801 "the populations of the central Fenland towns of March and Chatteris rose by around 140%, and that of Wisbech by over 280%" (Britain & Trudgill, 2005: 191). It is true that today the Fens still remain somewhat isolated and not very densely populated, relatively speaking. But the in-migration led to considerable dialect contact, dialect mixture and new-dialect formation, which has had interesting linguistic consequences, including changes in the location and nature of the major dialect boundary: the Fenland reclamation led to a certain amount of geographical expansion of the East Anglian dialect area.

Subsequently, the East Anglian dialect initially survived well as a distinctive variety, sheltered to a certain extent from outside influence by its relatively remote position and poor transport connections. Since World War II, however, the East Anglian linguistic area as a whole has been getting progressively smaller, and the dialect is now in a much weaker position than formerly. In places such as Braintree in Essex, for example, speakers who were born before World War I had East Anglian phonology, complete with the distinctive rhythmic pattern noted in 3.1, while those born after World War II have a phonology that is more typical of the Home Counties. Analysis of the data obtained by the Foxcroft-Trudgill survey in the mid 1970s (see 3.0) showed that the general diffusion of phonological features outwards from London was particularly noticeable in the case of the Essex towns of Colchester, Clacton, and Walton. In these towns, the older speakers sound like East Anglians, as an overall impression, while many younger speakers sound rather more like Londoners, as is often noted by lay observers.

---

124 The primary meaning of *soke* was 'area of jurisdiction'.

As we shall see shortly, this is a process which has been going on for very many decades, but a new factor has been the increasing in-migration into East Anglia of people from the Home Counties and "the Sheers",[125] due only in part to official governmental London overspill housing schemes whereby large numbers of Londoners have been settled in East Anglian towns such as Haverhill, Sudbury, Thetford and King's Lynn. This in-migration has proportionally reduced the demographic base of East Anglian dialect speakers.

The population of Norfolk almost doubled in the five decades from 1970 to 2020, from around 500,000 to over 900,000, something which was by no means entirely due to natural increase. The social-class distribution of East Anglian English is also diminishing. In the 1950s, nearly everyone in Norwich had some kind of Norfolk accent unless they came from somewhere else or had been educated at one of the more expensive private schools. Now, typically local speech variants are becoming less frequent in the speech of the younger members of the middle classes, so that the local dialects are under pressure socially from above as well as geographically from the south.

Unsurprisingly, then, a number of people in East Anglia in the first decades of the 21st century have started asking how much longer their distinctive variety of English can continue to exist; and there is a widespread perception amongst older East Anglians that East Anglian English is "dying out". Those who express this fear may couch their concerns in terms of young people – in Norwich, for instance – "talking Cockney". This is an interesting observation, but if pressed to give examples of what leads them to make this claim, complainers invariably make the same point: that young people tend to say *fing* and *muvver* rather than *thing* and *mother*.

As it happens, this is quite true: as in very many other parts of England – and indeed more recently even in parts of Northern Ireland and Scotland – London-origin TH-fronting, /θ/>/f/ and /ð/> /v/, is becoming increasingly common in East Anglia. The earliest recorded instance that I am aware of which captures the feature in southern East Anglia can be heard in Chapter 7, Text 10, on the 1950s SED recording of a speaker born in 1888 from Cornish Hall End in west Essex, the area of the region closest to London.

As far as northern East Anglia is concerned, we are able to date rather precisely the point at which this sound-change first reached Norwich, the East Anglian centre furthest away from London. Work reported on in Trudgill (1974) and Trudgill (1988) shows that the innovation was totally absent from the

---

[125] The counties to the west of East Anglia which, unlike Norfolk, Suffolk and Essex, have names ending in *-shire*.

phonologies of Norwich speakers born before 1950, but had started appearing in the speech of those born around 1960, thus 70 years or so after the rural western Essex speaker in Text 10. Urban centres in southwestern East Anglia would doubtless have started acquiring it earlier than that (Kerswill, 2003).

However, as will be apparent to anyone who actually compares the phonetics and phonology of younger Norwich speakers today with a true Londoner accent, the former could never be mistaken for the latter. This single London-origin feature, TH-fronting, has indeed made its way even into the urban East Anglian centres furthest away from London, but most other modern London features have not.

Looking at the whole sweep of the history of East Anglian dialects, moreover, we can see that there is nothing at all unusual about the spread of an individual linguistic feature outwards from London into even the furthest northeast of East Anglia. This is something which has been happening for centuries.

We can note a number of exogenous innovations which have, over the centuries, penetrated into East Anglian English from the south in precisely this way.

8.2 Exogenous innovations

8.2.1 The v-w merger

The phonological feature discussed in 3.2.2 involving the merger of /w/ and /v/ illustrates this point very well. The merger is still stereotypically associated with the traditional dialect of Norfolk, even though in the 21st century it has more or less disappeared, but it was very clearly a phenomenon which, like TH-fronting, spread into the East Anglia from London. In a very typical spatial diffusion pattern, the merger, having spread into East Anglia from London, then survived for many decades longer in Norfolk than it did in London. Wyld (1953: 292) wrote:

> this was formerly a London vulgarism, but is now apparently extinct in the Cockney dialect. Personally, I never heard these pronunciations, so well known to the readers of Dickens, Thackeray, and of the earlier numbers of Punch. My time for observing such points begins in the late seventies or early eighties of the last [i.e. 19th] century, and I never remember noticing this particular feature in actual genuine speech, though I remember quite well, as a boy, hearing middle-aged people say *weal* for *veal* and *vich* for *which*, jocularly, as though in imitation of some actual type of speech with which they were familiar.

Wyld then goes on to suppose that the London pronunciation was extant only until the 1840s or 1850s. But, as we saw in 3.2.2, the merger was still alive and well in rural Norfolk in the 1920s; and in the 1950s and 1960s SED materials, instances were recorded from all over Norfolk and Suffolk, as well as parts of

Essex. Because of its survival in (parts of) East Anglia for seven to ten decades after it had been lost in London, the merger eventually came to be regarded as an East Anglian feature.

The geography of this is illustrated very nicely in Map 8.1, from Anderson (1987), which is based on the SED materials. It can be seen that in the traditional dialects of the 1950s and 1960s, the merger was no longer found in London or in any of the Home Counties except Buckinghamshire, but that it did survive in the speech of older dialect speakers, even if in a few lexical items only, in a circle around London but – crucially – at some distance from it.

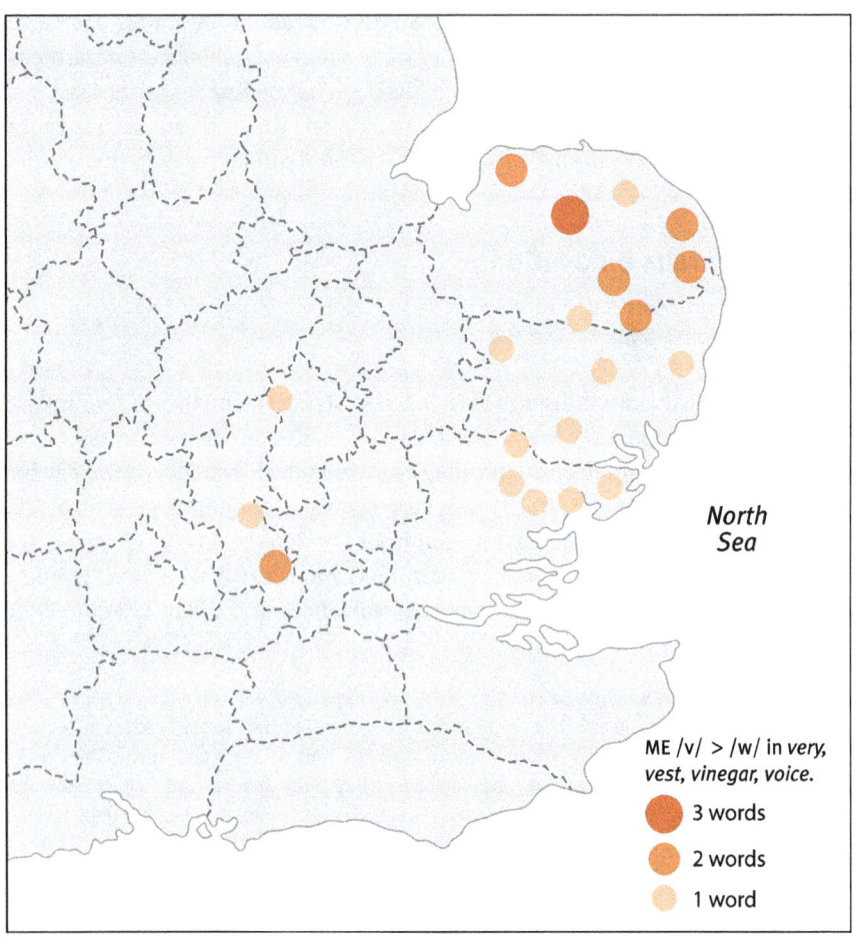

Map 8.1: The V-W Merger.

8.2.2 H-dropping

Another feature which clearly diffused from London outwards into East Anglia in the same kind of way is h-dropping. The term 'h-dropping' refers to the loss of word-initial /h/ in words such as *hill, house, hammer*, with the result that pairs such as *ill* and *hill*, *arm* and *harm*, become homophonous. Not to be considered as h-dropping is the absence of /h/ in unstressed grammatical words such as *him, his, he, her, have, has, had*, where all English speakers lack /h/. Neither can we use the term 'h-dropping' for the absence of /h/ in words which have orthographic <h> but which were borrowed from French without /h/, such as *heir, hour, honest*, and *honour* where, again, no English-speakers have /h/. However, care has to be taken in analysing the speech of older speakers in the case of a number of words in this category which used to lack /h/ but now have it as a result of a trend towards spelling-pronunciations, e.g. *hospital, humble, humour, herb* (though American English still lacks /h/ in this latter item). Other words in this class (see MacMahon, 1994: 477–8; Wells, 1982: 255) have had /h/ for so long that pronunciations of them without /h/ can safely be considered as h-dropping: *habit, heritage, homage, hospitable, host(ess), human*. Caution has to be exercised, though, with older speakers in the case of words such as *hotel, historic, hysteria* which have unstressed first syllables and which were treated in archaic RP like the unstressed forms of *h*-initial grammatical words, i.e. they also lacked /h/ (see Wells, 1982: 286). A final group of words in which absence of /h/ cannot be considered to be h-dropping, because no English speakers employ /h/ in such words consists of certain items with medial <h> such as *exhaust, exhilarate, exhibit, vehicle, vehement, shepherd* (plus, at least in England, place names such as *Durham, Birmingham*) (Gimson, 1962: 186).

H-dropping represents the end-point of a very long historical process in which the original Old English phoneme /h~x/ was gradually subjected to more and more phonotactic restrictions. It was lost word-initially before /r/ as in *hring* = *ring*, before /l/ as in *hlāf* = *loaf*, and before /n/ as in *hnutu* = *nut* in late Old English or early Middle English; it was lost in other preconsonantal positions after back vowels, as in *daughter, brought*, during the 1300s; and, during the 1400s it was lost after other vowels as in *night, sigh*, at least in the south of England, as discussed for Norfolk in 2.2 (McLaughlin, 1970: 110). The loss before /w/, as in *which*, is much more recent, and many conservative English varieties, e.g. in Scotland and Ireland, remain unaffected by this. And true 'h-dropping', as such – the loss of /h/ in absolute initial position, as in *hill* – is more recent still: Sweet (1888: 259) dates it to the late 1700s – "initial *h* began to be dropt everywhere in colloquial speech towards the end of thMn" [= third Modern period = 1700–1800], though Milroy (1983) has argued that it is an older development. Jones (1989: 268) also cites examples from

Lagamon's Brut, written in the 1200s. There are certainly a number of examples in *The Diary of Henry Machin*, written in the 1550s and 1560s (Jones, 1989: 268). The extent to which h-dropping had become the norm in the dialects of the greatest part of England by the 1860s also suggests a starting date earlier than that given by Sweet.

Map 8.2 (from Trudgill, 2004) shows that, in Ellis's data from the 1860s (Maguire, 2012), *h*-dropping was the norm at that time in all the dialects of England and Wales with the exception of those from the geographical peripheries: the far north of England; anglophone Wales and the far west of England; and East Anglia and neighbouring areas. H-dropping was absent from southeastern Lincolnshire, much of Cambridgeshire, all of Norfolk and Suffolk, most of Essex, and northeastern Kent (areas 1 and 2 on Map 8.2). From the map, based on the 1950s/1960s SED materials, it can be seen that, even a century later, Norfolk, Suffolk, northern Essex and the far north of Kent were still resisting the innovation (area 3 on Map 8.2). This was also true a couple of decades later of parts of Cambridgeshire, as we know from the 1970s/1980s work of Vasko (2010) and colleagues: much of rural Cambridgeshire was at that time transitional with respect to h-dropping. According to Vasko (2010), the Isle of Ely went with rural Norfolk and Suffolk in having /h/-retention, as did places further south close to the Suffolk and Essex borders such as Burwell, Wicken, Swaffham Prior, Swaffham Bulbeck, West Wickham, Castle Camps, Shudy Camps and Barlow. On the other hand, /h/ was frequently absent in the west of southern Cambridgeshire – for instance in Willingham, Rampton and Over (see the text in Chapter 7), as well as near the Hertfordshire border (Bassingbourn, Barrington) and the borders with Bedfordshire and Huntingdonshire (e.g. Gamlingay).

By the beginning of the 21st century, in the east of England it was only the dialects of Norfolk, Suffolk, eastern Cambridgeshire, and northeastern Essex – area 1 on Map 8.2 – which had not adopted h-dropping. An important factor here, however, is that this statement is valid only for rural dialects. The 1968 Norwich survey showed that some h-dropping was normal in Norwich;[126] Trudgill (1973) demonstrated that this was true also of other urban areas of East Anglia such as Ipswich, Yarmouth and King's Lynn (see below); and Vasko (2010) reports that h-dropping is the norm in the city of Cambridge and its immediate environs (see 3.2.2).

Insofar as it has arrived at all, then, h-dropping arrived in East Anglia relatively recently, and perhaps as much as three centuries after it had become

---

[126] As recently as the 1980s it was still a matter of common knowledge in the Norwich area that "city people drop their h's, country people don't".

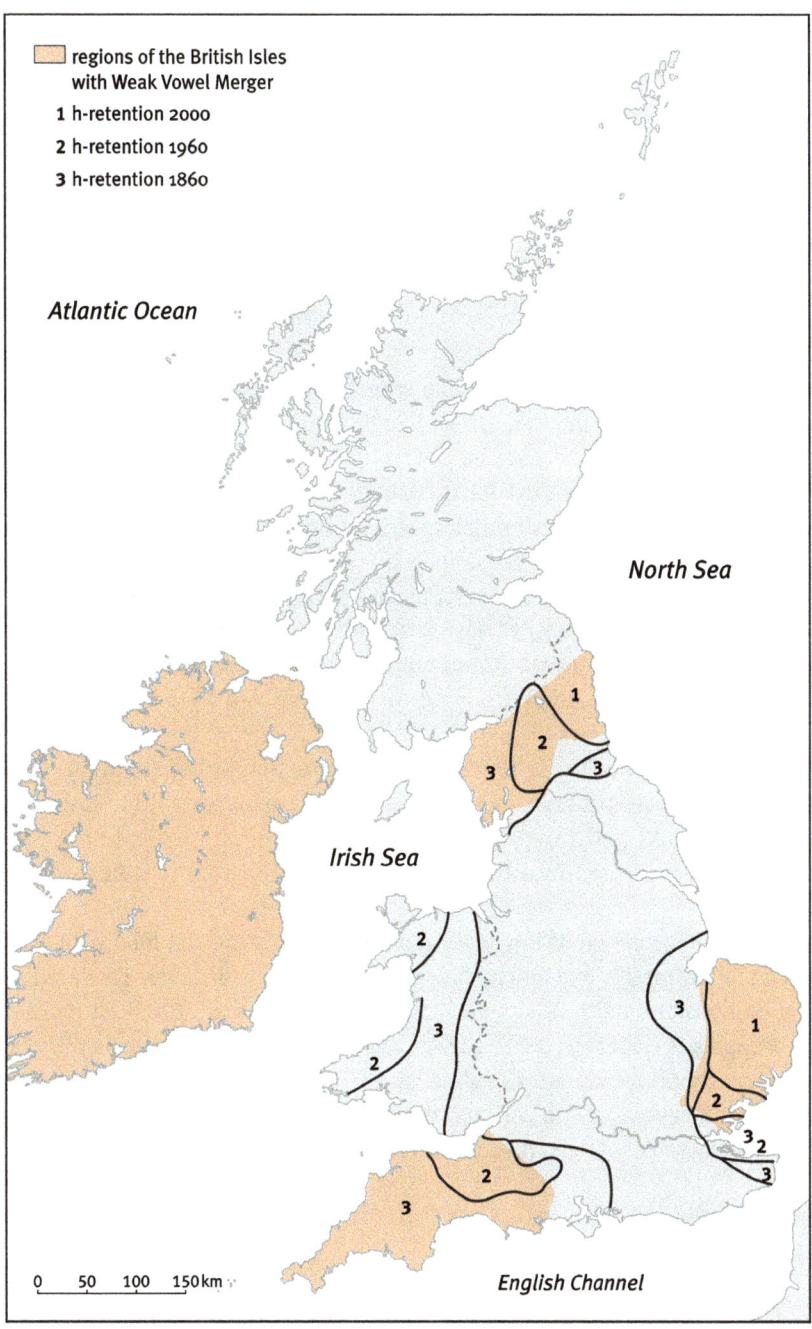

Map 8.2: H-retention & the Weak Vowel Merger.

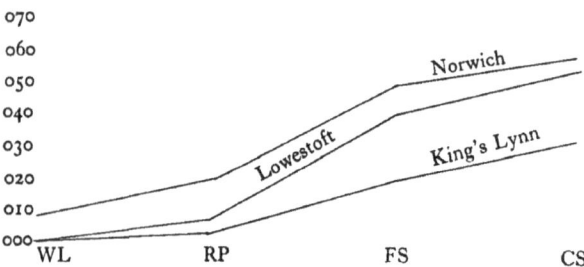

Figure 8.1: Percentage of h-dropping by teenagers in the 1970s.

established in London. In 1968, h-dropping in Norwich was still quantitatively at a much lower level than in other areas of England investigated by sociolinguists. Trudgill's (1974) study of Norwich has levels of h-dropping correlated with social class and style ranging from 0% for the Middle Middle Class (the highest social class group in the survey) in formal speech to no higher than 61% for Lower Working Class informants in casual speech – a level much lower than in most other parts of England. Hypercorrect forms, moreover, did not occur either.

As per the normal pattern of the spatial diffusion of linguistic innovations, h-dropping clearly first spread from London to the major urban areas of East Anglia, and only subsequently to rural areas dominated by particular towns and cities. Figure 8.1 shows the percentage of /h/-deletion in the speech of teenagers recorded by me in the 1970s in four contextual styles (reading word lists, reading a prose passage, formal speech, and casual speech) in Norwich, Lowestoft (Suffolk) and King's Lynn (Norfolk). The levels indicate the continuing diffusion of the innovation outwards from Norwich to other smaller urban areas.

There is no likelihood in the near future that h-dropping will follow the path taken by the v-w merger and end up being regarded as a distinctively East Anglian feature. But recent studies of London English (Cheshire et al., 2008) do indicate that *h*-dropping is currently receding there, and so it is not entirely impossible that the same geographical pattern as in the case of the v-w merger could eventually repeat itself in generations to come, with the innovation of h-dropping surviving longer in northern East Anglia than in the original London source dialect.

8.2.3 STRUT fronting

As we saw in 3.2.1.1, a vowel somewhat fronter than [ʌ] was the norm in the STRUT lexical set in RP around 1900. During the 20th century, it fronted to central [ɐ], though the practice continued on the part of linguists of employing /ʌ/ as the phonemic (as opposed to phonetic) symbol. In the English of London and other parts of the southeast, the fronting has now progressed further, giving "an open front vowel very close to cardinal [a]" (Gimson, 1962:103). As noted in Chapter 3, this diachrony is reflected in the contemporary geography of the vowel: the further one travels away from the English southeast, the further the vowel is located back along the trajectory the vowel has followed during the past five centuries (see Figure 3.1).

Map 8.3 (from Trudgill, 2004) shows the area of the southeast of England (labelled 4) for which Kurath & Lowman (1961: 17) found a "fully unrounded and lowered" STRUT vowel, i.e. the most advanced form in their data. It can be seen that this includes the whole of Essex plus areas of southern Suffolk.

My own research in the 1970s (Trudgill, 1986) showed that there was a clear phonetic gradient in the actual realisation of the STRUT vowel (see Map 8.4). Wisbech had [ɤ], and King's Lynn [ɜ], while older rural Norfolk speakers in most of the county had the back vowel [ʌ] (i.e. the unrounded equivalent of [ɔ]). Norwich, Cromer, Dereham, Yarmouth, Lowestoft, and Stowmarket all had an RP-like central [ɐ] for all age groups. The other urban centres in the south of the region, however, were undergoing change in that the fronting of this vowel typical of London and Home Counties speech was on the increase. These towns, that is, had vowel qualities for STRUT ranging from [ɐ] to [a] depending on the age of the speaker and the proximity of the town to London.

8.2.4 Long-mid diphthonging

Another change which made its way into East Anglia from the London area is one which has had important systemic phonological implications for East Anglian English, as we saw in 3.2.1.2. This is 'Long-Mid Diphthonging', a label which was introduced by Wells (1982) to describe "the change in FACE from [eː] to [eɪ] and in GOAT from [oː] to [oʊ]", which he dates to about 1800 in the precursor to RP. MacMahon (1994: 450, 459) cites references to it in 1711 for FACE and 1795 for GOAT.

In the regional dialects, however, it is remarkable that in 19th-century varieties as recorded by Ellis, Long Mid Diphthonging as a process had barely begun. Indeed, very many dialects all over England are shown by him as having falling diphthongs, such as [fɪəs, gʊət]. We can assume, though, that there would have been more long-mid diphthonging in urban speech and at higher social class levels: Ellis refers to the new rising diphthongs as a typically London feature.

204 — 8 The dynamics of East Anglian English: past, present and future

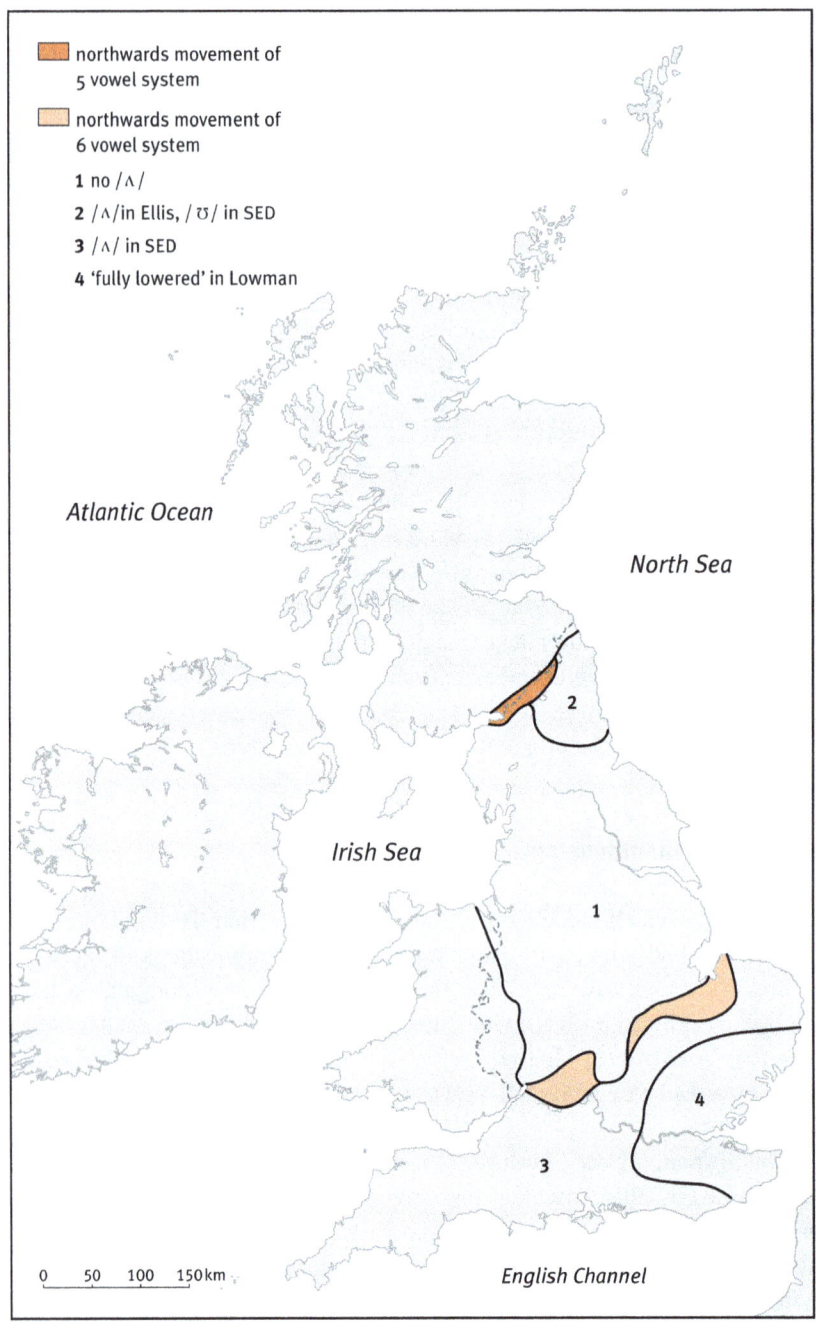

Map 8.3: The FOOT-STRUT split.

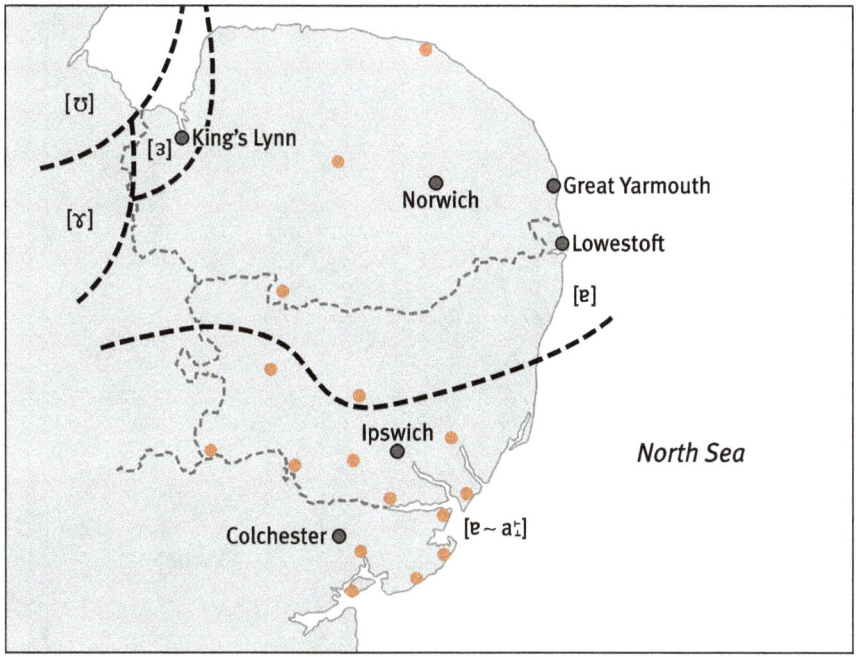

Map 8.4: East Anglian STRUT in the 1970s.

In East Anglia, as is still true to an extent in the 21ˢᵗ century, the vowels of the sets of *made* and *maid*, and of *moan* and *mown*, were still distinct in Ellis's records, with the former member of each pair being monophthongal descendants of the Middle English monophthongs long *a* and long *o* respectively, and the latter diphthongal descendants of the Middle English diphthongs *ai* and *ou*. The term 'Long Mid Diphthonging' obviously applies only to the original monophthongs, but the process eventually had the effect of producing a merger between the original monophthongs and original diphthongs, as described in 3.2.1.2: it will also be recalled that, in the 20ᵗʰ-century urban dialect of Norwich, the merger of *made* and *maid* was considerably more advanced than that of *moan* and *mown*.[127]

As far as FACE is concerned, Ellis says that rising diphthongal forms of FACE (1889: 226) are an innovation characteristic of the regional speech of Hertfordshire, Essex, and North and East London. Map 8.5 (from Trudgill, 2004) shows the extent of Long Mid Diphthonging for FACE in the 1870s (from Ellis, 1889), in

---

[127] I was born in Norwich in 1943, and I have the *made* and *maid* merger but retain the two sets of *moan* and *mown* as distinct, as mentioned in 3.2.1.2.

8 The dynamics of East Anglian English: past, present and future

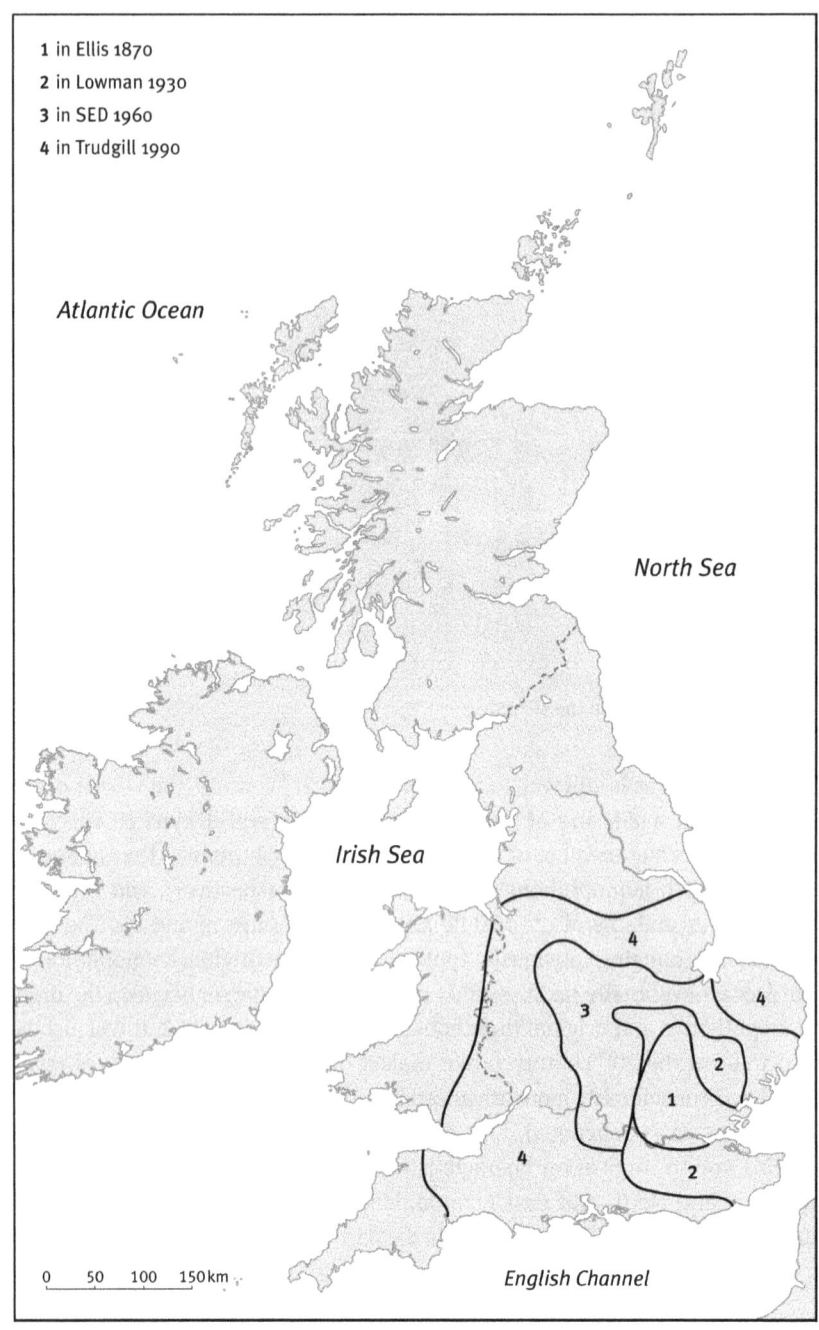

1 in Ellis 1870
2 in Lowman 1930
3 in SED 1960
4 in Trudgill 1990

Map 8.5: Long-mid diphthonging.

the 1930s (from Lowman), in the 1950s/60s (from the SED), and in the 1990s (from Trudgill, 1999). Ellis also cites diphthongal GOAT as being typical of (though recent in) the regional speech of his "Mid Eastern" D 16 area, i.e. Essex, Hertfordshire, Huntingdonshire, Bedfordshire and central Northamptonshire. He also shows that diphthonging is more advanced for FACE than for GOAT, which tallies well with what MacMahon says, as well as with the point just made about the relative dates of the two mergers in Norwich. In Chapter 3, we noted that in southern East Anglia the *moan-mown* distinction is now very recessive, so that for most speakers /ʌu/ is used in both lexical sets, and /uː/ has disappeared. As of the second decade of the 21st century, the distinction is now also beginning to disappear in the northern zone. When it has finally disappeared, this will complete a merger process which began in more central areas of England 500 years ago.

Map 8.6 from Trudgill & Foxcroft (1978) plots the northward progress of the loss of the *moan-mown* distinction up until the mid 1970s. South of line 1 on the map, the merger was total. Between 1 and 2 *go* occurred as /guː/ in the 1930s, but the distinction had gone by 1975. Between 2 and 3 *go* survived as /guː/, but that was all that was left of the distinction. Between lines 3 and 4, there were some traces of the distinction in all relevant lexical items, and between 4 and 5 the distinction was totally intact in the SED materials. Between 5 (4 in the west) and 6, our research showed some degree of merger in urban areas (King's Lynn, Yarmouth and Lowestoft) in 1975, while north of 6 the distinction was totally intact.

8.2.5 L-vocalisation

As discussed in 3.2.2, conservative rural East Anglian accents, at least in the north of the area, did not have 'dark l' as an allophone of /l/ after high-front vowels; that is, *hill, bell* were [hɪl], [bɛl] rather than the more modern [hɪɫ ~ ɪɫ], [bɛɫ]. On the other hand, the working-class accents of London and the Home Counties vocalise /l/ in the typical dark /l/ environments to give *hill, milk* as [ɪʊ], [mɪʊk] (see Wells, 1982); and even middle-class speakers from these areas usually have very marked velarisation/pharyngealisation and/or lip-rounding of [ɫ].

This London-area treatment of [ɫ] has also led to various interesting developments in the vowel system (Wells, 1982), notably the merger of vowels before [ɫ]. For many Londoners, pairs such as the following are no longer distinct:

doll   dole
pull   pool
fill   feel

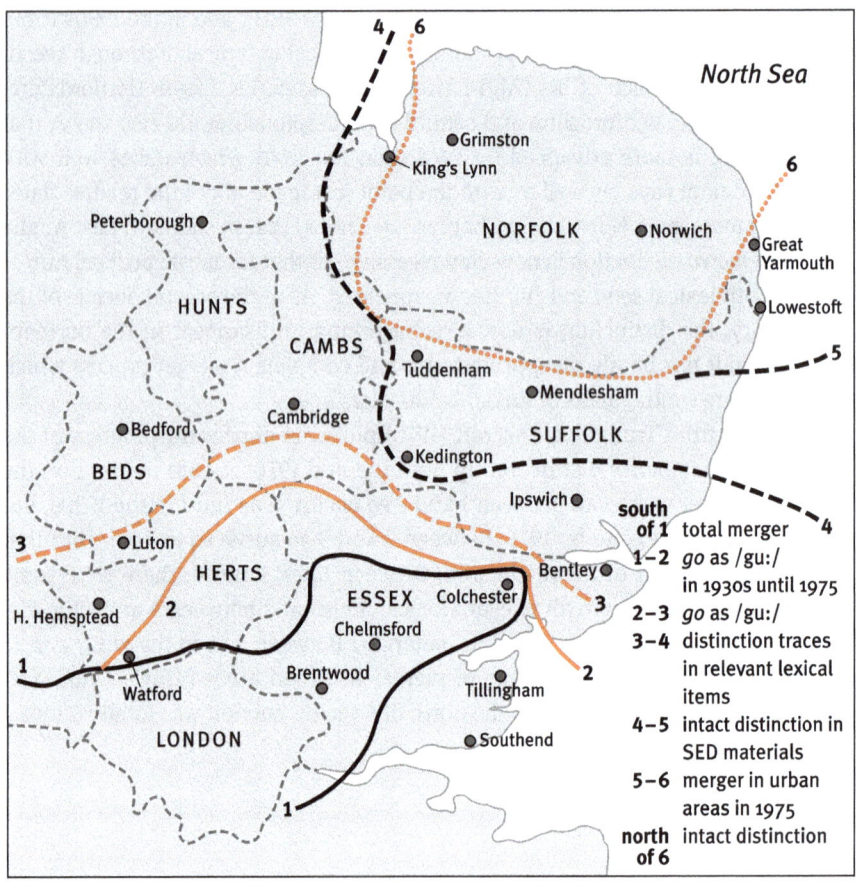

Map 8.6: The East Anglian *moan-mown* Merger.

Moreover, even in middle-class speech – and even if complete vocalisation of [ɫ] does not occur – some vowels may have radically different allophones before [ɫ] as compared to elsewhere:

rude [ɹʉːd]   *rule* [ɹuːɫ]
code [kʰɵʊd]   *coal* [kʰɒʊɫ]

The interaction of the older East Anglian treatment of /l/ with this newer London and Home Counties system makes for a complex pattern of change as the Home Counties system spreads. The situation in the 1970s, as revealed by the Foxcroft-Trudgill survey, is illustrated in Map 8.7 (southern lines apply to older speakers; northern lines to younger speakers).

Trudgill & Foxcroft (1979) showed that, of all the urban centres which they investigated, complete vocalisation had occurred only in the speech of some speakers in Clacton (Essex). However, strong velarisation and labialisation of the 'dark' allophones of /l/ had led to the mergers of FOOT and GOOSE and of LOT and GOAT in pre-/l/ position, such that *full=fool, doll=dole*, in Clacton and Walton-on-the-Naze as well as amongst younger speakers in Colchester, Wivenhoe, Felixstowe and, variably, Sudbury. Strong velarisation and labialisation, but without complete vocalisation, occurred in Clacton, Walton, Colchester, Wivenhoe (Essex), and Felixstowe and Sudbury (Suffolk) for all speakers, and for younger speakers in Bury, Ipswich, Woodbridge, and Hadleigh (Suffolk), as well as Harwich (Essex); and Potter (2014) has more recent – and very insightful – information on the progress of vocalisation in Woodbridge. Trudgill & Foxcroft (1979) also showed that phonetically distinct, i.e. backer, allophones of the GOOSE vowel occurred in all the Essex locations except West Mersea (on Mersea Island), and in all the Suffolk locations except Lowestoft in the far northeast – although in Hadleigh and Stowmarket the phenomenon was confined to younger speakers. It did not occur anywhere in Norfolk.

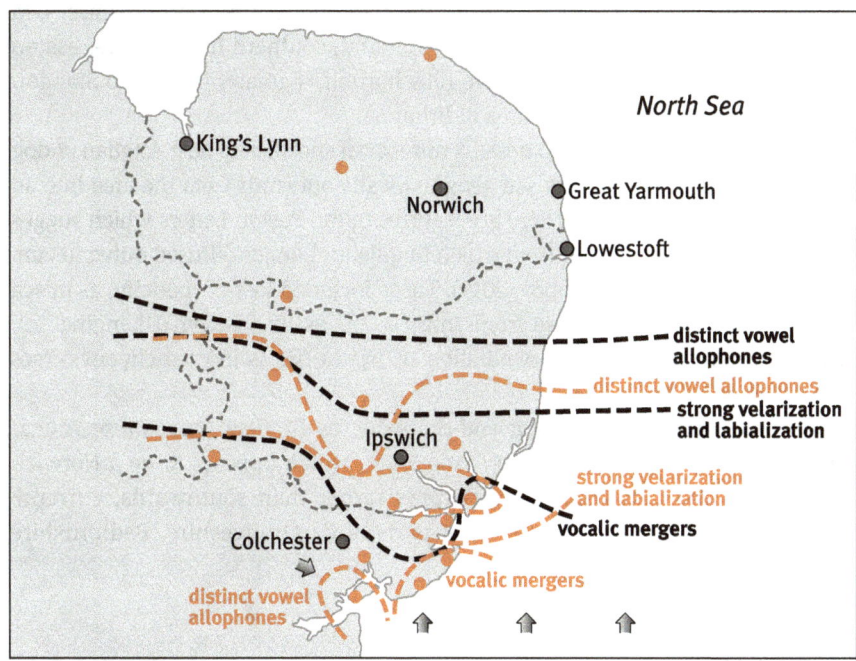

Map 8.7: L-vocalisation.

8.3 Endogenous innovations

There is, then, a very commonly recurring cyclical pattern whereby features thought of as being typically East Anglian, such as /h/-retention and long-mid monophthongs, are continually replaced over the generations by alien features moving into the region from the south, from the region around London.[128]

If this were the only existing pattern, we could suppose that East Anglian English is at any given time simply a repository of archaic features which have not yet been replaced by London-origin innovations. In fact, however, there are several counter-examples to this pattern. We noted in Chapter 1 that, in the medieval period, there was input from East Anglian dialects into the precursor of Standard English; and that there were claims that the social-class dialect differentiation which began to develop in London in the 14th century sometimes took the form of speech patterns derived from East Anglian dialects feeding into the incipient Standard English as higher class variants (Kristensson, 2001). These variants included forms such *street* instead of *strate*, *miller* rather than *meller*, *milk* instead of *melk*, and *old* rather than *eld*. East Anglian *again* also replaced London *ayaine*, and London *yeve* yielded to East Anglian *give*.

For later centuries, we also observed in 2.4 that Ellis's "Eastern" dialect area (Norfolk, Suffolk, Essex, Huntingdonshire, Cambridgeshire, Hertfordshire, Bedfordshire, Middlesex, Buckinghamshire, Rutland, southern Lincolnshire, eastern Northamptonshire) had, according to Ellis himself, a greater input into Standard English and RP than any other area of Britain.

In earlier chapters we also noted a number of specifically East Anglian endogenous innovations which diffused geographically outwards from the area into adjacent regions and beyond. There are features in the Paston Letters which suggest that East Anglia was an area from which linguistic changes diffused outwards into other areas (Hernández-Campoy, 2019). These included loss of rhoticity, as in <cadenall> 'cardinal'; the change from /ŋ(g)/ > /n/ as in <hangyn> 'hanging' and <hayryn> 'herring'; and the assimilation of /sj/ to /ʃ/, as in <sesschyonys> 'sessions' (see 2.3).

In more recent times, *total yod-dropping,* as in *view* /vʉː/, *muse* /mʉːz/, *cue* /kʉː/, *Bude* /bʉːd/, *Hugh* /hʉː/ (see 3.2.2), which appears to be a Norwich-based innovation, has spread westwards rather than southwards, currently being a feature of the phonologies of parts of Cambridgeshire, Bedfordshire,

---

128 For more examples of exogenous East Anglian changes, including LOT-unrounding and HAPPY-tensing, as also discussed in Chapter 3, see Trudgill (1999).

Huntingdonshire, Northamptonshire, Lincolnshire and Leicestershire as well as Norfolk.

We also saw in 3.2.2 that *t-glottalisation*, as in *later* [læitʔə], and *t-glottalling*, as in [læiʔə], are typical features of East Anglian English. In fact, East Anglia (see Trudgill 1974) may have been one of the main centres from which t-glottalling originally started diffusing outwards geographically into (much of) the rest of modern Britain.

Map 8.8, from Trudgill (1974), which is based on the SED materials, shows a heavy concentration of t-glottalling and t-glottalisation in the word *water* in Norfolk, Suffolk, Essex, Cambridgeshire and the immediately neighbouring counties. The SED researchers found it nowhere else. There is also interesting evidence from New Zealand about the early presence of t-glottalling in East Anglia. As reported in Trudgill (2004), data collected in connection with the Origins of New Zealand English project included a recording of a Mrs German, who we have already mentioned in 6.4. As explained there, the English she speaks is in many ways the dialect of mid-19th-century Bury St Edmunds (Suffolk). The fact that Mrs German had t-glottalling suggests that it has probably been a feature of East Anglian English since at least the 1850s.

East Anglian smoothing, too, is an endogenous change which is spreading, though not as yet in its most extreme form, beyond the borders of East Anglia. It will be recalled from 3.2.1.3 that this is a diachronic and synchronic process whereby triphthongs consisting of diphthongs plus schwa become monophthongs, giving pronunciations such as *seeing* /siːən/>/sɛːn/, *we're, we have* /wiːə/ > /wɛː/ (= *where*); *doing* /dʉːən/ > /dɜːn/, *do it* /dʉːət/ > /dɜːt/ (= *dirt*); *going* /guːən/ > /gɔn/; *playing* /plæiən/ > /plæːn/. As shown in Trudgill & Foxcroft (1979) and Trudgill (1986), this is a feature which is currently diffusing in a north-south direction within East Anglia, rather than northwards from London, as can be seen in Map 8.9 from Trudgill (1986). The towns in the northern part of the East Anglian region surveyed by Trudgill & Foxcroft – King's Lynn, Cromer, Dereham, Norwich, Yarmouth, and Lowestoft – have the MOUTH vowel as [æʉ]. In these northern towns, basilectal East Anglian smoothing thus gives /æʉ + ə/ > /ɑː/, as in *tower* /tɑː/, *ploughing* /plɑːn/. All the other (Suffolk and northern Essex) towns investigated in the 1970s Foxcroft-Trudgill survey have the MOUTH vowel as [ɛʉ] or [ɛʊ]. Older speakers in Ipswich, Woodbridge, Stowmarket, and Hadleigh had *tower* as /tɛʉə/, without smoothing, while younger speakers variably had smoothed monophthongal forms with /ɛː/.

Also, as we saw in 3.2.1.3, speakers with typical local phonology in northern East Anglia have the NEAR-SQUARE *merger*: words such as *here* and *hair* are total homophones. By the time of my 1968 Norwich survey, the normal pronunciation of the single vowel which applies to both these lexical sets was typically [ɛː].

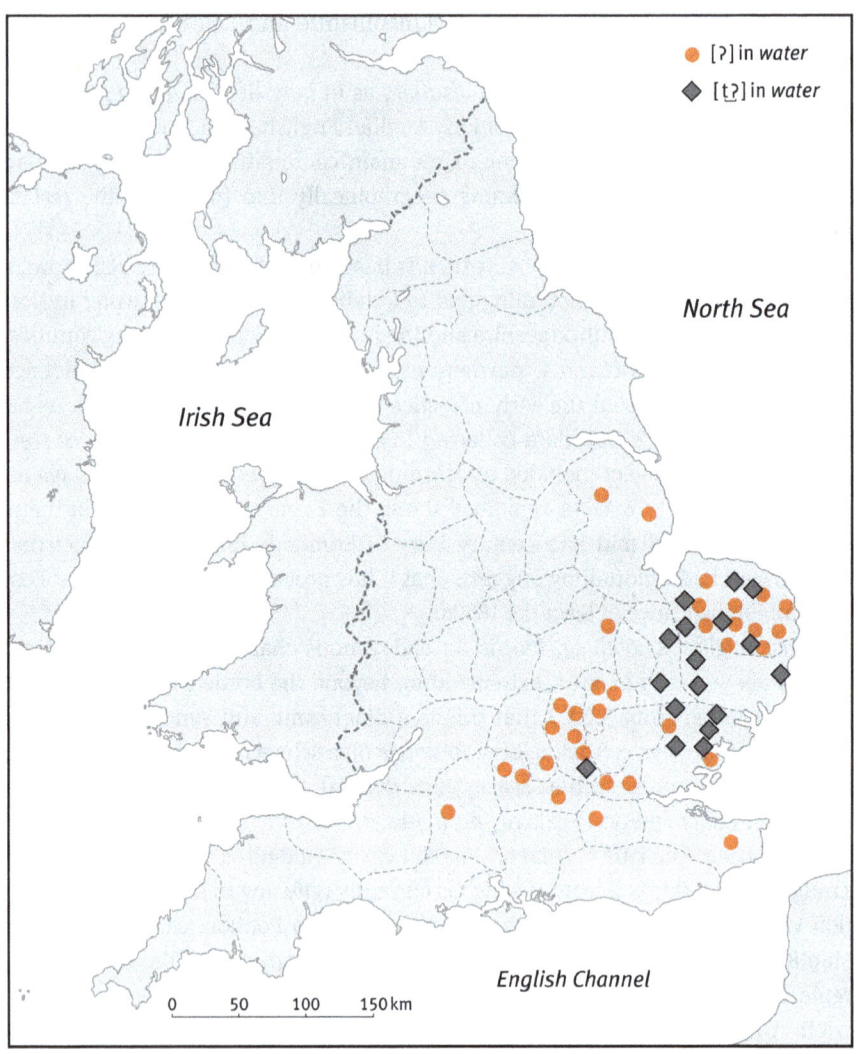

Map 8.8: T-glottalling and T-glottalisation in the SED

However, the very oldest informant in my sample, a woman born in the 1870s, used a diphthongal pronunciation [ẹə]. The 20-century monophthongisation of this vowel should be seen as related to the widespread south of England and RP monophthongisation trend involving the SQUARE vowel [ɛə] > [ɛː], the CURE vowel [ʊə] > [ɔː], and the FORCE vowel [ɔə] > [ɔː]. The merger itself, however, appears to be a Norfolk and therefore presumably Norwich-based innovation, having spread also into northern Suffolk and eastern Cambridgeshire (Butcher, 2021). It is

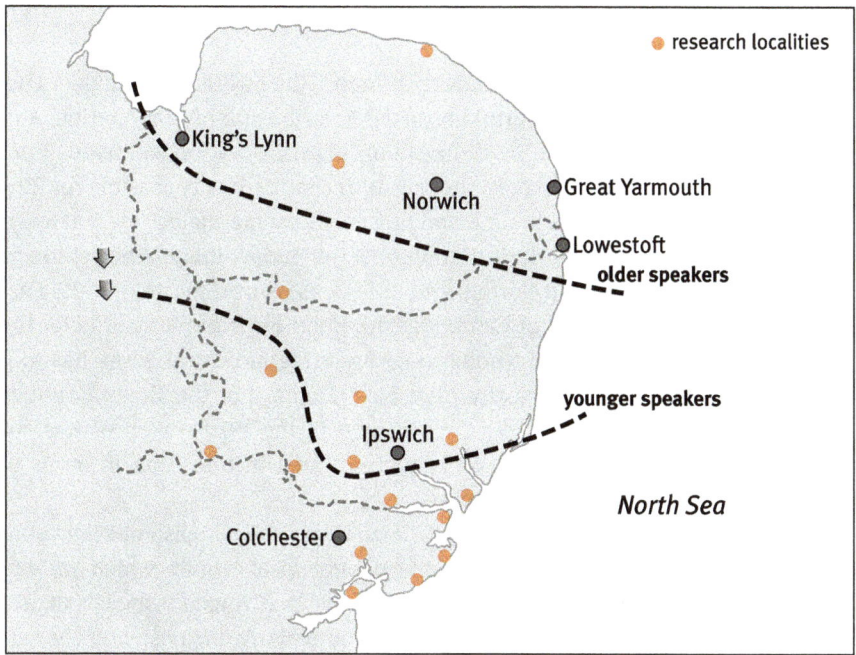

Map 8.9: Smoothing.

without parallel anywhere in neighbouring or metropolitan or national prestige varieties, so it is clearly an endogenous change. The change is not a surprising one in view of the low functional load of the distinction between the two vowels: similar changes elsewhere in the English-speaking world, such as the merger of the same two vowels in New Zealand English (see Wells, 1982: 608) and Newfoundland (Wells, 1982: 499), are likely to be spontaneous and historically unrelated. It is a change, moreover, which is taking Norfolk and northern Suffolk away from the Home Counties and the national linguistic mainstream. In view of the fact that it is typical of mergers to spread geographically at the expense of distinctions (Labov, 1994), it would be not at all surprising if this (probably 19th-century) innovation continued to expand further southwards into southern East Anglia. If so, it would be following the same route as the *East Anglian smoothing* which we have just discussed.

8.4 East Anglia versus the Home Counties

It is undoubtedly true that, as already mentioned, the East Anglian dialect area has for several decades been shrinking socially, as a result of in-migration, and geographically, as a result of the diffusion of linguistic features outwards from the Home Counties dialect area. In the mid-19th century it was possible for Ellis to regard Norfolk and Suffolk as belonging to the same dialect area as even parts of Buckinghamshire and Northamptonshire. Today, there is no reason to include any counties beyond Norfolk and Suffolk as being dialectologically East Anglian, with the exception of Cambridgeshire and Essex. And even here, the situation is a dynamic one: we noted how Braintree in central Essex has to a great extent moved phonologically from East Anglia into the Home Counties within living memory; and Vasko showed that in the 1970s much of western and central Cambridgeshire was very much an area in transition in terms of grammatical features and of h-dropping.

But all is not lost. East Anglian *that = it* survives in the English of even younger speakers in southern Essex. And one phonological feature which we employed as an important determining factor of the East Anglian English dialect area in 2.6 also seems likely to continue to be particularly diagnostic for the survival of the East Anglian dialect area in the future. This is the *Weak Vowel Merger* (see Map 8.2). The phonologies of eastern Cambridgeshire, Norfolk, Suffolk, and northern Essex are characterised by the absence of the KIT vowel from unstressed syllables: instead, as we saw, words and phrases such as *suet, wanted, horses, naked, David, do it, see'im, running, roses, Lenin* are pronounced with schwa in their second syllables. The contrast between the Home Counties and East Anglian pronunciations of *horses* as respectively [ɔːsɪz] and [hɔːsəz], and of *walking* as respectively [woːkɪn] and [wɔːkʔn̩], is very dramatic.[129] It is therefore encouraging for supporters of East Anglian English to note that the 21st century works of Spurling (2004) and Butcher (2015) on Ipswich, Potter (2018) on Woodbridge, and Simm (2019) on Yarmouth and Gorleston all attest to the strong survival into the contemporary dialects of young speakers of the Weak Vowel Merger well down into South East Anglia.

As I wrote in 2.0, East Anglia as an English-speaking region has always formed a distinctive linguistic area. Much of the evidence that has been presented in this chapter, and indeed in this entire book, suggests that this happy state of affairs is very likely to continue well into the foreseeable future.

---

129 This feature is also helpfully simple to test for in dialectological fieldwork: are *Rosa's* and *roses* pronounced the same or not?

References

Adams, James N. 2007. *The regional diversification of Latin 200 BC–AD 600*. Cambridge: Cambridge University Press.

Akire, Ti, and Carol Rosen. 2010. *Romance languages: a historical introduction*. Cambridge: Cambridge University Press.

Amos, Jennifer. 2011. *A sociophonological analysis of Mersea Island English: An investigation of the diphthongs [au], [ai], and [oi]*. Colchester: University of Essex Dissertation.

Anderson, Peter. 1987. *A structural atlas of the English dialects*. 1st ed. North Ryde: Croom Helm.

Anderwald, Lieselotte. 2002. *Negation in nonstandard British English: gaps, regularisations and asymmetries*. 1st ed. London: Routledge.

Avis, Walter S. 1961. The "New England short o": a recessive phoneme. *Language* 37 (4). 544–559.

Ayres, Harry Morgan. 1933. Bermudian English. *American Speech* 8 (1). 3–10.

Bailey, Beryl. 1965. Toward a new perspective in Negro English dialectology. *American Speech* 40. 171–177.

Bailey, Richard. 1996. *Nineteenth century English*. Ann Arbor: University of Michigan Press.

Baldi, Philip, and B. Richard Page. 2006. Review. Europa Vasconica-Europa Semitica: Theo Vennemann, Gen. Nierfeld. In Patrizia Noel Aziz Hanna (ed.), Trends in Linguistics, Studies and Monographs 138, Mouton de Gruyter, Berlin, 2003, pp. xxii + 977. *Lingua* 116 (12). 2183–2220.

Barringer, Chris. 2017. *A history of Norfolk*. Lancaster: Carnegie Publishing.

Baugh, Albert C., and Thomas Cable. 2002. *A history of the English language*. London: Routledge.

Beadle, Hilton Richard Leslie. 1978. *The medieval drama of East Anglia: studies in dialect, documentary records and stagecraft*. York: University of York.

Beal, Joan C. 1999. *English pronunciation in the eighteenth century: Thomas Spence's 'Grand repository of the English language'*. Oxford: Clarendon Press.

Benham, Charles. 1901. *Essex ballads*. Colchester: Benham Newspapers.

Blythe, Richard, and William Croft. 2012. S-curves and the mechanisms of propagation in language change. *Language* 88 (2). 269–304.

Briggs, Keith. 2011. Was Hægelisdun in Essex? A new site for the martyrdom of Edmund. *Proceedings of the Suffolk Institute of Archaeology and History* 63. 277–291.

Briggs, Keith. 2020a. *Suffolk place-names*. Martlesham.

Briggs, Keith. 2020b. The first girls in England. *Notes and Queries* 67. 200–202.

Briggs, Keith. 2020c. Two coastal terms of continental origin: shingle and dene. *Notes and Queries* 67 (3). 323–326.

Briggs, Keith. 2020d. The etymology of "girl": two more ideas. *Notes and Queries*. https://doi.org/10.1093/notesj/gjaa176

Briggs, Keith, and Kelly Kilpatrick. 2016. *A dictionary of Suffolk place-names*. Nottingham: English Place-Name Society.

Britain, David. 1991. *Dialect and space: a geolinguistic study of speech variables in the Fens*. Colchester: University of Essex Dissertation.

Britain, David. 1997. Dialect contact and phonological reallocation: 'Canadian Raising' in the English Fens. *Language In Society* 26 (1). 15–46.

Britain, David. 2001. Welcome to East Anglia!: two major dialect 'boundaries' in the Fens. In Jacek Fisiak and Peter Trudgill (eds.), *East Anglian English*, 217–242. Cambridge: Boydell & Brewer.

Britain, David. 2002a. Space and spatial diffusion. In J. K. Chambers, Peter Trudgill and Natalie Schilling-Estes (eds.), *Handbook of language variation and change*, 603–637. Oxford: Blackwell Publishing.

Britain, David. 2002b. Diffusion, levelling, simplification and reallocation in past tense BE in the English Fens. *Journal of sociolinguistics* 6 (1). 16–43.

Britain, David. 2002c. Phoenix from the ashes? The death, contact and birth of dialects in England. *Essex Research Reports in Linguistics* 41. 42–73.

Britain, David. 2005. Innovation diffusion, 'Estuary English' and local dialect differentiation: the survival of Fenland Englishes. *Linguistics* 43 (5). 995–1022.

Britain, David. 2014. Where North meets South?: contact, divergence, and the routinisation of the Fenland dialect boundary. In Dominic Watt and Carmen Llamas (eds.), *Languages, borders and identity*, 27–43. Edinburgh: Edinburgh University Press.

Britain, David. 2015. Between North and South: The Fenland. In Raymond Hickey (ed.), *Researching Northern English*, 417–435. Amsterdam: John Benjamins Publishing.

Britain, David. 2021. What happened to those relatives from East Anglia? A multilocality analysis of dialect levelling in the relative marker system. In Karen Beaman, Isabelle Buchstaller, Sue Fox and James Walker (eds.), *Advancing socio-grammatical variation and change: in honour of Jenny Cheshire*, 91–114. Amsterdam: John Benjamins Publishing.

Britain, David, and Peter Trudgill. 2005. New-dialect formation and contact-induced reallocation: three case studies from the English Fens. *International Journal of English Studies* 5 (1). 183–209.

Brook, G. L. 1958. *English dialects*. London: Andre Deutsch Ltd.

Browne, Thomas. 1683. *Certain miscellany tracts written by Thomas Brown*. London: Charles Mearn.

Burling, Robbins. 1973. *English in black and white*. New York: Holt, Rinehart and Winston.

Butcher, David. 2014. *Fishing talk*. Cromer: Poppyland Publishing.

Butcher, Kerri-Ann. 2015. *An exploration of the variables (t) and (ing) in Ipswich English: modelling linguistic variation in phonological theory*. Colchester: University of Essex Dissertation.

Butcher, Kerri-Ann. 2021. Revisiting the vowel mergers of East Anglia: correlations of MOAN, MOWN and GOOSE. In *Language variation: European perspectives VIII – selected papers from the 10th International Conference on Language Variation in Europe (ICLaVE 10)*, 54–77. Amsterdam: John Benjamins Publishing.

Campbell, James. 1975. Norwich. In Mary Lobel (ed.), *The Atlas of Historic Towns II*. London: Lovell Johns.

Charnock, Richard. 1880. *A glossary of the Essex dialect*. London: Trübner.

Cheshire, Jenny, Sue Fox, Paul Kerswill, and Eivind Torgersen. 2008. Ethnicity, friendship network and social practices as the motor of dialect change: linguistic innovation in London. *Sociolinguistica: International Yearbook of European Sociolinguistics* 22. 1–23.

Clarke, Sandra. 2010. *Newfoundland and Labrador English*. Edinburgh: Edinburgh University Press.

Claxton, Alic O. D. 1968. *The Suffolk dialect of the twentieth century*. Ipswich: Norman Adlard & Co.

Coates, Richard. 2017. Celtic whispers: revisiting the problems of the relation between Brittonic and Old English. *Namenkündliche Informationen* 109 (110). 147–173.

Coates, Richard, and Andrew Breeze. 2000. *Celtic voices, English places: studies of the Celtic impact on place-names in England.* Donington: Shaun Tyas.

Corrigan, Karen. 2010. *Irish English. Volume 1: Northern Ireland.* Berlin: de Gruyter

Corrigan, Karen. 2021. From Killycomain to Melbourne: historical contact and the feature pool. In Karen Beaman, Isabelle Buchstaller, Sue Fox and James Walker (eds.), *Advancing sociogrammatical variation and change: in honour of Jenny Cheshire*, 319–339. London: Routledge.

Cox, Barrie. 1975. The place-names of the earliest English records. *Journal of the English Place-Name Society* 8. 12–66.

Cozens-Hardy, Sydney. 1893. *Broad Norfolk: being a series of articles and letters.* Norwich: Eastern Daily Press.

Dance, Richard. 2014. Getting a word in: contact, etymology and English vocabulary in the twelfth century. *Journal of the British Academy* 2. 153–211.

Davidson, William. 1974. *Historical geography of the Bay Islands, Honduras: Anglo-Hispanic conflict in the Western Caribbean.* Birmingham: Southern University Press.

Davis, Norman. 1965. The language of the Pastons. *Proceedings of the British Academy* 40. 119–144.

Diessel, Holger. 2000. *Demonstratives: form, function and grammaticalisation.* Amsterdam: John Benjamins Publishing.

Dillard, Joey Lee. 1970. Principles in the history of American English: paradox, virginity and cafeteria. *Florida FL Reporter* 8 (1–2). 32–33.

Dillard, Joey Lee. 1972. *Black English: its history and usage in the United States.* New York: Random House.

Dobson, Eric John. 1968. *English Pronunciation 1500–1700.* Oxford: Oxford University Press.

Ekwall, Eilert. 1917. *Contributions to the history of Old English dialects.* Lund: Gleerup.

Ekwall, Eilert. 1928. *English river-names.* Oxford: Clarendon Press.

Ekwall, Eilert. 1960. *The concise Oxford dictionary of English place-names.* Oxford: Oxford University Press.

Ellis, Alexander J. 1889. *The existing phonology of English dialects, compared with that of West Saxon English.* London: Trübner.

Emonds, Joseph, and Jan Terje Faarlund. 2014. *English: the language of the Vikings.* Olomouc: Palacký University.

Eustace, S. S. 1969. The meaning of the palaeotype in A.J. Ellis's On Early English pronunciation 1869–89. *Transactions of the Philological Society* 68 (1). 31–79.

Evans, George Ewart. 1966. *The pattern under the plough: aspects of the folk-life of East Anglia.* London: Faber & Faber.

Fairclough, John. 2010. *Boudica to Rædwald: East Anglia's relations with Rome.* Ipswich: Malthouse Press.

Fasold, Ralph. 1972. *Tense-marking in Black English.* Arlington: Center For Applied Linguistics.

Fellows-Jensen, Gillian. 2000. Vikings in the British Isles: the place-name evidence. *Acta Archaeologia* 71 (1). 135–146.

Ferragne, Emmanuel, and Francois Pellegrino. 2004. Rhythm in read British English: interdialect variability. In *8th International conference on spoken language processing, Jeju, South Korea, October 4–8,2004*, 1573–1576. ICSLP.

Ferragne, Emmanuel, and Francois Pellegrino. 2007. An acoustic description of the monophthongs of East Anglia. In Jürgen Trouvain (ed.), *Proceedings of the16th International Congress of Phonetic Sciences*, 1513–1516. Saarbrücken Saarbrücken University.
Filppula, Markku, Juhani Klemola, and Heli Pitkänen, eds. 2002. *The Celtic roots of English*. Joensuu: University of Joensuu.
Fisiak, Jacek. 2001. Old East Anglian: a problem in Old English dialectology. In Jacek Fisiak and Peter Trudgill (eds.), *East Anglian English*, 18–38. Woodbridge: Boydell & Brewer.
Forby, Robert, George Turner, and Dawson Turner. 1830. *The vocabulary of East Anglia*. London: J.B. Nichols and Son.
Ford, Anne-Marie. 2018. *Gypsy countess*. London: Romany & Traveller Family History Society.
Fortson, Benjamin. 2010. *Indo-European language and culture: an introduction*. London: Wiley-Blackwell.
Francis, H. J. 1955. Being the autobiography of a Gypsy: part II vocabulary. *Journal of the Gypsy Lore Society* 34. 83–83.
Francis, W. Nelson. 1961. Some dialect isoglosses in England. *American Speech* 34 (4). 243–250.
Gepp, Edward. 1920. *A contribution to an Essex dialect dictionary*. London: Routledge.
Gil, Alexander. 1619. *Logonomia Anglica*. London: Beale.
Gimson, Alfred Charles. 1962. *Introduction to the pronunciation of English*. London: Edward Arnold.
Givón, Talmy. 1984. *Syntax: a functional-typological Introduction I*. Amsterdam: John Benjamins Publishing.
Goose, Nigel. 1982. The "Dutch" in Colchester: the economic influence of an immigrant community in the sixteenth and seventeenth centuries. *Immigrants and Minorities* 1 (3). 269–270.
Gordon, Elizabeth, Lyall Campbell, Jennifer Hay, Margaret Maclagan and Peter Trudgill. 2004. *New Zealand English: its origins and evolution*. Cambridge: Cambridge University Press.
Grapes, Sidney. 1974. *The Boy John*. Norwich: Wensum Books.
Green, Barbara, and Rachel Young. 1964. *Norwich: the growth of a city*. Norwich: Museums Committee.
Grose, Francis. 1790. *A provincial glossary, with a collection of local proverbs and popular superstitions*. London: Hooper.
Halliwell, James Orchard. 1881. *A dictionary of archaic and provincial words*. London: J.R. Smith.
Hammarström, Göran. 1980. *Australian English: its origin and status*. Hamburg: Buske.
Hancock, Ian. 1997. George Borrow's Romani. In Yaron Matras, Peter Bakker and Hristo Kyuchukov (eds.), *The typology and dialectology of Romani*, 199–214. Amsterdam: John Benjamins Publishing.
Hancock, Ian, Thomas Acton, and Donald Kenrick, eds. 1984. *Romani Rokkeripen To-divvus: The English Romani dialect and its contemporary social, educational and linguistic standing*. London: Romanestan Publications.
Härke, Heinrich. 2002. Kings and warriors: population and landscape from post-Roman to Norman Britain. In Paul Slack and Ryk Ward (eds.), *The peopling of Britain: the shaping of a human landscape*, 145–175. Oxford: Oxford University Press.
Heine, Bernd, and Tania Kuteva. 2002. *World lexicon of grammaticalisation*. Cambridge: Cambridge University Press.

Hernandez, Nuria, Daniela Kolbe and Monika Schulz (eds). *A Comparative Grammar of British English Dialects II: Modals, Pronouns and Complement Clauses*. Berlin: Mouton de Gruyter.

Hernández-Campoy, Juan Manuel. 2013. Ladylikeness and sociolinguistic submission in Late Medieval English society: gender-based use of negation in John Paston I and Margaret Paston. *Atlantis* 35 (1). 11–33.

Hernández-Campoy, Juan Manuel. 2016. Authorship and gender in English historical sociolinguistic research: samples from the Paston Letters. In Cinzia Russi (ed.), *Current trends in historical sociolinguistics*, 108–142. Warsaw: De GruyterOpen Poland.

Hernández-Campoy, Juan Manuel, Juan Camilo Conde-Silvestre, and T. García-Vidal. 2019. Tracing patterns of intra-speaker variation in Early English correspondence: a change from above in the Paston Letters. *Studia Anglica Posnaniensia* 54 (1). 287–314.

Hines, John. 1984. *The Scandinavian character of Anglian England in the pre-Viking period*. London: British Archaeological Reports.

Hines, John. 2013. The origins of East Anglia in a North Sea zone. In David Bates and Robert Liddiard (eds.), *East Anglia and its North Sea world in the Middle Ages*, 16–43. Woodbridge: Boydell Press.

Hoekstra, Jarich. 1995. Preposition stranding and resumptivity in West Germanic. In Hubert Haider, Susan Olsen and Sten Vikner (eds.), *Studies in comparative Germanic syntax*, 95–118. Dordrecht: Springer, dordrecht.

Holman, George Casper. 1962. *Sentiments and activities: essays in social science*. Glencoe: Free Press.

Holman, Katherine. 2007. *The Northern Conquest: Vikings in Britain and Ireland*. Oxford: Signal Books.

Holmberg, Anders, and Jan Rijkhoff. 1998. Word order in the Germanic languages. In Anna Siewierska (ed.), *Constituent order in the languages of Europe*, 75–104. Berlin: De Gruyter Mouton.

Hoskins, W. G. 1984. *Local history in England*. London: Longman.

Howe, Stephen. 2018. Emphatic yes and no in Eastern English: jearse and dow. In Laura Wright (ed.), *Southern English varieties: then and now*, 148–187. Berlin, Boston: De Gruyter Mouton.

Hughes, Arthur, and Peter Trudgill. 1995. *English accents and dialects: an introduction of varieties of English in the British Isles*. 3rd ed. London: Edward Arnold.

Hughey, Ruth, ed. 1941. *The correspondence of Lady Katherine Paston 1603–1627*. Norwich: Norfolk Record Society.

Ihalainen, Ossi. 1991. On grammatical diffusion in Somerset folk speech. In Peter Trudgill and J. K. Chambers (eds.), *English dialects: studies in grammatical variation*, 104–119. London: Longman.

Ihalainen, Ossi. 1994. The dialects of England since 1776. In Robert Burchfield (ed.), *The Cambridge history of the English language*, 197–274. Cambridge: Cambridge University Press.

Ishiyama, Osamu. 2008. *The diachronic relationship between demonstratives and first/second person pronouns*. Ann Arbor: University of Michigan Press.

Jackson, Kenneth. 1953. *Language and history in early Britain: a chronological survey of the Brittonic languages, first to twelfth centuries*. Edinburgh: Edinburgh University Press.

Joby, Christopher. 2012. Early modern records in Dutch at the Norfolk Record Office. *Dutch Crossing: Journal of Low Countries Studies* 36 (2). 132–140.

Joby, Christopher. 2014. Dutch poetry in early modern Norfolk. *Dutch Crossing* 38 (2). 189–203.
Joby, Christopher. 2015. *The Dutch language in Britain 1550–1702*. Leiden: Brill.
Johnson, Caleb H. 2006. *The Mayflower and Her Passengers*. Indiana: Xlibris Corporation.
Jordan, Richard. 1974. *Handbook of Middle English grammar: phonology*. Berlin: Mouton.
Jones, Charles. 1989. *A History of English Phonology*. London: Longman.
Kallen, Jeffrey. 1994. English in Ireland. In Robert Burchfield (ed.), *The Cambridge history of the English language V*, 148–196. Cambridge: Cambridge University Press.
Ketton-Cremer, Robert W. 1957. *Norfolk assembly*. London: Faber & Faber.
Kallen, Jeffrey. 2013. *Irish English Volume 2: The Republic of Ireland*. Berlin: de Gruyter.
Kerswill, Paul. 2003. Dialect levelling and geographical diffusion in British English. In D. Britain & J. Cheshire (eds.) *Social dialectology: in honour of Peter Trudgill*. Amsterdam: Benjamins, 223–243.
Kisbye, Torben. 1992. *A short history of the English language*. Aarhus: Aarhus University Press.
Kökeritz, Helge. 1932. *The phonology of the Suffolk dialect*. Uppsala: Uppsala University.
Kökeritz, Helge. 1938. Alexander Gill (1621) on the dialects of south and east. *Studia Neophilologica* 11 (1–2). 277–288.
Kontic, René. 1990. *Dialects in East-Anglia and the South-East of England*. Basel: Econom Druck.
Kristensson, Gillis. 1995. *A survey of Middle English Dialects 1290–1350: the East Midland Counties*. Sweden: New Society of Letters.
Kristensson, Gillis. 2001. Sociolects in fourteenth-century London. In Jacek Fisiak and Peter Trudgill (eds.), *East Anglian English*, 71–77. Woodbridge: Boydell & Brewer.
Kuhn, Hans. 1955. Zur Gliederung der germanischen Sprachen. *Zeitschrift für deutsches Altertum und deutsche Literatur* 86 (1). 1–47.
Kurath, Hans. 1928. The origin of the dialectal differences in spoken American English. *Modern Philology* 25 (4). 385–395.
Kurath, Hans. 1964. British sources of selected features of American pronunciation: problems and methods. In David Abercrombie, Dennis Fry and P. MacCarthy (eds.), *In honour of Daniel Jones*, 146–155. London: Longman.
Kurath, Hans. 1965. Some aspects of Atlantic seaboard English considered in their connection with British English. In Walter S. Avis and A. J. van Windekens (eds.), *Communications et rapports du Premier Congrès International de Dialectologie Générale*, 236–240. Louvain: Centre Inter-national de Dialectologie Generale.
Kurath, Hans. 1972. *Studies in Area Linguistics*. Bloomington: Indiana University Press.
Kurath, Hans, Miles Hanley, Bernard Bloch, Guy Lowman, and Marcus Hansen. 1939. *Linguistic atlas of New England*. Providence: Brown University.
Kurath, Hans, and Guy Lowman. 1961. *The dialectal structure of southern England: phonological evidence*. Tuscaloosa: University of Alabama Press.
Kurath, Hans, and Raven Ioor McDavid. 1961. *The pronunciation of English in the Atlantic states*. Ann Arbor: University of Michigan Press.
Labov, William. 1994. *Principles of Linguistic Change, Volume 1: Internal Factors*. Oxford: Wiley-Blackwell.
Laing, Margaret, and Roger Lass. 2019. Voiced or voiceless? Old english In Middle English <fd> Sequences. *Transactions of the Philological Society* 117 (1). 132–154.

Laker, Stephen. 2008. Changing views about Anglo-Saxons and Britons. In Henk Aertsen and Bart Veldhoen (eds.), *Six Papers from the 28th Symposium on Medieval Studies Held at the Vrije Universiteit Amsterdam on 15 December 2006*, 1–38. Leiden: Leiden University.

Larwood, Joshua. 1800. *Erratics: by a sailor; containing rambles in Norfolk, and elsewhere*. London: G. Auld, Greville-Street.

Lass, Roger. 1992. Phonology and morphology. In Norman Blake (ed.), *The Cambridge history of the English language II*, 23–155. Cambridge: Cambridge University Press.

Lass, Roger. 1999a. Introduction. In Roger Lass (ed.), *The Cambridge history of the English language III*, 1–12. Cambridge: Cambridge University Press.

Lass, Roger. 1999b. Phonology and Morphology. In Roger Lass (ed.), *The Cambridge history of the English Language*, 56–186. Cambridge: Cambridge University Press.

Lass, Roger, and Margaret Laing. 2009. Databases, dictionaries and dialectology – dental instability in Early Middle English: a case study. In M. Dossena and Roger Lass (eds.), *Studies in English and European historical dialectology*, 91–131. Frankfurt am Main: Peter Lang.

Lass, Roger, and Margaret Laing. 2016. Q is for What, When, Where?: the 'q' spellings for OE hw. *Folia Linguistica Historica* 37. 61–110.

Laver, John. 1994. *Principles of phonetics*. Cambridge: Cambridge University Press.

Lehmann, Christian. 1985. *Thoughts on grammaticalisation*. Munich: Lincom Europa.

Liddiard, Robert. 2013. The North Sea. In David Bates and Robert Liddiard (eds.), *East Anglia and its North Sea world in the Middle Ages*, 1–15. Woodbridge: Boydell & Brewer.

Lodge, Ken. 2001. The modern reflexes of some Middle English vowel contrasts in Norwich and Norfolk. In Jacek Fisiak and Peter Trudgill (eds.), *East Anglian English*, 205–216. Woodbridge: Boydell & Brewer.

MacMahon, Michael. 1994. Phonology. In Suzanne Romaine (ed.), *The Cambridge history of the English language vol. 4: 1776–1997*, 373–535. Cambridge: Cambridge University Press.

MacRitchie, David. 1894. *Scottish Gypsies under the Stewarts*. Edinburgh: D. Douglas.

Maguire, Warren. 2012. Mapping "the Existing Phonology of English Dialects". *Dialectologia et Geolinguistica* 20 (1). 84–107.

Markus, Manfred. 2021. *The English Dialect Dictionary online: a new departure in English dialectology*. Cambridge: Cambridge University Press.

Martin, Edward. 1999. Suffolk in the Iron Age. In John Davies and Tom Williamson (eds.), *Land of the Iceni*, 83–91. Norwich: Centre for East Anglian Studies.

Matras, Yaron. 2005. *Romani: a linguistic introduction*. Cambridge: Cambridge University Press.

Matras, Yaron. 2010. *Romani in Britain: the afterlife of a language*. Edinburgh: Edinburgh University Press.

McColl Millar, Robert. 2007. *Northern and Insular Scots*. Berlin: de Gruyter.

McDavid, Raven. 1955. The position of the Charleston dialect. *Publications of the American Dialect Society* 23 (1). 35–49.

McDavid, Raven (1968). Variations in Standard American English. *Elementary English* 45, 561–608.

McIntosh, Angus. 1976. The language of the extant versions of Havelok the Dane. *Medium Ævum* 45 (1). 36–49.

McIntosh, Angus, Michael Samuels, and Michael Benskin. 1986. *A linguistic atlas of late medieval English. Vol. 1.* Aberdeen: Aberdeen University Press.

McLaughlin, J. C., *Aspects of the History of English* (New York: Holt, Reinhart and Winston, 1970).

Milroy, James, 1983. On the sociolinguistic history of H-dropping in E.lish', in M. Davenport, E. Hansen and H.-F. Nielsen (eds), *Current Topics in English Historical Linguistics*. Odense: University of Odense Press,, 37–53.

Moens, William. 1888. *The Walloons and their church in Norwich 1565–1832. Vol. 1*. London: Huguenot Society of London.

Moor, Edward. 1823[1970]. *Suffolk words and phrases: or, An attempt to collect the lingual localisms of that County*. New York: Kelley.

Moore, Samuel, Sanford Meech, and Harold Whitehall. 1935. Middle English dialect characteristics and dialect boundaries. In *Essays and studies in English and comparative literature: language and literature XIII*, 1–60. Ann Arbor: University of Michigan Press.

Morris, John. 1973. *The age of Arthur: a history of the British Isles from 350 to 650*. New York: Charles Scribner's Sons.

Naismith, Rory. 2013. Coinage in pre-Viking East Anglia. In David Bates and Robert Liddiard (eds.), *East Anglia and its North Sea world in the Middle Ages*, 137–151. Woodbridge: Boydell & Brewer.

Nall, James Greaves. 1866[2006]. *Nall's glossary of East Anglian dialect*. Dereham: The Larks Press.

Nevalainen, Terttu, Helena Raumolin-Brunberg, and Peter Trudgill. 2001. Chapters in the social history of East Anglian English: the case of the third-person. In Jacek Fisiak and Peter Trudgill (eds.), *East Anglian English*, 187–204. Cambridge: Boydell & Brewer.

Nevalainen, Terttu, and Sanna-Kaisa Tanskanen. 2007. *Letter Writing*. Amsterdam: John Benjamins.

Newton, Sam. 1993. *The origins of Beowulf: and the pre-Viking Kingdom of East Anglia*. Woodbridge: Boydell & Brewer.

Nielsen, Hans Frede. 1998. *The continental backgrounds of English and its insular development until 1154*. Odense: Odense University Press.

Orton, Harold, Stewart Sanderson, and John Widdowson. 1978. *The linguistic atlas of England*. 1st ed. London: Croom Helm.

Orton, Harold, and Nathalia Wright. 1974. *Word geography of England*. London: Academic.

Page, Raymond Ian. 1999. *An introduction to English runes*. Woodbridge: Boydell & Brewer.

Parsons, David. 2001. How long did the Scandinavian language survive in England? Again. In James Graham-Campbell, Richard Hall, Judith Jesch and David Parsons (eds.), *Vikings and the Danelaw*, 299–312. Oxford: Oxbow Books.

Parsons, David. 2006. Field-name statistics: Norfolk and the Danelaw. In Peder Gammeltoft and Bent Jorgensen (eds.), *Names through the looking-glass*, 165–188. Copenhagen: Reitzel.

Peitsara, Kirsti. 1996. Studies on the structure of the Suffolk dialect. In Juhani Klemola, Merja Kytö and Matti Rissanen (eds.), *Speech past and present: studies in English dialectology in memory of Ossi Ihalainen*, 284–307. Frankfurt: Lang.

Peitsara, Kirsti. 2000. The prepositions "on" and "of" in partitive and temporal constructions in British English dialects: one on 'em of a night. *Neuphilologische Mitteilungen* 101 (2). 323–332.

Perridon, Harry. 1997. Is the definite article in Jutlandic a borrowing from Low German? *Multilingua* 16 (4). 351–363.

Pestell, Tim. 2013. Imports or immigrants?: reassessing Scandinavian metalwork in late Anglo-Saxon East Anglia. In David Bates and Robert Liddiard (eds.), *East Anglia and its North Sea world in the Middle Ages*, 230–255. Woodbridge: Boydell & Brewer.

Pettersson, Sofia. 1994. *A study of Dutch and Low German elements in the East Midland and East Anglian dialects*. Unpublished Paper: Stockholm University.
Pim, Keiron, Ellman Crasnow, and Bente Elsworth. 2013. *Into the light: the medieval Hebrew poetry of Meir of Norwich*. Norwich: East Publishing.
Pogatscher, Alois. 1888. *Zur Lautlehre der griechischen, lateinischen und romanischen Lehnworte im Altenglischen*. Berlin: Trübner.
Potter, Robert. 2014. *Investigating the social differentiation of language use in Suffolk*. Colchester: University of Essex Dissertation.
Potter, Robert. 2018. *A variationist multilocality study of unstressed vowels and verbal -s marking in the peripheral dialect of east Suffolk*. Colchester: University of Essex Dissertation.
Poussa, Patricia. 1997. Derivation of it from that in eastern dialects of British English. In Raymond Hickey and Stanislaw Puppel (eds.), *Language history and linguistic modelling*, 691–699. Berlin: De Gruyter Mouton.
Poussa, Patricia. 2001. Syntactic change in northwest Norfolk. In Jacek Fisiak and Peter Trudgill (eds.), *East Anglian English*, 243–260. Woodbridge: Boydell & Brewer.
Primer, Sylvester. 1888. Charleston Provincialisms. *American Journal of Philology* 9 (2). 198–213.
Prince, Hugh. 1962. Pits and ponds in Norfolk. *Erdkunde* 16. 10–31.
Ray, John. 1691. *A collection of South and East-Countrey Words*. London: English Dialect Society.
Roach, Peter. 1983 (4th ed. 2009) *English Phonetics and Phonology*. Cambridge: Cambridge University Press.
Ruano-García, Javier. 2016. When the provincial dialects were the subject of conversation: eighteenth-century Norfolk words. *Dictionaries: Journal of the Dictionary Society of North America* 37. 99–131.
Ryfa, Joanna. 2005. *Chavs and Grungers: the creation of distinct speech styles by two hostile communities of practice in Colchester, Essex*. Colchester: University of Essex Dissertation.
Sampson, John. 1930. *The wind on the heath: a Gypsy anthology*. London: Chatto & Windus.
Sandred, Karl Inge. 2001. East Anglian place-names: sources of lost dialect. In Jacek Fisiak and Peter Trudgill (eds.), *East Anglian English*, 39–62. Woodbridge: Boydell & Brewer.
Sandred, Karl Inge, and Bengt Lindström. 1989. *The place-names of Norfolk I*. Nottingham: English Place-Name Society.
Schiering, René. 2006. *Cliticisation and the evolution of morphology: a cross-linguistic study on phonology in grammaticalisation*. Ph. D. Konstanz University.
Schiering, René. 2010. Reconsidering erosion in grammaticalisation: evidence from cliticisation. In Katerina Stathi, Elke Gehweiler and Ekkehard König (eds.), *Grammaticalisation: current views and issues*, 73–100. Amsterdam: John Benjamins Publishing.
Schram, O. K. 1961. Place-names. In Frank Briers (ed.), *Norwich and its region*, 141–149. London: British Association for the Advancement of Science.
Schrijver, Peter. 2002. The rise and fall of British Latin: evidence fro English and Brittonic. In Markku Filppula, Juhani Klemola and Heli Pitkänen (eds.), *The Celtic roots of English*, 87–110. Joensuu: University of Joensuu.
Schrijver, Peter. 2014. *Language contact and the origins of the Germanic languages*. London: Taylor & Francis.

Schulte, Michael, and Henrik Williams. 2018. Den eldste tiden (–700). In Helge Sandøy and Agnete Nesse (eds.), *Norsk språkhistorie IV: tidslinjer*, 51–117. Oslo: Novus.

Seymour, M. C. 1968. A fifteenth-century East Anglian scribe. *Medium Ævum* 37 (2). 166–173.

Shrewsbury, J. F. D. 1949. The Yellow Plague. *Journal of the History of Medicine and Allied Sciences* 4 (1). 5–47.

Simm, Saskia. 2019. *A study of phonological patterns and change in Great Yarmouth English*. Cambridge: University of Cambridge Dissertation.

Skeat, Walter William. 1912. *English dialects from the eighth century to the present day*. Cambridge: Cambridge University Press.

Skipper, Keith. 1996. *Larn yarself Norfolk: a comprehensive guide to the Norfolk dialect*. Dereham, Norfolk: John Nickalls Publications.

Smith, Albert Hugh. 1956. *English place-name elements*. Cambridge: Cambridge University Press.

Spurdens, William Tylney. 1858. *The vocabulary of East Anglia by the Rev. R. Forby. Volume 3, Being a supplementary volume by the Rev. W.T. Spurdens*. United Kingdom: Nichols and Son.

Spurling, Juliette. 2004. *Traditional feature loss in Ipswich: dialect attrition in the East Anglian county of Suffolk*. Colchester: University of Essex Dissertation.

Stoker, David. 1981. Anthony de Solempne: attributions to his press. *The Library* s6-3 (1). 17–32.

Strang, Barbara M. H. 1970. *A history of English*. London: Methuen.

Sweet, Henry. 1888. *A History of English Sounds from the Earliest Period*, Oxford: Clarendon.

Teversham, Traviss Frederick. 1960[1958]. Get to the point – with dialect. *Amateur historian* 4. 7.

Thomas, Alan R. 1994. English in Wales. In Robert Burchfield (ed.), *The Cambridge history of the English language V*, 94–147. Cambridge: Cambridge University Press.

Thomason, Sarah, and Terence Kaufman. 1988. *Language contact, creolisation and genetic linguistics*. Berkeley: University of California Press.

Töpf, Ana L., and A. Rus Hoelzel. 2005. A Romani mitochondrial haplotype in England 500 years before their recorded arrival in Britain. *Biology Letters* 1 (3). 280–282.

Townend, Matthew. 2002. *Language and history in Viking Age England: linguistic relations between speakers of Old Norse and Old English*. Turnhout: Brepols Publishers.

Trudgill, Peter. 1974. *The Social Differentiation of English in Norwich*. Cambridge: Cambridge University Press.

Trudgill, Peter. 1985. The role of Irish English in the formation of colonial Englishes. In John Harris, David Little and David Singleton (eds.), *Perspectives on the English language in Ireland*, 3–7. Dublin: Centre for Language and Communication Studies.

Trudgill, Peter. 1986. *Dialects in contact*. Oxford: Basil Blackwell.

Trudgill, Peter. 1988. Norwich revisited: recent linguistic changes in an English urban dialect. *English World-Wide* 9 (1). 33–49.

Trudgill, Peter. 1990. *The dialects of England*. Oxford: Blackwell.

Trudgill, Peter. 1996a. Two hundred years of dedialectalisation: the East Anglian short vowel system. In Mats Thelander (ed.), *Samspel och variation*, 469–478. Uppsala: Uppsala Universitet.

Trudgill, Peter. 1996b. Language contact and inherent variability: the absence of hypercorrection in East Anglian present-tense verb forms. In Juhani Klemola, Merja Kytö and Matti Rissanen (eds.), *Speech past and present: studies in English dialectology in memory of Ossi Ihalainen*, 412–425. Frankfurt: Peter Lang.

Trudgill, Peter. 1996c. Dedialectalisation and Norfolk dialect orthography. In Irma Tavitsainen, Gunnel Melchers and Päivi Pahta (eds.), *Writing in nonstandard English*, 323–330. Amsterdam: John Benjamins Publishing.

Trudgill, Peter. 1997. British vernacular dialects in the formation of American English: the case of East Anglian do. In Raymond Hickey and Stanislaw Puppel (eds.), *Linguistic history and linguistic modelling: A festschrift for Jacek Fisiak on his 60th Birthday*, 749–758. Berlin/New York: De Gruyter Mouton.

Trudgill, Peter. 1998. The great East Anglian merger mystery. In R. Jolivet and F. Heussi (eds.), *Mélanges offerts en hommage à Mortéeza Mahmoudian*, 415–423. Lausanne: Université de Lausanne.

Trudgill, Peter. 1999a. Norwich: endogenous and exogenous linguistic change. In Paul Foulkes and Gerard Doherty (eds.), *Urban voices: accent studies in the British Isles*, 124–140. London: Edward Arnold.

Trudgill, Peter. 1999b. *The dialects of England*. 2nd ed. Oxford: Blackwell.

Trudgill, Peter. 2001. Modern East Anglia as a dialect area. In Jacek Fisiak and Peter Trudgill (eds.), *East Anglian English*, 1–12. Woodbridge: Boydell and Brewer.

Trudgill, Peter. 2003. *The Norfolk dialect*. Cromer: Poppyland.

Trudgill, Peter. 2004. *New-dialect formation: the inevitability of Colonial Englishes*. Edinburgh: Edinburgh University Press.

Trudgill, Peter. 2011. *Sociolinguistic typology: social determinants of linguistic complexity*. Oxford: Oxford University Press.

Trudgill, Peter. 2016. *Dialect matters: respecting vernacular language. Columns from the 'Eastern Daily Press'*. Cambridge: Cambridge University Press.

Trudgill, Peter. 2017. The spread of English. In Markku Filppula, Devyani Sharma and Juhani Klemola (eds.), *The Oxford handbook of World Englishes*, 14–34. Oxford: Oxford University Press.

Trudgill, Peter. 2018. I'll git the milk time you bile the kittle do you oon't get no tea yit no coffee more oon't I": phonetic erosion and grammaticalisation in East Anglian conjunction-formation. In Laura Wright (ed.), *Southern English varieties then and now*, 132–147. Berlin: De Gruyter Mouton.

Trudgill, Peter. 2019. Bermudian English as a North American dialect: a note on the segmental phonology. https://www.researchgate.net/publication/330180330

Trudgill, Peter, and Christina Foxcroft. 1979. *A sociolinguistic study of linguistic change in urban East Anglia*. London: Social Science Research Council.

Trudgill, Peter, and Tina Foxcroft. 1978. On the sociolinguistics of vocalic mergers: transfer and approximation in East Anglia. In Peter Trudgill (ed.), *Sociolinguistic patterns in British English*, 69–79. London: Edward Arnold.

Trudgill, Peter, Elizabeth Gordon, Gillian Lewis, and Margaret MacLagan. 2000. The role of drift in the formation of native-speaker southern hemisphere Englishes: Some New Zealand evidence. *Diachronica: International Journal for Historical Linguistics* 17 (1). 111–138.

Trudgill, Peter, Daniel Schreier, Daniel Long, and Jeffrey P. Williams. 2003. On the reversibility of mergers: /w/, /v/ and evidence from lesser-known Englishes. *Folia Linguistica Historica* 37 (Historica 24-1-2). 23–46.

Tynch, Milton. 1994. *Analysis of the verb system of the AAVE of Edenton, North Carolina.* Unpublished Paper: North Carolina State University.

Vasko, Anna-Liisa. 2005. *Up Cambridge – prepositional locative expressions in dialect speech: a corpus-based study of the Cambridgeshire dialect.* Helsinki: Société Néophilologique de Helsinki.

Vasko, Anna-Liisa. 2010. *Cambridgeshire dialect grammar.* Helsinki: Varieng.

van Riemsdijk, Henk. 1978. *A case study in syntactic markedness: the binding nature of prepositional phrases.* Breda: Peter de Ridder Press.

Viereck, Wolfgang. 1975. *Regionale und soziale Erscheinungsformen des britischen und amerikanischen Englisch.* Tübingen: Niemeyer.

Viereck, Wolfgang. 1980. The dialectal structure of British English: Lowman's evidence. *English World-Wide* 1 (1). 25–44.

Wakelin, Martyn. 1984. Rural dialects in England. In Peter Trudgill (ed.), *Language in the British Isles*, 70–93. Cambridge: Cambridge University Press.

Wakelin, Martyn Francis. 1972. *English dialects: An introduction.* London: Burns & Oates.

Walker, James. 1791. *A critical pronouncing dictionary.* London: A. Wilson for T. Cadell.

Walton-Rogers, Penelope. 2012. Continuity within change: two sites in the borders of the former Iceni territory in East Anglia. In Rica Annaert, Tinne Jacobs, Ingrid In't Ven and Ste Coppens (eds.), *The very beginning of Europe? Early-Medieval migration and colonisation*, 109–122. Brussels: Flanders Heritage Agency.

Wells, John. 1982. *Accents of English.* Cambridge: Cambridge University Press.

Williamson, Tom. 1993. *The origins of Norfolk.* Manchester: Manchester University Press.

Williamson, Tom. 2013. East Anglia's character and the 'North Sea World'. In David Bates and Robert Liddiard (eds.), *East Anglia and its North Sea world in the Middle Ages*, 44–62. Woodbridge: Boydell & Brewer.

Winroth, Anders. 2014. *The age of the Vikings.* Princeton: Princeton University Press.

Wright, Joseph. 1905. *The English dialect grammar.* Oxford: Froude.

Wright, Laura. 2001. Some morphological features of the Norfolk guild certificates of 1388/9: an exercise in variation. In Jacek Fisiak and Peter Trudgill (eds.), *East Anglian English*, 79–162. Woodbridge: Boydell & Brewer.

Wyld, Henry C. 1953. *A history of modern colloquial English.* 3rd ed. Oxford: Blackwell.

Index

abear 176
abed 188
Abridge 46, 48
Acle 33–34
acrost 166
Adams, James 6
addle 126
adverbials 108
adverbs 90
Ælfwald, King 12
Æthelberht I, King 12
Æthelberht II, King 12
Æthelred, King 12
Æthelstan, King 12
Æthelweard, King 12
Æthelwold, King 20
afore 159, 163
African American English 144–147
after 157, 180, 183
aftermath 116
again 22
agin 161, 167
agin 173
agricultural terms 134
ah 137, 154, 172, 180, 188, 191
Akethorpe 15
Alconbury 46
Aldeby 15
Alfred, King of Wessex 13
allus 185
alonga 109, 177
alveolar flap /r/ 44
American (Southern) English 144–147
American English 46, 89, 141–144, 199
Amos, Jennifer 72–73, 77
anaphoric pronouns 107
Anderson, Peter 59, 78, 198
anend 191
Angles 8, 14, 27
Anglo-Frisian 9
Anglo-Norman 20–22, 128
Angloromani 26
answer particles 137, 154
anti-languages 26

approximants 44, 85, 140
archaeological evidence 2–3, 4, 8, 14, 30
archaic forms 94, 117, 134, 210
Are y'alright? 137
aren't 99
Ashby 15, 17
Ashwellthorpe 15, 71
aside 191
Aslacton 15
assart 134
assimilation 38
Australian English 148, 180
auxiliary *do* 96
auxiliary reduction 34
a-verbing 92, 156, 160, 167, 169, 173, 177, 189, 191
Avis, W. S. 142
Ayres, Harry M. 140

back-formations 104
Bailey, Beryl 147
Bailey, Richard 44
bairn 126
Baldi, Philip 2
Barringer, Chris 134
be 95, 99, 186, 188, 191
Beadle, Richard 31–33, 35, 152
beaker 154
Beal, Joan 45
Beccles 32–34
beck 14, 127
Bedfordshire
 – 1930s dialect area 46
 – 1950s dialect area 56
 – 19th century dialect area 45
 – h-dropping 200
 – possessive pronouns 107
 – *Survey of English Dialects* 50
beefing 129
beergood 136, 155
Belgium 22
Benham, Charles 101, 175–178
Beonna, King 12
Beowulf 12

Berliner Lautarchiv 179
Bermuda and the Caribbean 140–141
Besthorpe 15
bidialectalism 13, 17
biffin/biffen 129
bilingualism 4, 13, 17–18
Binham 10
bishoprics 30
blast! 80, 138, 188
blee 120
blood libel 21
Bloom, Alan 187–189
blow 185
boke 120
bor 136, 159, 176, 191
Borrow, George 25, 136
borrow/lend 97
borrowings 82
Boudica, Queen 2
boundaries
– Brittonic dialect boundaries 3
– cultural division 30
– East Anglia 193
– ethnolinguistic dividing lines 17, 193
– isoglosses 31, 40, 42, 46, 56, 73, 116, 193–194
– Norfolk-Cambridgeshire 31
– Norfolk-Lincolnshire 33
– Norfolk-Suffolk 14, 30–31, 48
– northern and southern English dialects 51
– religious boundaries 30
– rivers 11, 30, 193
– Suffolk-Essex 11, 31
boy 137
Boy John Letters 120, 137, 158–161
Braintree 195, 214
Brancaster 7, 29
breaking 28
breast 116
breck 134
Breckland 134
Breeze, Andrew 3–5
Bret- 5
Breton 20–21
Brettenham 5
Breydon Water 15
Briggs, Keith 5, 7–8, 12, 119, 123

Brindred, Michael 86
Britain, David 44, 51, 56, 65, 72, 77, 107–108, 194
Brittonic 1–5, 119–120
broad 120
Brook, G. L. 42
Brown, James 188
Browne, Sir Thomas 120–121, 123, 125, 134, 137
Buckinghamshire 41, 214
Bulcamp 7
Bure, River 17
Burgh Castle 4
Burling, Robbins 147
Burnt Fen 46
Bury St Edmunds 12, 32–35
Butcher, David 132, 138, 168–170
Butcher, Kerri-Ann 74, 78, 213–214
Buxhall 46
by 15

caddow 120, 155
Caister 7, 29
Caistor St Edmund 2, 7, 10, 29
Caistor-by-Norwich 7
Calthorpe 15
Calvert Street 24
Cam, River 11
Cambridge 11, 67, 84, 90, 200
Cambridge, University of 40, 193
Cambridgeshire
– 1930s dialect area 46
– 1950s dialect area 56
– as part of dialect area 39, 41, 214
– as part of East Anglia 1
– border with Norfolk 31
– Brittonic in 2
– Celtic tribes in 2
– *do* 111
– East Anglia dialect area 45
– *een't* 99
– *freeze* 93
– h-dropping 200
– *have* 96
– imperatives 95
– NEAR/SQUARE set 78
– nouns plurals 99

– part of dialect area 43
– place names 7, 29
– possessive pronouns 107
– pronouns 102
– rhoticity 87
– *set* 97
– *Survey of English Dialects* 50
– third-person singular zero 51, 90
Campbell, James 16
Campsey 7
campus 7
Camulodunum (Colchester) 2, 7
Canada 142
Canadian English 72
Canadian Raising 72
Canute, King 20
Caribbean English 140–141
Carlton 46
carnser 128
carr 127
castra 29
Catholic church 23
Catuvellauni 2
causative/non-causative pairs 97, 169, 185
Celtic languages 1–2, 3, 21, 119–120, see also Brittonic, see also Breton
Celts 1, 5–6, 30
Charles V, Emperor 22
Charleston, South Carolina 140
Charnock, Richard 136, 182
Chaucer, Geoffrey 31
Cheshire, Jenny 202
chester 7
Chesterton 7, 29
Chet, River 4
CHOICE vowel 73
Christianity 10
church 53, 68, 80, 148, 156
Civitas Icenorum 30
Clare, John 125
Clarke, Sandra 141
Clarke, W. G. 134
Claxton, A. O. D. 93
clear /l/ 86, 164
clip 172
CLOTH vowel 79
Coates, Richard 4–5

cockey 119
Cockney 71, 85, 148–149, 196
codification 19
coins 28
Colchester 2, 7, 23, 29, 175–178
Colne, River 4
Colonial Englishes 140–149
conjunctions 110–115, 144
conservative features 53, 87, 115, 210, see also archaic forms
continuous aspect verb-forms 92
conversational style 139
Cooper, Ernest R. 165
cooshie 132
cor blast! 138
Corieltauvi 2
Cornish Hall End 181–183, 196
Cornwall, Alfred 179–180
Corrigan, Karen 44, 149
Coslany 5
cosset 117
cothish 135
cothy 155
couch 128
Cox, Barrie 9
Cozens-Hardy, Sydney 125
cran 133
Crostwick 30
crowd, to 131
Cruso, Jan 24
culch 129

d and t merger 83
d for /ð/ 34, 86, 104, 122, 152
Daines, Simon 42
Danelaw 13–14, 18, 22
Danish (modern) 14–15
Danish invasion 10, 12–13
dannocks 131
dare 97
daren't 97
dark /l/ 86, 183, 206
dative 26
Davidson, William 141
Davis, Norman 37
Dawson, Edward J. 162–164
de Guader, Ralph 21

deaf 70
dedialectalisation 62, 143, 148, 161
deek 131
deen 127
defences 11
definite article 100, 177
demonstratives 101, 106, 160, 167, 173, 177, 188
dene 119
design 185
Devil's Dyke 11
dialect contact 17–18, 21, 73, 195
dialect mixture 73, 195
Diary of Henry Machin 200
dibles 135, 155
Dickens, Charles 89, 121, 129
dickey 120, 159, 161
Dictionary of American Regional English (DARE) 145
Diessel, Holger 106
diffuse linguistic communities 19
digby 133
Dillard, J. L. 147
Diphthong Shift 148
diphthongisation 38, 63, 160, 173
diphthongs
– Australian English 149
– fast vs. slow 48, 71
– *here* 163
– ingliding 78
– long o 65
– Low Mid Diphthonging 205
– upgliding diphthongs 47, 77
discourse features 136–139
do 93, 95–96, 114, 144
Dobson, E. J. 34
dodman 116, 155
Doegen, Wilhelm 179
dog 67
dorn't 161
double comparatives 90, 108
double negation 98, 191, *see also* multiple negation
doubt 176
douw 155
dow 138
down (in relation to North Sea) 134

draw 172
DRESS vowel 63, 174, 180
driddling 182
duller/dullor 128
Dunwich 31–34
durst 97
Dutch 7, 19, 23–25, 129–132
dwainy 121
dwile 131
dykes 11

Eadmund, King 12
Eadwald, King 12
Ealdorman Aelfred 13
Ealdwulf, King 12
earldom of East Anglia 20–21
Early British 5
Early Modern English 37–40, 193
East Anglia
– as earldom 20–21
– definition of region 1, 10, 21, 47, 51
– East Anglian lexis 116
– first kingdom of 10–11
– name of 8
– Northern vs. Southern dialect variation 29–31, 35–36, 39, 48, 57
– topography 11
East Anglian short *o* 53, 64–66, 75, 79, 89, 142, 148, 163, 169, 173, 183, 189, 192
East Anglian vocabulary of Romani 25
East Midlands 31, 35, 188
East Winch 33
Eccles 4
Edgefield 17
Edward I, King 21
Edward the Elder, King 20
Edwards, William Henry 190
een't 99, 188
egles 4
Ekwall, Eilert 3–4, 17, 22, 28, 32
Ellis, A. J. 40–42, 46, 53, 59, 73, 84–85, 101, 123, 200, 203, 210, 214
Ellis, Stanley 50, 171, 184–185
Elmham 162
Ely 10, 31, 95
Emerson, Peter Henry 119

Emneth 90
Emonds, Joseph 19
emphatic contexts 138
English Dialect Dictionary 60, 77, 82, 98, 103–104, 110–112, 117–120, 124, 126–132, 135–136, 145, 157, 161, 176
en't 169, 188
Essex Ballads 86, 101, 175–178
Essex
– 1930s dialect area 46–47, 50
– and Alexander Gil 39
– as part of East Anglia 1
– Australian English 149, 180
– Brittonic 2
– CHOICE vowel 73
– dialect area 27, 39, 45
– dialect 28
– *do* 111
– GOAT vowel 76
– h-dropping 53
– Kingdom of Essex 11
– l-vocalisation 209
– lexical differences within East Anglian region 116
– linguistic boundaries 194
– long open e 49
– Long-Mid Diphthonging 205
– LOT vowel 67
– MOUTH vowel 77
– New England settlements 142
– noun plurals 100
– place names 29, 35
– possessive pronouns 107
– PRICE vowel 72
– pronouns 102
– rhoticity 87
– shift towards London variants 195
– *Survey of English Dialects* 50
– *that* 103
– third-person present-tense singular zero 90
– typical East Anglian features 47
– yod-dropping 89
ethnolinguistic dividing lines 17, 193
Evans, George Ewart 25
exes/exies 139

f to v 35, 39
Faarlund, Jan Terje 19
FACE vowel 70–71, 157, 163, 177, 186, 203, 205
Fairclough, John 3
Falkland Islands English 67
fang, to 121
fantail 133
far (father) 159
fare, to 121, 155, 159, 166, 176
faring 121
Fasold, Ralph 147
fast speech phenomena 86
fate (adj.) 155
Fellows-Jensen, Gillian 3, 14–16
fen 22
Fens 1, 5, 10–11
– CHOICE vowel 73
– foot-strut split 65
– *frit* 94
– h-dropping 53
– impassibility 194
– linguistic boundaries 193–194
– Long Mid Merger 75
– MOUTH vowel 77
– NURSE vowel 53
– past tense of *be* 96
– possessive pronouns 107
– PRICE vowel 72
– third-person present-tense singular zero 90
– transitional nature of 56, 66
Ferragne, Emmanuel 61, 144
field-names 16–17
Filppula, Markku 5
find up 118, 121
fire 80
first 80
fishing vocabulary 132, 168–170
Fisiak, Jacek 28, 31
fit 121
five-and twenty 100
flax 22
FLEECE vowel 70–71, 74
Flegg 14–15, 16, 17, 37, 150
Flemings 8
Flemish 20, 22–25, 130

Flempton 8
flit 185
focussed linguistic communities 19
fogger 155
foldcourse 134
folk memory 85
folk-etymological forms 129
fool 75
FOOT vowel 64–66, 73, 75, 142, 148
FOOT-STRUT split 42–43, 47, 62, 66, 204
Forby, Rev. Robert 39, 45, 59, 65, 68, 93, 99, 104, 106, 118, 120, 123, 126–127, 129, 131, 134, 136, 142, 154, 193
Fortson, Benjamin 2
Foxcroft, Tina 59, 70, 76, 81, 89, 195, 206, 209, 211
Foxcroft-Trudgill Survey 59, 195, 208
Francis, W. Nelson 59, 64, 71, 76–77, 79, 84, 142
Fransham 34
Freethorpe 15
freeze 93
French 20, 23–24, 73, 82, 91, 128–129, 134
Freston 8
Frisian 7, 9, 19
Frisians 8
Friston 8
frit 94
fule 161
fule 167
furze 116
fye out 131
fystey 155

Gamlingay 188
Gariannum 4
gat 166
gate 16
Gaul, Celtic languages of 3
gay (noun) 117
gears 185
genetic evidence 25
genitive case 26
Gepp, Edward 90, 100–102, 107, 122, 136
German 7, 23
German, Mrs 147, 211
Germanic 3–5, 13, 118, 121

gerunds 38, 89, 160
Gil, Alexander 29, 35, 38, 47
Gimson, A. C. 66, 203
Gipeswic 12
Gipping, River 30
girl 123, 137
git 161
give 22
Glosthorpe 15
glottal stops 83
glottalisation 55, 83, 148, 164, 180, 183, 186
GOAT vowel 64, 73, 75–77, 143, 149, 180, 203, 206
Godmanchester 7
Godwinson, Harold 20
golt 191
Goose, Nigel 23
GOOSE vowel 73–75, 209
Gordon, Elizabeth 147
Gorleston 123, 214
gorse 116
gosgood 136
gotch 155
grammatical gender 18
grammaticalisation 106, 110, 146
granfar 159
Grapes, Sidney 158–161
Great Ouse, River 4, 195
Great Vowel Shift 38, 82, 160
Great Yarmouth 34, 119, 132, 203, 206, 211, 214
greetings 136–137
Grimston hybrid 15
Grim's Ditch 3
grosher 155
grup 127
guild certificates 22, 91
Gunilduscroft 17
Gypsies 25

hackle 122
Haddenham 95
Haddiscoe 30
Hadleigh 209–211
Hægelisdun 12
hain, to 122

hake 127
half 81–82
Hallam, Thomas 43
Halliwell, J. O. 45, 194
Hallstatt culture 2
ham 5, 17
Hammarström, Göran 148
Hancock, Ian 25–26
Happisburgh 17
HAPPY-tensing 70, 180
haps 182
Hardingham 25
hardly 98
Härke, Heinrich 13
harnser 117
Haslam, Marie 50
have 34, 86, 99, 156, 160, 163, 169, 172, 182, 185
have 96
hazelt 182
h-dropping 48, 52, 84, 183, 186, 189, 192, 199–201
Hebrew 20
heft 133
Heigham 82
hem 22
hem 152
here 101, 173
Here go! 137
Hernández-Campoy, Juan Manuel 37, 210
Hertfordshire 41, 45–46, 56, 85, 107, 205
Hethincroft 17
Hindi-Urdu 132
Hines, John 8, 10
hodmandod 116
Hoekstra, Jarich 19
Hoelzel, A. R. 25
hogget 172
holl 122
Holman, George C. 8, 13
Holmberg, Anders 19
holmr 15
Holt 16
home 65, 148, 192
Home Counties 196, 203, 213–214
Honington 46, 49
horse 67, 100, 149, 182, 214

Hoskins, W. G. 140
hour 80
housen 99
how 16
Howe, Stephen 138
howsever 166
Hoxne Hoard 6
huckle 155
Huguenots 24
hulver 127
humour 139
Hundred of Happing 17
Hundreds 16
Huntingdonshire 7, 29, 41, 43, 45, 50, 56, 107
Hurston, Zora Neal 145
hutkin/hudkin 131
hw- 32, 37
hypercorrect forms 84, 91, 186, 202

Iceni 2–3, 4, 5, 30
Icknield way 27
Ihalainen, Ossi 38, 42, 67, 73, 101, 122, 157, 194
Ilketshall 46, 49
imperatives 95, 160
Indo-European 2, 104
inflectional languages 26
informal speech 69, 84
ing suffix 5, 38, 89, 92, 186
Ingham 33–34
ingliding diphthongs 78
Ingoldisthorpe 15
inhospitable areas 14, 194
initial-fricative voicing 36, 39
intensifiers 108, 138
interjections 138, 188
interrogatives 98
intonation 40, 61
intrusive /r/ 87, 109
in't 99, 163, 188
Ipswich 12, 16, 57, 62, 84, 211
irregular verbs 93–94
Ishiyama, Osamu 106
isoglosses 31, 40, 42, 46, 56, 73, 116, 193–194

Jackson, Kenneth 6
Jamestown settlement, Virginia 140

jearse 138
Jewish communities 20
Joby, Christopher 24
Jocelin of Brakelond 35
Johnson, Caleb 142
jokes 139
Jones, Daniel 199
Jordan, Richard 141
Jutes 8
Jutland 18

k- 29, 31, 84
Kallen, Jeffrey 44
kedge/kedgy 135
Kennett, River 11
Kent 23
Kentish 27, 31
Kett, John 98
Ketton-Cremer, R.W. 24–25
Kilpatrick, Kelly 7–8
kin suffix 131
Kingdom of East Anglia 10, 12, 27
Kingston 46
King's Lynn 4, 43, 202–203, 206, 211
Kirby 14
Kirby Bedon 16
Kirby Cane 16
kirk 14
Kirkley 14
Kirstead 14
KIT vowel 55, 62–63, 149, 164, 169, 173, 214
kl- 83
knacker 136, 155
Kökeritz, Helge 38–39, 59, 64, 70–71, 75–77
Kontic, René 118
köslönnī 5
Kristensson, Gillis 22, 27–29, 35, 37, 210
Kuhn, Hans 13
Kurath, Hans 45–47, 59, 65–67, 142–143, 147, 203
kw- 32, 37, 84

l (phoneme) 86, 164, 183, 206–209
Labov, William 72, 213
Lagamon's Brut 200
Laing, Margaret 32–33, 122, 151
Lake Lothing 15

Laker, Stephen 4
Langland, William 31
language contact 4, 17, 21–22, 195, *see also* dialect contact
language shift 6, 105
Lark, River 11, 30
Larwood, Joshua 67, 82, 135, 153–157
Lass, Roger 21, 32–33, 37, 105, 122, 151–152
Late British 5
Late Middle English 31, 34
Late Spoken Latin 6
later dental hardening 122
Latin 2, 4, 6–7, 127
Laver, John 72
lay 97, 169, 173, 189
Le Page, Robert 19
learn 97
Leicester 2
Leighton Bromswell 46
lenition 44
Liddiard, Robert 22, 29
ligger 127
Lincolnshire
– border with Norfolk 33, 193
– dialect area 38, 41, 46, 56
– possessive pronouns 107
– *Survey of English Dialects* 50, 64
Lindström, Bengt 16, 119
linen 118
lingua francas 6
linking r 87
little boat 169
Little Downham 49, 87, 90, 184–186, 189
Little Ouse, River 4, 30
Little Sampford 46
Littleport 46
Loddon 4
Lodge, Ken 67, 70, 74, 77–78, 82
Logonomia Anglia (Gil, 1619) 38
loke 122
London
– dialect contact 21
– East Anglian dialects in 22
– h-dropping 202
– l-vocalisation 206
– northwards variant spread from 81, 195
– refugees 23

– rhoticity 45, 148
– Southern East Anglia linked to 30
– th-fronting 197
– v-w merger 197
– vowel fronting 66, 203
– yod-dropping 89
Long Melford 32
Long Mid Merger 70, 75, 177, 180
long monophthongs 78
long o 65
Long Stratton 7
Long-Mid Diphthonging 203
lop 133
LOT vowel 48, 66–67, 81–82, 140, 148, 183
Lothingland 14–15
love 133
Low Countries 22
Low German 7
Lowestoft 14, 61, 202–203, 206, 211
Lowman, Guy 45–48, 50, 53, 57, 59, 64, 67, 71, 76, 84, 87, 180, 203, 206
lucam 128
Ludham 71
Lutton 55
l-vocalisation 86, 206–209
Lynn 4, 33–34

MacMahon, Michael 199, 203, 206
made 78
Magna Steyndale 17
Maguire, Warren 84, 200
Maldon 12
Mallender, Ned 168
mand 133
March 43
mardle 122
maritime vocabulary 129, 132, 166
markets 16
Markus, Manfred 130
marram 127
Marshall, Sybil 186, 190–192
marshy areas 14–15, 30, 72, 194
Martin, Edward 3
Martin, Fred 181–183
Martlesham 46, 71
mash 133
master 109, 138

Matras, Yaron 25–26
matter 98
Mautby 37, 150
mawther/mauther 122, 136, 155
McDavid, Raven I. 48, 59, 65, 141–142, 144
McIntosh, Angus 31, 39
Meir ben Elijah of Norwich 20
Mercia, Kingdom of 10–12
Mercian dialect area 27–28, 31
Mersea Island 72–73, 77, 209
mice 39, 70
Middle Angles, Kingdom of the 10
Middle English 151
– dialect areas 31
– East Anglia as dialect area of 31–32
– GOAT vowel 76
– GOOSE vowel 74
– Middle English period 20–22, 29
– NURSE/CURE vowel 79
– vowel system 42
middle-class speech
– 19th century 148
– FACE vowel 70
– GOAT vowel 74
– h-dropping 84, 202
– l-vocalisation 206
– local dialects 196
– *moan-mown* 76
– monophthongisation 81
– third-person zero 91
Middlesex 11, 39, 46, 48
migration
– and the Fens 72, 195
– and zero-marking 91
– from East Anglia to London 22
– from Home Counties 196
– from the Low Countries 22
milches 123
milk 22
miller 22
million 129
Milroy, James 199
moan-mown distinction 76, 137, 167, 177, 183, 205, 208
mob, to 132, 159
Moens, William 23
moise/moize 118, 155

monophthongal ā and diphthongal ai distinction 161, 163, 169
monophthongisation 80, 170, 212
monophthongs 70, 78, 82, 205
Moor, Edward 123, 129, 154
Moore, Samuel 31
more 115
morphology 26, 49–50, 87
Morris, John 5
Morton, H. V. 139
Mousehold Heath 21, 26
mouse-hunter 132, 163
MOUTH vowel 47, 77, 173, 180, 183, 186, 211
multiple negation 98, 172, 182, 186, 191
mutual intelligibility 13
Myklecrundell 17
mylner 29

nacker 136
Naismith, Rory 12
Nall, James Greaves 129
narbor 155
Nashe, Thomas 122
nautical terms 129, 166
NEAR/SQAURE set 78, 173, 183, 212
Necton 46
negation 98–99, 172, 191, *see also* multiple negation
Nelson, Lord 95
Nene, River 4, 27
Netherlands 22
Nevalainen, Terttu 37, 91
New England 65, 75, 141–144
New Zealand 67, 148–149, 211, 213
Newfoundland 141, 213
Newton, Sam 12
Nielsen, Hans Frede 8, 10, 13
nigh 166
no 76, 137
Norfolk Biffin apples 129
Norfolk Broads 120, 127
Norfolk
 – /d/ pronunciation 83
 – /tr/ 84
 – 1930s dialect area 46
 – as part of East Anglia 1
 – Brittonic place names 4
 – Brittonic 2, 4–5
 – Celtic tribes in 2
 – *do* 111
 – English-Danish dialect contact 17
 – FACE vowel 71
 – FOOT-STRUT split 44, 148
 – Germanic place names 8
 – GOAT vowel 76
 – GOOSE vowel 74
 – lexical differences within East Anglian region 116
 – linguistic boundaries 193
 – LOT vowel 67
 – Mercian dialect area 28
 – Middle English 31
 – MOUTH vowel 77
 – NEAR/SQUARE set 78
 – New England settlements 142
 – Norse place names 14
 – Northern vs. Southern East Anglia dialect variation 29–31, 35, 39
 – Old Danish place names 15–16
 – Old Danish vocabulary 126
 – Old English place names 16, 29
 – Old English 10, 27
 – population growth 196
 – possessive pronouns 107
 – rhoticity 87
 – Roman place names 7
 – short o 64
 – typical East Anglian dialect features 47, 49, 51–52
 – v and w 85
Norman French 20–21
Normans 20–22
norms, agreed language 19
Norse 12–14, 105, 126, *see also* Old Norse
Norsified English versus Anglified Norse 19
North Creake 4
North Elmham 30, 49, 162–164
North Erpingham 16
North Germanic 13, 19, 105
North Sea 4, 8–9, 11, 18, 22, 30, 51, 193
Northamptonshire 2, 41, 43, 45–46, 107, 214
north-south diffusion of dialect features 81, 211
Northumbrian Old English 27

Northwest Germanic 13
Northwestern Romance 6–7
Norwegian 14–16
Norwich Castle 21
Norwich Cathedral 16
Norwich City 57
Norwich School 24–25
Norwich
– /ð/ 86
– and English across the world 140
– bilingualism 18
– Brittonic place names 5
– Danish rule 16
– diffusion of variants from 194, 202, 211, 213
– GOOSE vowel 74
– Gypsies 26
– h-dropping 84, 200
– intervocalic /t/ 83
– Jewish communities 21
– loss of /x/ before /t/ 34
– lot vowel 67
– MOUTH vowel 211
– multilingualism 20, 23–24
– NEAR/SQUARE set 212
– *no* 76
– Norwich a 157
– PRICE vowel 71
– printing presses 24
– refugees from the Low Countries 23, 91
– regional capital 22
– short *o* 65
– smoothing vowels 82
– street names 16, 24
– th-fronting 197
– trade and commerce 14
– urban centre 1, 57, 193
– variants spreading from 91
– vowel lowering 203
noun plurals 99, 182
now 108
numerals 100
NURSE vowel 53, 62, 68, 79, 87, 156, 161, 167, 173, 177, 180, 183, 186

object pronouns 101, 103, 152
of 109
off 67, 183

Offa, King 12
old 22, 28, 138
Old Danish 12–20, 34, 105, 116, 126–128
Old English
– Celtic influence 5
– contact with Old Danish 17
– dialects 27
– East Anglia as dialect area 27–31
– Germanic history 9–11
– h-dropping 199
– influence on Old Danish 18
– lexical influences 119–120, 124
– Norsified English versus Anglified Norse 19
– place names 5, 15, 30
– river names 3
Old French 7
Old Norse 14, 17–18, 22, 29, 34, 105, 119, 126
Old Welsh 4
older speakers 34, 72, 76, 86, 92, 148, 203, 211
ol' partner 137
on 109, 160, 167, 173, 182, 185
on the huh 125
only 98, 172, 182, 189
open syllables 70, 76, 79, 82, 143, 156–157
orf 167
Origins of New Zealand English project 147, 211
orthography
– Boy John Letters 161
– Cooper's *Mardles from Suffolk* 167
– dialect spellings 68, 78, 80, 101, 122
– ght words 33
– h-dropping 199
– Middle English 33, 37
– NURSE/CURE vowel 79
– Old English 34
– Paston Letters 151
– PRICE vowel 72
– rhoticity 122
– w for v 84
– yod-dropping 89
Orton, Harold 35, 39, 116
Oswald, King 12
ought 98, 123
Oulton Broad 15

Ouse, River 11, 27, 30
Outwell 90
Over 187–189
Oxborough 34
Oxford English Dictionary 120–121, 124, 126–132, 135–136, 154, 160

p, t, k 55, 83, 164, 183, 186
paddock 127
Page, Richard 2, 10
paigle 176
painting words 129
Pakefield 168–170
palatalisation 84
Palsgrave, John 125
Parsons, David 15–16, 18
partner 80
paryard 136, 155
passive bidialectalism 13
past participles 93, 169, 185
Paston, Lady Katherine 37
Paston Letters 34, 37–38, 84, 105, 122, 150–152, 210
Paston, Margaret 33, 37, 84, 150
past-tense forms 93, 96, 177, 180, 191
past-tense negation 90
peak 159
ped 133
Peitsara, Kirsti 93, 109
Pellegrino, Francois 61, 144
pent 123
perk 129
Perridon, Harry 18
personal names 15, 17, 28–29
personal pronouns 101
Pestell, Tim 14
Peterborough 41, 65, 195
Pettersson, Sofia 130
Philip II, King 23
phonetic reduction 60
Pie, Iona and Peter 139
pightle 117, 155
Pilgrim Fathers 142
pit 123
place names
– Brittonic 4, 119
– Essex 35

– evidence for Old English dialect area 27–28
– Grimston hybrids 15
– Latin/Roman 7, 9
– minor Scandinavian names 16
– New England 141
– Norse 12, 14–15
– Old Danish 15, 17
– Old English 15, 30
– *plains* 130
– West Germanic 5, 8
– woodland 29
plains 130
plancher 155
plat 116
plurals 90, 99, 182
Pockthorpe 15
poetry 12, 24
Pogatscher, Alois 6
population density 1, 15, 22, 29
porny 191
possessive pronouns 50, 107, 191
possessives 26
Potter Heigham 158–161
Potter, Robert 62, 209, 214
Poussa, Patricia 104, 106
pre-fricative lengthening 79
preposition stranding 19
prepositions 100, 109
present participles 89, 92, 156
presentative *be* 95
present-tense plurals 152
present-tense verb forms 33
preterite 156, 172
preterites 163, 169, 173, 177, 182, 185, 188, 191
price vowel 48, 71–73, 183
Primer, Sylvester 140
Prince, Hugh 123
printing 23
progressive aspect 92, 156
Promptorium parvulorum 122
Pronoun Exchange 101, 177, 182
pronouns 95, 101–108, 152
Pulham 64
pur 136, 155
push 130
PVI [Pairwise Variability Index] 61

qu- spellings 32, 37
quant 119
Quarles 33
qw- spellings 37

r (phoneme) 38, 44, 46, 78, 87, 173
Rædwald, King 10–11
raihan 'roe deer' 10
Ramsey Heights 190–192
ranny 127
rare 109, 138
Ray, John 122, 136
R-Dropping 44
reallocation 72
Received Pronunciation (RP) 41, 44, 71, 210, 212
reflexive pronouns 107
refugees 23, 91, 128
relative pronouns 108, 160, 167, 177, 182
relly 129
Rendlesham 12
Repps 17
retrodiction 28, 31
retroflection 44, 183
reverse acculturation 4
reverse spellings 34
Revolt of the Earls 21
rhoticity 44, 46, 62, 87, 120, 122, 148, 161, 173, 180, 186
rhythm 60–62, 144, 146
Riemsdijk, Henk van 19
right 108
river names 3, 17, 30, 119
r-loss 186
roads 7, 29
roightle 191
Romani 25–26, 132
Romans 3–4, 6
Ruano-García, Javier 121
rudle 123
rum 132, 155, 191
runic inscriptions 10
rural speech 74, 76, 82, 86, 117, 200
Rutland 41

sailing, travel via 29
sammodithee 137

Sampson, John 25
Samson of Bury, Abbot 35
Sandred, Karl Inge 4, 14, 16, 119
Saxham 8
Saxons 8, 27
Schiering, René 60, 146
Schram, O. K. 27
Schrijver, Peter 2, 6
Schulte, Michael 34
schwa 55, 60, 70, 78, 86, 149, 163, 183, 214
Sco Ruston 30
Scott, Bill 171–174
Scottish Gaelic 4, 133
scud 133
second-person pronouns 137, 160
set 97, 177
seven vowel system 68
Seymour, M. C. 33–34, 152
shack 134
shannock 133
Sharrington 17
Sheringham 133
shew (preterite of show) 94
short *a* 53, 68, 183, 189
short *o* 53, 64–66, 75, 79, 89, 142, 148, 163, 169, 173, 183, 189, 192
Shrewsbury, J. F. D. 29
shrines 12
shud 118
shummaker 156
sibrit 135
Sigeberht, King 12
sight 155, 176
Simm, Saskia 214
sj to ß assimilation 38
Skeat, Walter 120, 135, 161
skep 163
Skipper, Keith 129, 135
slower speech styles 139
Smith, Albert 28
smoothing 78, 80–82, 86, 92, 170, 211
snack 128
Snackegate 24
snail 116, 155
Snailgate 24
snasty 156
Solempne, Anthony De 24

some 42–43
sosh 125
South Creake 4
South Walsham 46, 84
Southern (US) drawl 144
Southern Hemisphere Englishes 67
Southwold 165
Spain 23
spelling. *see* orthography *splinters*, 199
splinters 116
Spong Hill 10
spreet 166
Spurdens, William 122
Spurling, Juliette 214
squat 117
squit 117
St Helena English 72
staithe 14, 128
stam 125
Stamford 41–42
Standard English 41, 123, 210
START/BATH/PALM vowel 54, 79, 149, 180
Steeple 46
stetch 182
Stiffkey 46
stingy 125
Stockholm Codex Aureus 13
Stoke Ferry 193
Stoker, David 24
Stour, River 4, 11
Stowmarket 76, 203, 210–211
Stradbroke 7
Stradishall 7
Stradsett 7
Strang, Barbara 42, 44
Strangers 23, 25
Strangers 82, 91, 128, 130
strata 7
Stratford St Mary 7
Stratton Strawless 7
street 22, 28
street names 16, 24, 82
stress 60–62, 144
stress-timedness 60–61, 111, 144, 146
stroop 128
STRUT vowel 56, 66, 180, 202, 204, *see also* FOOT-STRUT split

Stuston 34
sty 16
stylistics 65
subject pronouns 101
such 178
Suffolk
– /d/ pronunciation 83
– /tr/ 84
– 1930s dialect area 46
– Anglo-Saxon East Anglian boundaries 10
– as part of East Anglia 1
– Brittonic place names 5
– Brittonic 2
– Celtic tribes 2–3
– *do* 111
– FACE vowel 71
– FLEECE vowel 70
– FOOT-STRUT split 148
– Germanic place names 8
– GOAT vowel 76
– GOOSE vowel 75
– Gypsies 25
– irregular past tenses 93
– Kingdom of Essex 11
– lexical differences within East Anglian 116
– LOT vowel 67
– Mercian dialect area 28
– NEAR/SQUARE set 78
– Norse place names 14
– Northern vs. Southern East Anglia dialect variation 29–31, 35, 39
– Old Danish place names 15
– Old Danish vocabulary 126
– Old English 10, 27
– Roman place names 7
– Romans in 3, 6
– typical East Anglian features 47
– yod-dropping 89
sunk 117
Survey of English Dialects 39, 50–52, 59, 65, 69, 71, 76–78, 80, 85, 87, 90, 102, 116, 148, 159, 162–164, 171–174, 176, 180–181, 183–184, 186, 197, 200, 211
Sutton Hoo 10
Swabians 8
swad 125
Swaffham 8, 34, 43

Swanton Morley 153–157
Swedish 15
swingletree 116
syllable stress 60, 62, 76, 81, 144
syntactic data 19

T'is true 104
Tabouret-Keller, Andrée 19
tag questions 104
tempest 117
temporal adverbials 108
Tendring Hall 25
terms of address 80, 136–137
terrier 134
t-glottalisation 211
t-glottalling 56, 148, 173, 180, 211
thackster 136, 156
thape 125
thapes 156
that 103–107
that 166, 169, 173, 177, 182, 185, 188, 214
the 100, 177
theirn 50, 191
them 22, 101, 177, 188
there 101
Therfield 53
theta /θ/ 33
Thetford 16, 33–34
th-fronting 183, 196
third-person singular present-tense -s 50
third-person singular present-tense zero 51, 90–91, 147, 156, 160, 169, 173, 176
third-person singular -t 33, 90
Thorkell the Tall, Earl 20
Thornham Parva 3
thorpe 15
THOUGHT vowel 78, 177, 180
Thrandeston 15
thurck 135
Thurlston 15
Thurne, River 17
Thwaite 29, 84
thwaite 30
tidy 185
Tillingham 72, 179–180
Tilney 34
time 110

time-telling 100
to be 95, 99, 186, 188, 191
toft 14
Toft Monks 34
together 101, 137, 160
Tombland 16
ton 15
Töpf, A. L. 25
topography 11, 29, 51, 193
tother 156, 159, 186
Tottington 35
towel 82
Townend, Matthew 13, 18, 105
tr- 84, 161
trade and commerce 6, 12, 14, 16, 22, 129
transitive verbs 92, 156
TRAP vowel 63, 82, 157, 174, 180, 186
trilingualism 24
Trinovantes 2–3, 30
triphthongs 80, 92, 211
troll 117
troughings 118
truce terms 139
Trudgill, Peter 44, 51, 56, 59–60, 62, 63–65, 67–73, 76–77, 81, 83–84, 86–87, 89, 91, 104, 111, 121, 130, 137, 140, 146–147, 149, 194, 196, 200, 203, 206, 209, 211
Trunch 4
Tuddenham 49, 77, 87, 171–174
tumbril 182
tusk 133
Tynch, Milton 145

un- as on- (prefix) 34
Undley 10
univerbation 188
unrounded vowels 48, 63, 66–67, 140, 148, 203
unstressed syllables 81, 83, 86, 164, 214
up (in relation to North Sea) 134
upgliding diphthongs 47, 77
upper-class language 21–22
urban areas
– conversational style 139
– dialect areas 57
– diffusion from 130
– GOAT vowel 74

– h-dropping 202
– l-vocalisation 209
– Long-Mid Diphthonging 206
– made and maid merger 205
– *moan-mown* 76
– shift to London variants 195
– STRUT-fronting 203
– third-person zero 90

Vange 35
Vasko, Anna-Liisa 52, 90, 92–93, 95, 97, 99, 102–103, 109, 187, 200, 214
velar consonants 84
velar fricatives 152
venta 2
Venta Icenorum 2
Verlamion (St Albans) 2
vestigial dialect variants 85, 87
vicus 7
Viereck, Wagner 49, 107
Vikings 12–20, 104, 126
Vocabulary of East Anglia, The (Forby, 1830) 39
vowel fronting 54, 66, 73, 75
vowel lengthening 79, 81
vowel lowering 34, 66, 81, 152, 174, 203
vowel mergers 38, 47, 55, 70, 74–75, 77–78, 84, 213
vowel raising 38, 62, 161, 164, 167, 169, 173
vowel reduction 60, 87
vowel retraction 63
vowel rounding 48, 66, 73, 78, 148
vowel shortening 75
vowel system in modern East Anglian 62
vullike 188

w and v merger 84–85, 140, 161, 167, 197
Wader, Ralph/Waders, Radulf 21
Wakelin, Martyn 85, 92
Wal- 5
Walcott 5
Walker, James 44
Walloons 22–25
Walsham Hundred 17
Walton 5
Walton Rogers, Penelope 3–4, 30
war 191

was 148
Wash 11, 27, 30, 38, 51
wash 185
water words 4
Waveney, River 15, 30, 83
Way Dike Bank 46
Way's vocabulary 26
weak forms of pronouns 102
Weak-Vowel Merger 55, 62, 81, 149, 173, 183, 186, 201, 214
weeson 156
Wells, John 42, 44, 55, 64, 66–67, 70, 79, 81, 87, 144, 148–149, 199, 203, 206, 213
Welsh 2–5
wem/wame 126
weren't 96, 166
weren't 188
Wessex 8, 13, 20
West Frisian 9
West Germanic 4–5, 7–11, 13, 19, 130
West Saxon 27, 31
wh- words 32, 151, 199
what 108, 160, 177, 182
while 110
whin 116
Whinburgh 32
Whiter, Rev. Walter 25–26
wholly 108, 138, 176
Wickham Market 62
Wickhams 7
Wiggenhall 34
Wilby 15
William the Conqueror 21
Williams, Henrik 34
Williamson, Tom 3, 5, 10–11, 30
Winroth, Anders 18
Wisbech 34, 90, 203
wit and repartee 139
wong 16
Woodbridge 62, 209, 211, 214
woodland 29
Woolverston 32
Word Geography of England 116, 123, 126–127, 130
Word Geography of England 116
word-initial /w/ 89
working-class speech

– GOAT vowel 74, 76
– h-dropping 84, 202
– l-vocalisation 206
– LOT vowel 67
– short *a* 69
– short *o* 65
– triphthongs 80
Wright, Joseph 60, 85, 141
Wright, Laura 22, 91, 105
Wright, Nathalia 116
written language 10, 21
Wuffingas dynasty 10, 12
wuz 160, 169, 173, 182, 191
Wyld, H. C. 79, 84, 197
Wymondham 33–34, 150

x before t loss 33, 152

y (French) 73
y (Old English) 35, 39

yar 160
Yare, River 3, 14–15
ye 102, 151
Yellow Plague 29
yes 137
yes-no question intonation 61
yet 114
yod-dropping 49, 73, 80, 87, 143, 160–161, 211
yoll 133
you 101
you ... together 101, 137, 160
younger speakers 62, 63, 71, 76, 83, 117, 183, 195–196, 209, 214
yourn 50, 107, 191
yow 160

zero marking 51, 90–91, 147, 156, 160, 169, 173, 176

www.ingramcontent.com/pod-product-compliance
Lightning Source LLC
Chambersburg PA
CBHW072111170426
R18158500001B/R181585PG43191CBX00010B/1